MW00355502

Design for People

AUTHOR Likeminds [reads]

TITLE Scott Stowell

DATE DUE Design for people

BORROWER'S NAME

Design for People

stories about how
(and why) we all can
work together
to make things better

foreword by
Douglass G. A. Scott

essay by
Karrie Jacobs

edited by
Chappell Ellison,
Bryn Smith,
and Scott Stowell

an Open book

published by
Metropolis Books

Hi. Scott here. Before we get started, I just wanted to let you know what's in this book.

Up front, you'll find these instructions, the contents page, the dedication, a foreword by Doug Scott, a preface by me, and an essay by Karrie Jacobs. It's an honor for me to be able to share Doug's and Karrie's words with you.

Most of the rest of the book—192 out of 256 pages—is made up of 12 chapters. Each one tells the story of a big design project (or two) in the words of lots of different kinds of people, edited together from hundreds of interviews that were done for this book, plus some original correspondence—emails, faxes, etc., like this:

Elsa Stowell:
I don't know if this is unique, but it is good.

Scott Stowell to Alice Twemlow:
17 October 2005
I've had more thoughts about that book idea—I'd love to talk.

On the first page of each chapter, I introduce that story—and everybody who appears in that chapter introduces themselves. On the last page of each chapter, you'll find a very short essay on an idea (related to that chapter in some way) that I invited a client, colleague, or friend to write about.

Whenever you see anything underlined, anywhere in the book (like this: pay attention), that means you can find out more about that thing in the glossary, which starts on page 225. After that, there's an appendix with some outtakes (one extra quote from every person who was interviewed, whether they made it into a chapter or not), the index, some other things—books, movies, etc.—that I think you might like, and of course, the credits.

I hope you stay until the end.

This is for Mom and Dad.

Douglass G. A. Scott:
I was a graphic
designer at WGBH in
Boston for 35 years,
leaving as creative
director in 2009. I now
design books, identities,
and exhibits, and teach
at the Rhode Island
School of Design, Yale,
and Northeastern.

Always Open

Scott Stowell is my kind of designer. His work, and that of his colleagues and collaborators at Open, is about the creation of effective visual communication. This means the work has a job to do, and gets on with it in an efficient and intelligent manner.

I have admired both Scott's concerns and his graphic design work for 25 years. I first met him when he was a student in several of my courses at the Rhode Island School of Design. I often save examples of my best students' work so that I can show it to encourage excellent work from others. I still have Scott's typography work from the late 1980s. As a student, he not only demonstrated a mature understanding of the process of making design, but also the ability to make things that worked—formally, semantically, and functionally.

I also preserve examples from graphic design history to exhibit and use in my history of graphic design courses. When Scott moved to Rome to work on *Colors* magazine, he proudly sent me his first issue. I, of course, still have that copy and show it often. I also have the envelope imprinted with *Oops! Colors 6*.

I enjoyed teaching Scott the design student and was amazed at his knowledge of the design profession and his ability to recall examples of contemporary work and designers that supported his ideas and design decisions. I challenged him. He challenged me. I learned much from him. Since 2000, Scott has been a fellow faculty member with me in Yale's graduate program in graphic design. His ability to encourage and enlighten has only strengthened over the years. I always look forward to his critiques of student projects. His manner is conversational, direct, friendly, often humorous, and always helpful.

As a designer, Scott is a generalist. He can make work in many different forms and media. He understands how to distill a complex problem into a simple, clear statement of purpose. He is able to respect the needs of clients and users, the constraints of budget and production, and his own personal aesthetic needs.

I feel that Scott is always prepared. He enjoys the challenge of finding the right idea upon which to build. However, his preparedness does not rule out serendipity. Scott does things he has never done before, nor has he seen before. Open's work is not trendy, but it does possess the quality of inventiveness. The work does not call attention to itself. Rather it sends a message and expects the audience to understand it and respond.

Scott is generous to everyone concerned—those who work with him at Open, his collaborators, clients, editors, writers, illustrators, photographers, printers— everyone associated with the projects. He uses the word *our* when discussing the work at Open. He wants people to know why Open did something, how they did it, the story behind the decisions, where things went wrong, and how problems were overcome.

This book is proof of Scott's generosity. It is earnest, illuminating, unpredictable, and funny. Just like Scott Stowell and just like Open.

Scott Stowell:
I've wanted to be a
graphic designer ever
since I found out that
they existed. In 1998,
I started my studio,
Open. Ten years later,
I won a National Design
Award for some reason.
I've been trying to
figure out what to do
next ever since.

You Are Here

I can't think of a job I would like more than being a designer. My job consists of getting to know interesting people who do interesting things, learning about what they do (and a bunch of other stuff), and then figuring out how to help them succeed. That usually involves making things: logos, movies, signs, websites, etc. It always involves coming up with ideas. I get to do this almost every day. It's fun. And now I get to tell you about it.

↑
Scott making a
writing and design
presentation,
September 1980

As a designer (and as a person), I want the things I make to tell you about themselves. I like bright colors, clean shapes, and friendly words. Big type. Hard edges. No fuss. I try to be clear, whether I'm making a philosophical argument, a set of instructions, or a joke. *What is it? It's this.* I don't want to waste anybody's time. I just want to be as direct as possible. Then what you think about it is up to you.

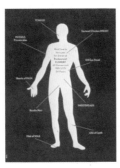

↑
magazine ads for Restaurant Florent designed with M&Co., 1992

Being direct has power. It's forceful. It's easy to understand. And when different people understand something, they have at least one thing in common. Making a connection with people helps me think about things from their point of view, and that's the most important part of making design for people. If you can get people to work together on something they all understand, the result will be better than anything they could do on their own.

I run a design studio in New York City. It's called Open. I started Open because I wanted to work with other people. I called it Open because I didn't want to name it after myself (and had rejected hundreds of other possible names, including finalists like All-Purpose, General Assembly, and Butter). As a word, open is an adjective and a verb, but not usually a noun. So its job is to change the way we see things. As a designer, that's my job, too.

↑
a poster titled "Poster," 2004

One of my favorite projects we've ever worked on is a magazine called *Good*. You can find out more about it in chapter 9 of this book, starting on page 161.

Just like *open*, *good* is a very common word. You see it everywhere. So we tried to have some fun with it whenever we could.

↑
a *Good* magazine
subscription card,
2006

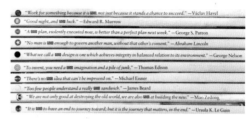

↑
issues of *Good*,
2006–2008

For instance, for the spine of each issue of *Good*, we'd pick a quote that had something to do with the theme of that issue. Our only rule was that the quote had to contain the word good.

The theme of the fifth issue of *Good* was "For the People." That issue was full of articles about how we relate to each other and our government here in the United States. So for the spine of that issue, we picked a quote from Abraham Lincoln: "No man is good enough to govern another man, without that other's consent." That time, I happened to be the one to actually set the type, so I made it look the way it was supposed to look, and sent it off to the printer.

We had designed the spine of *Good* to look a certain way, and we stuck to it every time. The quote itself was set in a typeface called Sabon Italic, and the attribution (in this case, Abraham Lincoln's name) was in Sabon Roman. I'm pretty sure I had set up that rule myself, and this time I got it wrong: I set Lincoln's name in Sabon Italic, too. But I didn't notice. Nobody else at Open noticed. And nobody at *Good* noticed either. So it's printed that way.

Of course, this was a tiny detail that hardly anybody at all would ever notice. But when I realized what I had done, it really bothered me. I'm the kind of person who might save all the issues of a magazine (like *Good*) and line them up on my bookshelf. And I'd probably notice that mistake, or at least wonder why that one issue looked just a little bit different from all the others. But mostly I was mad at myself for not getting it right.

So I asked the editors if we could run a correction in the magazine, just like we would if we had misspelled Lincoln's name, or if we had printed a quote that he actually hadn't said. The editors thought that was a funny idea, so we printed it in the next issue along with a couple of other more normal corrections.

> on an article at *goodmagazine.com.*
>
> seventh-grade honors-math teacher had developed a popular unit that used baseball statistics to teach percentages and decimals. He used
>
> **Oops ISSUE 005:** In our article **PAPER NOT PLASTIC**, we incorrectly stated that Ross Mirkarimi's San Francisco district includes Lombard Street. On **THE SPINE**, Abraham Lincoln's name was typeset incorrectly. It should have been in roman, not *italics*.
>
> **14**
> GOOD Jul/Aug 07
> Hello

↑
the correction in *Good* issue 006, July/August 2007

The nice thing is that the next issue's theme was "Design Solutions." It was all about how even the smallest decisions create the world around you.

I don't know if anybody ever read that correction. I don't know if anybody cared. But I was thrilled to turn my mistake into an opportunity to reveal

one small decision: in this case, italic instead of roman. The design issue of *Good* was about pulling back the curtain to show how things get made. By printing that correction and explaining that mistake, we offered the readers of *Good* what might have been their first chance to see behind that curtain.

That situation—that client, that idea, those rules, that mistake, that opportunity—was special. It had never happened before and will never happen again. It was a unique set of circumstances that happened because a unique group of people had crossed paths and started working together. So is this book. (Speaking of which, I included that little story in this preface because it didn't fit in the chapter about *Good*.)

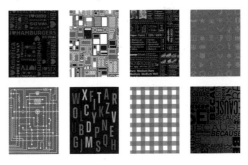

↑
Good intro pages (which also didn't fit in the *Good* chapter), 2006–2008

About 10 years ago, after Open had been open for a while, I wanted people to see the work we'd done. But mostly I wanted to share the stories behind it. I hadn't done the work alone, so I couldn't share the stories alone. That idea became this book. I'm happy it took a while, because there are more stories to share— like when a logo made people cry (pages 150 and 153), or the day we spent with Danny DeVito (page 172), or all the times Rob was worried about getting fired (pages 78, 110, and 213). This is a book for people and by people.

WE'RE ALL
IN THIS
TOGETHER

↑
a button designed
for a Glenn Gissler
Design holiday card,
2005

Those people include a fifth- and sixth-grade teacher in Arkansas (chapter 2), a security supervisor in Connecticut (chapter 3), and a medical student in Kenya (chapter 11). This is my book, but it's also a lot of other people's book.

A lot of people came together to make it. But it's not comprehensive, definitive, or objective. We couldn't talk to every person involved in every project, and we couldn't fit every one of their stories. (We also couldn't print some of the stories people told, but that's another story.)

Open is a

_____ _____
(adjective)   (noun)

in _____. We
   (place)

_____ _____
(verb)   (adjective)

_____ for people
(noun)

who _____,
      (verb)

_____,
(verb)

and _____.
    (verb)

↑
a "visual portrait"
of Open made
for the Image of
the Studio
design exhibition
at Cooper Union,
September 2013

This book has 12 chapters. Each one is 16 pages long. Some of the projects in those pages happened 15 years ago. We're still working on at least one of them today. Any of them could fill a whole book. They're all unique situations that connected a lot of different people. As a designer, it's my job to do the best I can in those situations. Running a studio means it's also my job to help construct them, so other people can do the best they can, too.

Every project is full of opportunities to make things better. *Could we do more with less money? Let's give the project a clearer name. Hey, we rewrote your copy! How about a website instead of a sign?* I think it's our job to keep coming up with ideas like these. And if we get shot down, it's our job to keep trying. There's always a way to make things better, even if it's just getting ready for the next thing that you can make better.

The things we have to deal with every day don't usually happen on purpose. Most of them are the result of a multitude of unpredictable coincidences. We can't control what happens to us. But we can control what we do about it. We take what we get and make the best of it. And then what we make of it becomes the reason it happened in the first place. The world we live in` is the result of the choices we

make, so we can always make things better—by making the best of things, no matter what.

This book is by far the hardest thing I've ever done. It's the hardest situation I've ever put myself in. And of all the work I've put into it, writing this preface has been the hardest part. Now I'm almost finished. So you and I find ourselves in our own special situation: Me, writing these words at this point of my life. Now. You, reading this, at exactly this moment. This has never happened before and will never happen again. What will you do next? It's your turn. Go.

↑
wine bottles
designed for
(Carmen +) Scott's
wedding party,
28 September 2013

I'm lucky to have worked with all these people at Open: some for a day, some for years. All the work that's in this book—and a lot more that isn't—would not have happened without them. This book wouldn't have, either. Thanks, everybody!

Dominic Amatore
Niko Arranz
Heather Asencio
Su Barber
Tim Barber
Andrea Beaudry
Debra Bergman
Josh Berta
Elliot Blanchard
Chase Booker
Cara Brower
Andrew Brown
Mo Caicedo
Rob Carmichael
Jenny Carrow
A. Purcell Carson
Julia Cassell
Jason Jude Chan
Lu Chekowsky
Yussef Cole
Annabel Coleman
Tomás De Cárcer
Erin Dean
Rob Di Ieso
Moreno DiMarco
Jessica Disbrow

Rimma Dreyband
Ken Edge
Gary Fogelson
Rosie Garschina
Elizabeth Goodspeed
Jon Gorman
Erica Gorochow
Hope Hall
Matt Hanson
Carol Hayes
Drew Heffron
Bala Heller
Sabrina Henley
Amelia Hennighausen
Tina Hornung
Yoshié Hozumi
Miranda Hughes
Tian Hughes
Ian Hutchinson
Gemma Ingalls
Zak Jensen
Matt Johnson
Bayard Jones
Adam Katz
Bryan Keeling
Patricia Kelleher
Monika Kim
Cat Kirk
Kate Kittredge
Michelle Kratchman
Matthew Lane-Smith
Erika Lee
Jun Lee
Josh Levi
Bethany Liebman
Eric Linn
Walter Lubinski
Louise Ma
Dennis Mabry
Peter Mannes
Tom Manning
Nicci Martinez
Martha Kang McGill
James Mckinnon
Leslie Mello
Sam Mestman
William Morrisey
Jolie Newman
Neda Niaraki
Naz Şahin Özcan
Şerifcan Özcan
Uroš Perišić
Simone Pillinger

Cynthia Ratsabouth
Scott Reinhard
Chad Roberts
Nicholas Rock
Danny Rosenbloom
Rob Sabatini
Tamar Samir
Zoë Scharf
Rich Scurry
Jiri Seger
Mohammad Sharaf
Trevor Shimizu
Karin Soukup
Scott Stowell
Dave Stoy
DeDe Sullivan
John Surdakowski
Jules Tardy
Pedro Tarrago
Julie Teninbaum
Ryan Thacker
Chris Thomas
Anna Tribelhorn
Lindsay Utz
David Van Riper
Lucia Vera
Emre Veryeri
Corinne Vizzacchero
Garry Waller
Lauren Wang
Rich Watts
Peter Wegner
Amit Werber
Chris Wilcha
Emily Wilson
Christian Wolfe

Karrie Jacobs:
I've been a writer
and editor for most
of my life. I write
about cities, build-
ings, and other
man-made things.
I was the founding
editor in chief of
Dwell magazine.

I Was in the Room:
Graphic Design,
Loose Talk, and
Heisenberg's
Uncertainty Principle

Here's how Scott Stowell, proprietor of Open, explains the profession to which he's devoted pretty much his entire life: "Graphic design—or, communication design—is just the way we talk to each other."

True, up to a point.

But talk is, as they say, cheap. Talk is loose. Talk can be mumbo jumbo. Talk is the stuff that comes out of our mouths whether we want it to or not.

Graphic design is something different. It's talk that has been pared down to its rudiments, and rethought a thousand times. It may appear simple, but it's almost never unpremeditated. It's rarely loose or cheap, even if it's meant to look that way. It is, for sure, a language, but it isn't exactly talk. It is language born of process, one that is sometimes deep and, intentionally or not, mysterious.

I'm pretty sure that Scott knows this. After all, the mission of this book is to distill design into talk, to demystify the process by having everyone involved in the making of a batch of signs for a park or a logo for a cable net-work tell their stories. The hope is that readers will gain some insight into how and why designs happen. The question I have is whether the eyewitness-to-history approach gets it right. Does it reveal the things that make certain graphics great, those little mnemonic triggers and cultural associations that fall loosely under the heading of inspiration? You tell the story of how a design happened. You were in the room. You were there. But the mystery, the source of the spark... it's very hard to pin down.

For example, I knew Scott back in the day, at pretty much the only other job he's ever had. As a 19-year-old undergrad at the Rhode Island School of Design (RISD), he landed an internship at M&Co., a New York City firm that was legendary in the 1980s and early 1990s for its work with Talking Heads, its quirky sense of humor, and the antics of its founder, Tibor Kalman, a master of the talk that isn't talk.

↑
Scott at M&Co.,
July 1993

Upon graduation, Scott returned to M&Co. and worked there until Tibor shuttered the company and moved to Rome with *Colors*, the Benetton-owned magazine that he'd helped invent. Scott, at 24, moved to Rome for a year and art directed three issues of *Colors*, including the award-winning 1994 issue on AIDS, before returning to New York.

↑
Colors issue 7,
June 1994

In the early 1990s, I worked for *Colors*, which then shared a Manhattan office floor with M&Co. Scott was just a kid, fresh out of RISD, but he was possibly the smartest, most talented kid on the premises. There are a number of stories I could tell about him from that period. But if I'd been interviewed for this book, if I'd been asked to help demystify, I would have said this:

Karrie Jacobs: Tibor and I were invited to give a lecture together at the Edge of the Millennium conference, staged by the Cooper Hewitt Museum in 1992. The division of labor that we'd agreed upon was that I would write the talk and Tibor would produce the visuals. What this meant, in practice, was that one of M&Co.'s employees, in this case Scott, researched and supplied the visuals. I wrote, Scott dug up images, and Tibor gave both of us a hard time. In the talk, which was about the end of design as a meaningful discipline, there was a section about how toasters, once uniformly stainless steel, had been reshaped in a fantastic range of styles, colors, and materials. We argued that this was an example of corporate cynicism rather than true design. To illustrate this point, Scott and an intern went out and bought every model toaster they could find and lined the auditorium stage at the Cooper Union, where the conference was held, with a parade of small appliances. This was my favorite thing about that lecture, the one aspect of it with which I was unreservedly happy. So when I think of Scott, I think this: He's the guy who bought the toasters.

But, of course, I don't really know why that happened. What was the impulse that sent him shopping for toasters? Maybe Scott knows. Or maybe he doesn't.

In fact, when he read the earliest draft of this essay, the first thing Scott did was shoot off an urgent email to another M&Co. alum, Keira Alexandra:

Scott Stowell to Keira Alexandra: 06 September 2015 *Circa 1992, Tibor and Karrie Jacobs did a lecture that involved showing a ton of meaninglessly different models of toasters. Actual toasters were bought at Kmart or wherever. Who bought them?*

Keira then emailed a mass query to anyone who had been on the premises in 1992, but no one could quite remember. The implication is clear: I thought of Scott as the guy who bought the toasters, but he might not have. A day or two after his missive to Keira, he sent me an email in response to the essay which noted:

Scott Stowell to Karrie Jacobs: 07 September 2015 *Buying the toasters (even if I bought them) was definitely not my idea. It was Tibor's. I don't want to claim credit for his idea. It was funny, but also super showy and pretty wasteful. Fun fact: Did you know that all of those toasters are also in the Cooper Hewitt permanent collection? Ridiculous.*

I was there. I have vivid memories of all the discussions and arguments that went into every aspect of the making of this lecture. I was in the room. But, apparently, I was mistaken. Or else Scott is mistaken. (And, by the way, I searched for the toasters in the Cooper Hewitt's collection, but couldn't find them.) It isn't that memories are flawed or that, as any criminal defense attorney will tell you, eyewitness accounts are unreliable—although both things are true—but that design is a highly collaborative, inherently messy process, born of meetings, earnest arguments, and goofy offhand remarks. When the design process is working as it should, it's impossible to sort out who did what.

Scott likes to tell the story of the most epic creation of his M&Co. years, the giant EVERYBODY sign that was erected in Times Square in 1993 as part of the 42nd Street Art Project: "It was one of those things where Tibor said, 'Hey, we've got to put something on this thing. Go up there and figure it out.'"

↑
Scott's sketchbook, 1993

Scott spent days sitting on the pavement on 42nd Street, thinking and sketching, trying to decide how best to use a blank wall in front of a temporary police station. He finally came up with a

massive, street-level, taxicab-yellow billboard that he thought of as "an advertisement for people." It said in jumbo letters: EVERYBODY.

↑
EVERYBODY sign, 1993

But it wasn't just populist propaganda. The billboard had a function. It had chairs attached to it so you could sit on the south side of 42nd Street and gaze at Times Square. The chairs, I believe, are what makes the piece important because they were the earliest indication that it might be permissible to stop and contemplate this amazing place instead of scurrying through, a precursor to the reddish glass bleachers that were later erected in the center of Times Square. However, Scott says the chairs weren't his idea. They were suggested by Andy

Jacobson, at that time M&Co.'s business manager. Scott initially shrugged it off as just another flawed concept. "It was one of those things where I said, 'Yeah, yeah, Andy...'" Later it dawned on Scott that it was actually a great idea.

The point is this: Each design studio has a culture and the work it produces is more the product of that culture than it is the work of any given person, even if that person is the studio's marquee name. So every time an interviewee in this book lauds Scott's genius, they're actually lauding the collaborative genius of Open—the hard work and the dumb jokes. The true product of Scott's imagination is Open itself, the fact that he founded this studio, nurtured it, and has kept it growing and evolving for 17 years.

↑
Su Barber and
Gemma Ingalls
(then Corsano) at Open,
26 September 2001

In an attempt to probe the mechanics of the talk that isn't exactly talk, I recently spent a day at Open. I thought that by watching and listening—by simply being in the room—I would gain a deeper understanding of the studio's process. Open is housed in one of those stolid buildings on Varick Street, in Lower Manhattan, that used to be full of printers, until the printers moved to cheaper boroughs or went bust.

↑
the lobby of
180 Varick Street,
9 July 2002

Now the buildings are crammed with design firms, architecture firms, ad agencies, and publishers. Open occupies a very white room, about 1,000 square feet, tucked into a corner of the eighth floor. There's a reception desk near the door, but no receptionist. It's furnished with tables and desks that look oddly handmade without being the least bit rustic. There's a conference table, a pair of desks on the left, and another pair on the right, facing the center of the room.

Scott, who's now 46, has been working out of this office since 1998. He originally rented it with illustrator Chip Wass. The two got together to create a poster promoting Chip's astonishingly obsessive collection of dingbats, little illustrations that we'd likely refer to today as emoji. The poster, structured like the Periodic Table of Elements, quickly led to other work.

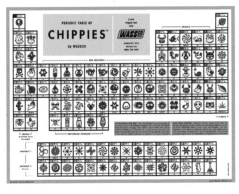

↑
the Periodic Table
of Chippies,
1997

"We did periodic tables for all kinds of clients," Wass recalls. "We did them for *Entertainment Weekly*, and the *New York*

Times." The collaboration led to a job redesigning Nickelodeon's Nick at Nite. But first it led to the rental of room 822.

↑
Scott and Chip
working on
Nick at Nite,
24 October 2000

"The space is very open," Wass says. "You know, there's a literal-ness to the studio name. We were really looking at each other all the time. Scott and I had divided the office space right down the middle, in a mirror image in terms of how the space was organized. And our desks faced each other, and we sort of looked at each other's things around each other's desks. So we were really in each other's stuff, in a lot of ways."

A set of four eastward-facing windows frame a view dominated by large NYU apartment towers and a motley assortment of buildings on

SoHo's fringe. What's important isn't so much the view, as the sunlight streaming in. At the opposite end of the office, behind the conference table is a solid wall of books, every volume on graphic design you'd ever want. Every necessary monograph is there: Paul Rand. Alvin Lustig. Charles and Ray Eames. Irma Boom. Tibor Kalman. (Of course.) There's also a copy of the 1977 edition of *Standard Alphabets For Highway Signs and Pavement Markings, Metric Edition*.

↑
behind Scott's desk,
August 2015

Every decorative touch and tchotchke, like the YES, WE'RE OPEN shop signs that fill a wall near the entrance or the APERTO sign that Scott keeps near his desk seem to be chosen to reinforce or comment on the firm's culture. (Well, maybe not the can of hot dogs Scott has, or the tubes of condiments he's amassed.) It's all very casual seeming without actually being casual. It completely exemplifies the talk that isn't talk.

Wass, who relocated to Baltimore, abandoned his chair in room 822 in 2005. It's now occupied by a young designer named Martha McGill. The office, I suspect, now has a different dynamic, one that's calmer, less driven by knotty entanglements.

Indeed, Open, on the day I visit, strikes me as a very quiet place. Contemplative. It's less like a business and more like a research center: The Scott Stowell Institute of Visual Language.

(Upon reading the paragraph above, Scott said in an email, *It's never that quiet here, we're usually talking and/or laughing all day and we were all sitting quietly at our computers because you were going to come around to talk to us. And some of the others were pretty nervous.* So you should probably keep in mind Heisenberg's Uncertainty Principle—in which the observer always has an impact on the observed— while reading the following.)

Open's studio is occupied by a small cadre of very smart, thoughtful people—six on the day I visited—most of whom were once students of Scott's at either Yale or the Cooper Union. Like Scott at M&Co., designers Catherine Kirk (better known as Cat) and Martha were interns at Open before they became full-fledged employees. Two of the six on the day I visit are still in school: Elizabeth Goodspeed attends Brown and RISD, and Chase Booker attends Yale, but they are interning at Open for the summer, helping out on jobs, just like everyone else.

The one bit of drama I witnessed on the day I spent at Open involved Elizabeth. She'd just returned from a trip to Seattle and noticed copies of a project she worked on back from the printer:

Elizabeth Goodspeed: I haven't seen it yet. Oh my God, it looks so good! Do I get a copy of this? This looks so much better than the printed copy I made for myself.

The project in question is an eye-catching poster and other materials for the New York City Department of Education's translation program. It helps parents who don't speak English find a translator to allow them to communicate with their children's teachers.

↑
New York City Department of Education Translation and Interpretation Unit outreach postcard, 2014

"The problem was, all their advertisements for this service were in English," Elizabeth explains. Her design has the word hello in myriad languages, colorfully arrayed. It's eye candy for the greater good. I especially liked that this example of Open's work is entirely and literally about talk.

Aside from Elizabeth's happy outburst, the weekly meeting is perhaps the noisiest event of the day. It's certainly the talkiest event. At 10 am, everyone gathers around the conference table. Jason Jude Chan, the studio manager who came to Open three years ago, after a series of business development and marketing jobs, distributes a project list divided into three categories: *today, tomorrow,* and *yesterday.* Naturally, most conversation focuses on the *today* projects, the ones that have real deadlines and up-coming client presentations.

↑
Open's job list,
29 July 2015

These include posters and brochures for the American Academy in Rome, best known for its Rome Prize, a website for an environmental non profit called the Blue Moon Fund, a variety of graphics and signage for the Riverdale Country School, signage for Brooklyn Bridge Park, market-ing materials for Changing Course (a competition intend-ed to help restore the Lower Mississippi River Delta), an annual report for the Hudson

Square Business Improvement District and, no surprise, the design of this book.

↑
Design for People
page layouts
in progress,
4 September 2015

Most of the discussion about the *today* projects takes place in spoken shorthand. The direction of each project has been long settled and if there is a debate about aesthetics to be had, it will happen later, perhaps at a group crit. This meeting is mostly logistics, Jason saying things like: "Rome stuff. Tomorrow at 1:30. Presen-tation." Or Martha comment-ing on the problematic state of a client's website: "When you resize, there's this choppiness."

After the meeting, the room gets very quiet. Six people. Six computers. Music play-ing, but almost too softly to be noticed. (Again, Scott: *The music was very low because you were going to record us.*)

At 10:58 am there's a noise.

"Did the H fall off?"
asks Elizabeth.

Scott investigates. Indeed, the letter H part of a sign at the studio entrance that says HI has fallen off the wall.

"A plot point for Karrie's essay," Scott remarks.

The only way for me to find out what people are actually doing behind their big computer screens is to go ask them, one by one.

For example, Cat is working on a presentation of proposed solutions for Changing Course. The objective is to make the Lower Mississippi River Delta more sustainable. Her job is to come up with a visual language that makes each team's approach to rerouting the river comprehensible to an audience of non-hydrologists. Which means she's got to understand the solutions herself. I ask her if she's been assigned this task because she's the resident deep thinker:

Cat Kirk:
I think we're pretty much all deep thinkers. The part I like about this is the storytelling. What

I'm trying to do is find a way to translate this into human terms. I think that's very interesting. And very hard.

And Martha is designing a presentation that needs to be completed for a meeting with the American Academy in Rome the following day:

Martha Kang McGill:
I think a lot of it comes down to how it's presented. Obviously how we think about the task at hand begins with strategy, but then we figure out how we're going to sell our ideas or explain our ideas in

a way that other people can understand. I think that matches a lot with the general attitude that Open has about graphic design, that people can understand and get something out of it: Just speak in clear, plain language.

In truth, watching Open at work, listening to the designers talk about what they're up to, and eavesdropping on the occasional conversation is not especially enlightening. If big creative breakthroughs are taking place, they're taking place silently, invisibly. A watched pot, as my mother would say, never boils. The day I observe, the pot is slowly simmering. I wonder whether things that are creatively meaningful are more likely to emerge from a group of people quietly—too quietly—going about their business or from a more tempestuous group.

As far as I can tell, Scott is largely a benevolent presence, steering his designers with dialogue, rather than giving orders. For example, he sits down next to Martha, and chats amiably with her about the logo and identity of the American Academy in Rome. Ultimately he suggests, "I think the way to solve it is to not change the logo and change everything else." Very civilized. Very respectful. Perhaps when I'm not there watching, affecting the dynamic, Scott is a tyrant.

When I ask him what he's working on, he explains to me the politics of signage at Brooklyn Bridge Park (BBP):

Scott Stowell: Basically, there's been this long difference of opinion. On one side there's the people running the park, who want everybody to know exactly what they need to know at all times. *Don't climb on the rocks because you'll break your neck!* And on the other side there's Michael Van Valkenburgh and the rest of the park's designers saying, *We just want people to enjoy this place. The landscape tells you where to go. You don't need signs getting in your way.* So we just try to do things that are just enough but not too much, you know?

In Brooklyn Bridge Park Open has, for years, been developing and installing a signage system that is pared down, accessible, and wonderfully direct. It's a perfect illustration of the studio's approach. And a walk in the park is more revealing than a day at the studio. In fact, I started to notice and appreciate the BBP signage system while running along the waterfront or walking my dog, long before I had a clue who designed it.

↑
Brooklyn Bridge Park,
May 2015

Prior to the opening of this 85-acre park along a two-mile slice of Brooklyn's edge, the model for a waterfront park in New York was Manhattan's Battery Park City, with its fussy esplanade shaped by an allegiance to a 1980s postmodern idea of history. Even when it was newly completed, Battery Park City felt a little stilted. A year or so ago, I began running and walking in Brooklyn Bridge Park almost daily. And I was struck by the fact that this very consciously designed and fabricated land-scape felt extremely contem-porary and not too terribly precious. It feels like a place where people can have fun, where people do have fun.

I especially love the graph-ics on Pier 2, a giant expanse of recreation areas, like a vast open-air, public health club. Icons hand painted (by Colossal Media) in deep blue on the pier's <u>concrete</u> dividers and pillars illustrate the available activities. One is of a person jumping, indicating the "play turf" area. Another is a simple pictogram of someone on roller skates, one leg up in the air, indicating the skating rink.

↑
painting the
Pier 2 icons,
2 May 2014

The icons are very literal, very representational, but they're not nostalgic. They just say

exactly what needs to be said. They're warm, and they're a little cute. But they never reach the point of being too cute.

I was thrilled when I learned that the firm behind these icons, as well as the park's other signage, was Scott's. (To be more precise, the icons were designed by a former Open employee named Ryan Thacker. *I can't remember whose idea it was to have icons*, notes Scott, *but he made them.*)

↑
sketches by
Ryan Thacker,
March 2014

Sure, I'd admired Open's work in the past, like its seven years of weekly covers for *The Nation*, or its wickedly dense <u>info-graphics</u> for *Good* magazine, or its occasional *New York Times* <u>Op-Ed page</u> illustrations. But, for me, the park signage is the work that expresses the es-sence of Open, that telegraphs

Open-ness. Of course, while I read the design of Brooklyn Bridge Park as a rebuke to Battery Park City, Scott sees it differently. He thinks of the park as "the opposite of the High Line" and Open's signage as an example of "municipal design."

↑
Citi Bike kiosk, 2015

Wendy Leventer, the former president of the Brooklyn Bridge Park Development Project, tells a story. She originally brought Scott to the project and, early on, he came up with a phrase to try and convey the value of the park to a somewhat hostile surrounding community. "Very clear. Very simple. I remember being absolutely bowled over by the idea," Leventer recalls. Scott proposed a URL for an introductory website and language for a sign to be used at public announcements: *This is your park*. The phrase is, of course, another way of saying EVERYBODY, another expression of the cheerful populism that Scott has injected into his practice. Or, as Leventer observes, "He is so down to earth, but super clever."

Actually, it's *pro forma* for clients to marvel at the simplicity and directness of Open's work. For example, Jason Klarman, who worked with Open on the identity for the cable network Bravo says: "I would say that I have never been more blown away by a pitch in my career. Scott just came in with an idea. He put Bravo in a talk bubble. He said, 'Shows on Bravo are things that people talk about.' He created this entire pitch around buzz and what people talk about."

There's only one network with a name that's a word that people yell on a semi-regular basis. So why not take that word right out of their mouths? The tag line says Bravo is "on" new trends, celebrities and technology. It reminds you Bravo is "on" right now, so you might be missing something. And it announces Bravo's transformation from arts network to entertainment powerhouse.

↑
Bravo presentation, 21 October 2004

From the way clients like Leventer and Klarman talk about the crispness of the ideas Scott presents at meetings, you'd think they were inspirations that came to him as he was riding up in the elevator. You might envision Scott as a singular figure, the Don Draper of Varick Street. But the magic is more elusive than that. It somehow emanates from that white room, and the people in the white room, but it's hard to put your finger on, even if you're in the room... Especially if you're in the room.

↑
in the studio,
October 2012

In an interview a couple of years ago, Scott explained his approach this way: "If we can make something look like what it's about, that's when I think we've done our job." That's a very succinct description of Open's work. It's also deceptively simple. It's not easy to make visual language that's obvious without being clichéd, just as it's not easy to talk in a way that's both intelligent and clear.

If I were one of the myriad enthusiastic clients interviewed for this book, I'd still wax poetic about the toasters. Granted, Scott now dismisses the gesture as "super showy and pretty wasteful." He swears it wasn't his idea. But I was there. Filling the stage with toasters was such an eloquent and funny way of conveying the point of the lecture that it made the words we were speaking almost superfluous. I'd insist that on that evening in 1992, Scott succeeded in making something that looked "like what it's about." I'd contend that Scott's design philosophy had triumphed before he even knew that he had one. He might argue otherwise. And I may, in fact, be mistaken. But I saw what I saw. I was in the room.

When *The Nation* magazine hired us to design their covers, *us* was just me. I finished the first one between signing the lease on our studio and moving in. I knew I was excited to make basically a new poster every week that would be printed and sent to thousands of people. But I didn't know that working with a client every week meant I was also making a relationship. And I never thought about how that relationship might end.

1.

in order
of appearance

Scott Stowell:
Hello.

Karen Rothmyer:
I was managing
editor at the time.

Chip Wass:
I'm an illustrator. I
shared a studio with
Scott and worked on
several *Nation* covers.

Milton Glaser:
I was an occasional
hired hand. The
relationship devel-
oped over a long
period of time.

Katrina vanden Heuvel:
I'm editor and pub-
lisher of *The Nation*.
I've been editor and
publisher since 1995.

Hal Siegel:
I was sort of free-
lancing around and
The Nation seemed
like a fun gig.

Roane Carey:
I was copy chief at *The
Nation* in 1998, when
Open started doing
the covers. Now I'm
managing editor.

Cara Brower:
The Nation was an
Open client before I
was an Open designer.

Ryan Thacker:
I was an Open intern
commuting from
Philly and Jersey for
the summer of 2003.

Su Barber:
When I started as
an intern at Open in
1999, *The Nation* was
already a client.

Rob Kimmel:
My dad is an old activ-
ist lefty. When I was a
kid, there were stacks
of *The Nation* piled
on the coffee table.

Bob Stowell:
I'm a retired printer
in North Chelmsford,
Massachusetts.

Elsa Stowell:
Bob and I have been
married for a long
time. We're very proud
of both of our sons,
Stephen and Scott.

Christoph Niemann:
Scott hired me to
illustrate a few covers.

Carol Hayes:
My title at Open, if I
remember correctly,
was designer. I was
Scott's first employee.

**Amelia
Hennighausen:**
At Open I was an office
manager/archivist/
production person and
probably a bit more.

Gemma Ingalls:
I was the studio/proj-
ect manager at Open.
I helped crack the
whip on the design-
ers as they painstak-
ingly designed the
Nation covers.

Alan Kimmel:
I spent most of my
working life as an
encyclopedia and
textbook editor,
mainly in the social
studies. Except for
a short time in the
U.S. Army Air Force,
I have lived all my 88
years in Chicago.

The Nation
↑
The Nation
in 1865, 1984,
and 1997

Scott Stowell:
The Nation is the oldest continuously published weekly magazine in America. It has come out basically every week since 1865.

Karen Rothmyer:
It was founded by progressive political thinkers—abolitionists at the end of the Civil War—and that has always been its tradition.

Scott Stowell:
I probably got *The Nation* as a client in November or December of 1997. And my friend Chip and I moved in to our studio at the beginning of 1998.

Chip Wass:
I really don't remember whose idea it was, but we started to talk about sharing a space. We were kind of in complementary careers, where we could ask each other for help all the time. Like Scott ended up having this in-house illustrator and I had this in-house designer.

Scott Stowell:
The job was to make the covers—I mean literally. I think it was 500 bucks a week, and if I added the 500 bucks up over a month, it literally paid the rent. I was like, *Cool, I'm all set!*

Milton Glaser:
As a political instrument, as a way to express ideas, *The Nation* has almost no peers in this country.

Scott Stowell:
Milton Glaser and Walter Bernard did the format for it, in the 1970s. It was basically a newspaper all the way up through the '70s, '80s, '90s. The covers were all text. The articles started on the front.

Katrina vanden Heuvel:
The old design was brilliant. The editorial would start on the cover, but the danger was that *The Nation* looked the same each week.

Scott Stowell:
A couple years before I got involved, Milton started doing graphic covers, but then they were looking for somebody to take over.

Karen Rothmyer:
Katrina came in with a much more visual approach, being younger and more aware.

Milton Glaser:
We really were not interested in the idea of having *The Nation* as a weekly client. We knew they'd have to ultimately get art directors involved.

↑
Scott's cover sketches,
January 1998

Katrina vanden Heuvel:
We were interested
in something that
would be a little
more irreverent.

Hal Siegel:
The Nation was
hunting around for
another designer.

Katrina vanden Heuvel:
I felt it was important
to highlight a state-
ment each week as to
what we considered
the story and to be
more visual in doing
that. Though we re-
mained, and remain
to be, a magazine
of words, of writers,
you want to enhance
that experience.

Hal Siegel:
Carl Lehmann-Haupt
and I worked on a few
covers together, but
then I decided I want-
ed to focus on digital
media. Carl didn't
want to keep doing the
covers on his own. Not
wanting to leave *The
Nation* in the lurch,
we thought we should
recommend another
designer. Open imme-
diately sprang to mind.

Katrina vanden Heuvel:
With Open, there
was a great clever-
ness as well as a
humanity, which are
often hard to fuse.

Hal Siegel:
Scott had been the art
director at *Colors*, and
while the two maga-
zines aren't exactly in
the same space, they
share a certain type of
worldview and spirit.

Scott Stowell:
When you get a job
like that, it's like, *Wow,
this is the most amaz-
ing opportunity*. It's
so prestigious, and
it's been around for
so long, and *Oh my
God you've given me
the keys to this thing*.

Hal Siegel:
I only knew that Open
had gotten the work
after I saw their first
cover on the stands.

↑
Open's first cover
for *The Nation*:
"The Gift of Time,"
2/9 February 1998

Roane Carey:
That issue was 72
pages—our usual was
40—and Jonathan's
article, which took
up the entire feature
section and ran
around 15,000 words,
if I recall, became
a book, a prescient
warning about the
danger of nuclear war
after the end of the
Cold War, when most
of the public was not
paying attention.

← an early draft
for "Israel at Fifty,"
April 1998

**Scott Stowell
to Katrina
vanden Heuvel:**
13 April 1998
*Everything I tried with
the landscape photos
turned out flat; so I
went in this new direc-
tion, which I'm very
excited about. Colors
are as follows: the map
prints in light blue,
the Nation logo and
list of contributors
are in a darker blue,
the large type and
the over-the-logo line
are black, and the "A
Special Issue" box is
red with red type.*

↑
"Israel at Fifty,"
4 May 1998

Karen Rothmyer:
Katrina and I would
decide what the
cover story would be;
there's always vari-
ous competitors for
that position. I would
usually be the one
to talk to Scott and
send him the story.
Sometimes we didn't
have anything brilliant
and we relied on him
to come up with ideas.

Cara Brower:
Scott would get a
summary of the main
story they wanted to
illustrate on the cover.
Then the pressure was
on to come up with
cover ideas to present.

Ryan Thacker:
We'd typically show
three or more.

Katrina vanden Heuvel:
The problem with a
weekly is some weeks
you're really excited
about the cover story
or the issue, and other
weeks, you're not.

Karen Rothmyer:
It was very much a
collaborative process.

Cara Brower:
I would usually have a
go at coming up with
ideas and then show
them to Scott and
discuss. Scott would
always have ideas that
made them better.

Su Barber:
We must have de-
signed around 200
covers. The beauty of
a project like that is it
can't be too precious.

Scott Stowell:
This image comes
from an old atlas that
I have. It's from 1947,
so it says Palestine in
it. And we negotiated
with the editors for
a long time to figure
out what we could call
the border of Israel
at that time, and then
just put one on top of
the other. I remem-
ber they got hate
mail on both sides.

Karen Rothmyer:
Readers would scream
that something was
tasteless or anti-
feminist or racist or
whatever. They would
read things into cov-
ers that I never even
noticed were there.

Scott Stowell:
This was one of my
favorite covers ever.
Because it was totally
like, *We're just putting
it out there, and you
guys, the readers, are
bringing all that to
it,* and I loved that.

Karen Rothmyer:
Katrina and I were always thinking that there were various elements that needed to be emphasized on the cover.

Scott Stowell:
But it was not like, *We have to use a famous person*, or *It has to be blue*, or any of that junk. Ninety-something percent of their sales is subscriptions, so there was never a marketing reason to do anything on the cover.

Karen Rothmyer:
I never felt like that gave us any more freedom. It's no different than an editor who has the newsstand model, which is, *I want people to read this.*

Scott Stowell:
I would present directly to Katrina. At first it was in person, then it was like, *OK, you don't need to come in every time, just send a fax.*

Su Barber:
We had the teeniest art budget, next to no time, and one type family, but something great could always be assembled from those bits and pieces.

Cara Brower:
We always used Knockout for the type. It was very liberating as it gave all of our designs a cohesiveness that gave *The Nation* its look and identity.

Scott Stowell:
The Nation is printed on newsprint and it has this kind of strident content. When it was full bleed, it looked like some kind of religious pamphlet you get at the airport. So the only real, systematic decision I made early on was to never bleed. It always had this white border hooked up with the logo in a box.

Su Barber:
Working on those covers was like school. How to sell an idea. How to visualize metaphor. How to make something out of almost nothing.

Rob Kimmel:
It was pretty amazing to see *The Nation* transformed just as I was studying graphic design. I wasn't aware of Open as a firm, but the covers they were churning out every week were an ongoing case study in communicating visually.

Bob Stowell:
I can remember saying, *Wow, what is this?*

Elsa Stowell:
There were many interesting articles in it. We looked forward to getting it in the mail. It was very exciting.

↑
"Oversexed,"
21 May 1998

←
Scott's fax to Katrina explaining the "Oversexed" cover, 4 May 1998

Scott Stowell:
I always describe this photo as "the least sexy stock photo ever in the world." It's unsexy people in an unsexy environment with an unsexy plant and furniture and clothing. It's terrible, but you put this word on it, and then all these details come out of the image that make it really weird.

Katrina vanden Heuvel:
Scott had his own ideas about images. I don't think he was as interested in using cartoonists and illustrators as much as we had been doing.

Scott Stowell:
Our fee was $500 and then I think a $250 art budget. So we would just try to do the art, or I would try to do the art myself as much as possible. We wouldn't get the $250, but I would save it up and then be able to go to some big illustrator and be like, *Here's $1,000.*

Christoph Niemann:
This was the classic newspaper or magazine assignment. I either got a synopsis or the whole article and then I would come up with sketches and we would discuss the concept. We would also discuss the style, then go back and forth and decide which concept worked.

Chip Wass:
Scott gives an enormous amount of creative freedom to illustrators and photographers. It's this kind of window that he makes where you do your thing.

Scott Stowell:
Sometimes we would have three weeks to do it. Sometimes we would have three hours to do it.

Karen Rothmyer:
When you run a weekly magazine it's like every moment is a crisis. At the last minute a cover would change because something had happened and some story would be put in that we hadn't expected.

Carol Hayes:
The schedule was always tight and there was always a frenetic energy in the studio when the issue was closing.

Amelia Hennighausen:
It was very cool to be around when the covers were coming together, even at the last minute, which was almost every issue.

Chip Wass:
I've never worked for an art director who was a few feet away from me. Any revisions or anything could just happen very, very efficiently.

Katrina vanden Heuvel:
I do think the disadvantage, designwise, is that often you don't have much time for thought or different drafts. There was diplomacy involved at times.

← "Beyond Monica," 7/14 September 1998

Scott Stowell:
We used the official photo of Bill Clinton from the White House website because it was free. But that photo was very low resolution, so we put it into Photoshop and made it blurry to make it high resolution enough to print.

Milton Glaser:
Fuzzying up Clinton's face is amusing. When you squint you actually see him looking forward and that's always an illusion that's compelling. When you have a designer talking about another designer's work, that's like a musician complimenting another musician's work. I wouldn't have done it that way, but that, in most cases, is irrelevant.

→
draft and final cover
for "More Democracy,"
26 October 1998

**Scott Stowell
to Katrina
vanden Heuvel:**
5 October 1998
*This is an idea I've
been dying to try all
year: to use the ad-
dress label as an inte-
gral part of the cover
message and design.*

↑
"Politics '98,"
2 November 1998

Scott Stowell:
There's no mention of
the Monica Lewinsky
scandal or anything in
this issue, but this is all
anybody talked about
in politics at the time.

←
"Come Together,"
7 December 1998

Milton Glaser:
"Come Together." In
many of these cases,
these elements don't
come together, but
the effect of the white
and the flag in the
middle is attractive,
and the idea of the
flag itself being in
color is a nice idea. So
I think that looks fine.

→
"Students for Sale,"
27 September 1999

Chip Wass:
I tend to get a lot of
projects that are for
children, or very whim-
sical, and it was great
to have some things
with a little more
gravitas. Scott and I
would often describe
the tone of something
as being a joke told
with a serious face.
Sometimes with *The
Nation*, we were doing
the opposite of that.

Scott Stowell:
Michael Tomasky wrote this piece about the *New York Times* Op-Ed page. I said, "I just want to put the *New York Times* Op-Ed page on the cover of *The Nation*." And so we had to talk to the legal department and they said it was totally fair use.

Katrina vanden Heuvel:
"The Savaging of the President" was a classic. Because it's a case of a cover that drove me crazy.

Scott Stowell:
All we did was scan in a copy of the *Times*, and then surprinted the type in red.

Katrina vanden Heuvel:
Just looking at it now, you know it's not going to turn out right.

Carol Hayes:
Printing on newsprint was always a bit of a crapshoot.

Scott Stowell:
There were no proofs, no press checks, no nothing. The thing is, the background image was full color, and a newspaper is a warm color, right? And everything prints really dark on newsprint. The people on press were like, *We can't read the red type, so we'd better put more red ink on the press.* But that made the background even darker. So it just became this mush.

Katrina vanden Heuvel:
I was so upset because it was something I had worked on, and I valued the writer and the subject.

Scott Stowell:
I remember the exact moment: I'm riding in a cab going home to Williamsburg at like two in the morning, and I get a call from Katrina, who's livid. She says they have to pulp the entire run of the magazine at a cost of I don't know how many thousands of dollars.

Katrina vanden Heuvel:
I threw that issue around the room.

Scott Stowell:
Basically I convinced her not to do it. I said, "Don't bother. The cover looks dark. Why are you going to waste all that money? Just don't. Don't reprint it." I explained to her why we screwed up, and how there was no way to really avoid it.

Katrina vanden Heuvel:
The wacko thing was it did really well. Our newsstand sales were not serious, but in our end-of-year review, it was the best-selling issue because of the power of the story.

Scott Stowell:
The worst possible thing happened, and it was fine. There's another one next week, you know?

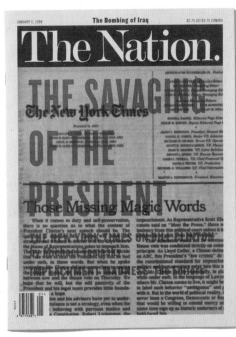

↑
"The Savaging of the President,"
4 January 1999

→
how it was
supposed to look

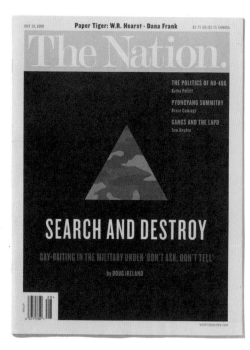

"Search and Destroy,"
8 July 2000

Su Barber's
camouflage shorts

Su Barber:
I think the first sketch
of mine that went
through was for the
"Search and Destroy"
story, about gays in
the military. It was
thrilling. The camo
pattern was scanned
off my shorts.

Christoph Niemann:
Whether you're an art
director or an illustra-
tor, you have to be
in the story the mo-
ment the assignment
comes. Especially with
tight deadlines—that's
the only way you can
do interesting work.

Scott Stowell:
I was moving from
working on my own
to having the studio
and working with
other people. It was
so liberating to have
a weekly deadline.
The art had to ship
by Tuesday morning.
We would get our
copy in the mail on
Thursday or Friday.

Su Barber:
You send a file out and
just days later a stack
of beautifully printed
newsprint arrives.

Scott Stowell:
As the studio grew and
I felt like I had done
enough of these, and
I didn't feel like I had
to do everything in the
world anymore, this
was a great project
to have in the studio.
Because it would be,
OK, you do it this week,
or, *Everybody come
up with some ideas.*

Cara Brower:
I think everyone at
Open had their time
of designing cov-
ers—for a while I did
them every week, and
I think Su before me,
and then when Ryan
joined us, I remember
him working on them.

Ryan Thacker:
I worked on two cov-
ers as an intern. I
remember thinking, in
retrospect, that Scott
was way too gener-
ous for giving me
credit. One was really
weird. It was about
George W. Bush and
the illustration was
this giant hand with
a magnifying glass,
frying him like an ant.

Scott Stowell:
I'm a big fan of clichés,
actually, because ev-
erybody gets them.
And they came in
handy in this job.

Karen Rothmyer:
What Scott taught
me was that you
really need to have
one big idea.

Scott Stowell:
The money was not
astronomical, but
it was plenty. And
because it wasn't
so astronomical, it
wasn't so weighty.

Ryan Thacker:
I guess it's pretty
cheap to have
the intern do vec-
tor drawings.

Milton Glaser:
It's not a way to make a
good living, but it is a
vehicle that you really
feel has some effect
on culture. I have to
say that most work in
graphic design doesn't
have such an effect.

Roane Carey:
The cover that stands out most for me, for obvious reasons, is the 9/11 cover, "A Hole in the World." That week, and the weeks that followed, were a crazy time in New York City and at *The Nation*. Trying to report on the catastrophe, even as we lived in the middle of it, was very moving.

Su Barber:
September 11, 2001, was a spectacularly beautiful morning. The sky was perfectly clear and bright blue. Scott and I were both in the office early, working side by side at our desks, listening to the radio.

Scott Stowell:
WNYC was on, and they reported a plane flew into the World Trade Center.

Su Barber:
For a few minutes it sounded like maybe a hoax or just a horrible accident, then the second plane hit and we recognized the gravity of the scene.

Scott Stowell:
So we went outside onto Varick Street, and the whole street was just cars stopped at weird angles.

Gemma Ingalls:
I remember a car parked outside the building with the doors open and the radio blaring.

Scott Stowell:
We wandered and bumped into people from the office out on the street, and then we watched the towers fall down. I just remember people standing next to me who buckled and fell at the same time.

Karen Rothmyer:
Like with so many things that happen in one's life, one's mind takes a while to catch up with reality.

Scott Stowell:
I didn't know you weren't supposed to go back to work during a terrorist attack. So we came back to work and everyone called their parents.

Elsa Stowell:
How should I put it? It was such a terrible day.

Karen Rothmyer:
I was like, *I guess we'll do a strip across the cover recognizing the event*.

Scott Stowell to Karen Rothmyer:
11 September 2001
Perhaps we should do a solid black cover or something like that. I also just shot pictures of the Twin Towers as they were collapsing, so maybe I could find a one-hour photo place and we could use one of those. Let me know. The phones are jammed but our email is fine.

Karen Rothmyer to Scott Stowell:
11 September 2001
yes, we had already concluded we have to scrap the cover we were planning on. If your pictures come out well, yes, let's go with one of those. If not, we can just go with a black cover with type.

Katrina vanden Heuvel:
It was just a fraught, horrifying moment.

Karen Rothmyer:
Everything was out except for one phone line attached to the fax machine.

Scott Stowell:
Jonathan Schell wrote the cover story that day. Literally two hours after it happened, Katrina faxed over the first paragraph.

Katrina vanden Heuvel:
We knew we had to move forward with something of the moment.

Karen Rothmyer:
Scott came over in the afternoon and he opened his computer and he showed me what he'd come up with on screen, and it was the dark outline of the buildings against the blue sky.

Scott Stowell:
I thought it needed a little something. I remember trying A Hole in the World on the image, and it felt like too much.

Karen Rothmyer:
We were racing around getting everybody writing pieces, throwing everything out of the magazine, so I had a lot on my mind. But when I saw what Scott had done I was sort of breathless with admiration. It was just exactly right.

Katrina vanden Heuvel:
There was no back and forth. *This is the tone we wish to convey. This is the image.*

Karen Rothmyer:
He and I talked there and I don't know if he said or I said, "Maybe it's just a little empty?"

Scott Stowell:
I was like, "Let's just put the date on it."

Katrina vanden Heuvel:
We knew we wanted to make this almost like a monument. An enduring statement.

Gemma Ingalls:
It's still pretty badass. The only rival to it was the all-black *New Yorker* cover.

Scott Stowell:
It's a weird thing to say, but the constraints and limitations—*We have to stay in here, it's the day it happened, we're still in crisis mode and we can't deal with it, we have no access to any media whatsoever*—made the cover way better. After this the covers got dark for a while, in more ways than one.

OCTOBER 1, 2001

$2.95 US/$3.95 CANADA

The Nation.

September 11, 2001

A Hole in the World
On Tuesday morning, a piece was torn out of our world. A patch of blue sky that should not have been there opened up in the New York skyline. In my neighborhood—I live eight blocks from the World Trade Center—the heavens were raining human beings.... Our world was changed forever. **By Jonathan Schell**

WWW.THENATION.COM

↑
"Bush Goes Nuclear,"
1 April 2002

Christoph Niemann:
That was probably my
favorite one. I think it's
a fun image and also
it's a little absurd.

Christoph Niemann:
Shaking the system
doesn't mean chang-
ing opinions. I often
find that a lot of political art is being done as
if this could change
your opponent's
view, which I think
in the history of the
world has probably
never happened.

Katrina vanden Heuvel:
Do I agree with ev-
erything that's in *The
Nation* every week?
No. But if you have
antipathy toward the
ideas that we're lift-
ing up, I think it's a
problem. We need to
have some simpatico.

Christoph Niemann:
What's important for
me is that you have to
be a political person
to do the relevant
work. But I still think
when you actually
do the art, you must
not get carried away
with your opinion.
The idea is to get a
point across to the
reader. It's journalism.

Karen Rothmyer:
It was a unique pe-
riod in terms of what
was happening in the
magazine world in
general. During the
period that Scott was
there, design became
an integral, everyday
part of *The Nation* in a
way that it hadn't been
a few years before.

Rob Kimmel:
My dad actually kept
years of the covers, in
a manila file folder in a
standing file cabinet.

Alan Kimmel:
I don't recall why I kept
all those back issues of
The Nation for so long.
Perhaps it was in case
I wanted to refer to an
article some nostalgic
day—or, as it seren-
dipitously happened,
to hand off some of the
old covers to my son. It
may simply be that I'm
a pack rat who hates to
throw anything away.

↑
Open's last cover
for *The Nation*:
"California Chaos,"
1/8 September 2003

Cara Brower:
I had the design
formed in my head
as soon as we found
out the cover story.
It was just there, in
my mind's eye!

Ryan Thacker:
It was about the crazy
California recall elec-
tion or something.

Cara Brower:
I was trying to do a
contemporary version
of a 1940s film noir
poster. Most of them
have highly illustra-
tive collages of their
characters with really
expressive poses and
they always have the
classic condensed
type with the names
of the stars running
along the bottom.
Scott had the idea
to put Gary Coleman
offset on his own,
which really makes
the cover, I think.

Scott Stowell:
They broke up with
me in the end. I was
sitting at my desk and
I got a phone call from
Katrina. It wasn't even,
*Can I take you out to
lunch*, or something.
It was totally, *We
would like to see other
people*. I was like, *I
can change*. And she
said, *It's not you, it's
me*. That whole thing.

Karen Rothmyer:
There was no argu-
ment or anything that
caused the change.
I think there was a
feeling on both sides
that we had a good
run and it was time for
seeing what a fresh
eye could bring to it.

Katrina vanden Heuvel:
I think we decided
that Scott was ready
to do some other
things. We continued
with the idea of an
image-based cover.

Scott Stowell:
I was totally shocked.
I think that we were
not quite as attentive
as we were at the be-
ginning, and I think the
covers near the end
don't feel as urgent or
something. I don't feel
as invested in them.

Karen Rothmyer:
Probably what happens
is after a few years
everybody gets sick of
each other. There's a
return to similar topics
repeatedly, so who-
ever is doing the cov-
ers may be running out
of fresh ideas anyway.

Scott Stowell:
You do something
together every week
for almost six years,
and I didn't realize how
rewarding that could
be. Because you get
to know somebody,
and you end up in a
personal relationship.

Katrina vanden Heuvel:
When we were work-
ing together, a weekly
had a sense of more
urgency. A few years
ago we brought in a
creative director for the
first time. That's new.

Scott Stowell:
To this day, I get a
free copy every week.
And so I read it. But
it's a little bit like your
ex-girlfriend bringing
her latest idiot boy-
friend over to visit.

**Amelia Hennighausen
to *The Nation*:**
10 November 2003
*I don't really like
the new covers.
Your content, as
always, is great.*

Rob Kimmel:
I read *The Nation*
online now, much to
my father's dismay.

Scott Stowell:
Working with a client
and developing a rela-
tionship that's not ad-
versarial after a while
was a revelation to
me. That's actually the
most rewarding part
of the work. And the
work is the evidence
of the relationship.

Pierre Bernard:
I'm a French graphic designer inspired in Poland by Henryk Tomaszewski's teaching. I worked for 20 years in the Grapus collective before founding the Atelier de Création Graphique in Paris.

Designers today are public interrogators. By creating a new form for each subject we are entrusted with, we raise questions. Each of our proposals finds its visual expression in the examination of its subject. We can open doors, rouse minds and sensibilities, and participate in the rediscovery of the world as it is.

If our questions are sincere, without preconceived ideas, our images can break free of their content. They can help all of us reflect, appreciate other points of view, and provoke as many reactions as there are people to provoke.

When they are successful, they help us all to speak.

Au boulot, les graphistes!

Art21, or *Art in the Twenty-First Century*, was the first national public tv show in the United States about contemporary art and artists. It was also the first tv show we got hired to do the graphics for. *Art21* isn't made by PBS or any tv station. It's made by an independent nonprofit (also called Art21), and they do things their own way. Getting this job and figuring it out was hard. Then we had to figure it out a few more times.

2.

in order
of appearance

Susan Dowling:
I created Art21 with my old friend Susan Sollins a long time ago.

Eve Moros Ortega:
I do two things at Art21. I oversee all the film production and I oversee the running of the entire nonprofit.

Scott Stowell:
Thanks for reading.

Wesley Miller:
I'm the associate curator of Art21.

Tobias Frere-Jones:
I design typefaces. This was the first serious project I did with Scott—that is, something not drawn on a bar napkin.

Kate Davis Caldwell:
I'm a visual artist from New Jersey, living and working in LA.

Su Barber:
This was my first huge project as a designer at Open.

Mo Caicedo:
I was the animation director on season four.

Cat Kirk:
When season seven came along, I was kind of Open's film editor.

Bryan Keeling:
On seasons one and two, I was Open's lead motion graphics guy.

Rich Scurry:
I did the animation for *Art21* season three.

Christina Milan:
When I learned about *Art21*, I was an administrative assistant in an art gallery.

Jack Watson:
I teach visual art and art history at Chapel Hill High School in North Carolina.

Peter Foley:
I have composed, produced, and performed the music for *Art21* since its inception in 2001.

Zak Jensen:
I was an Open intern for summer 2004.

Ryan Thacker:
Open worked on *Art21* for years before I did. I made the Art21 logo.

Jason Jude Chan:
I was Open's producer for season seven.

Jonathan Munar:
I oversee Art21's presence across all digital platforms.

Uroš Perišić:
For a couple seasons, I've animated the interstitials.

Nikki Kalcevic:
I teach grades five and six in northwest Arkansas.

Linda Montanaro-Kramer:
I discovered *Art21* while attending New World School of the Arts in Miami, Florida.

Don Ball:
I am an art educator in Mississauga, Ontario, Canada.

↓
host segments
from *Art21*
season one,
2001

Susan Dowling:
The host segments
required by PBS were
not always success-
ful. Thank goodness
we were finally able
to drop them.

Eve Moros Ortega:
Being a thinker, to
really think, that's
what artists teach us.
They teach us to look.
And pay attention.

Scott Stowell:
Art21 fits in perfectly
with stuff I'm inter-
ested in, which is like,
*Hey America, do you
know about these
weird art people?*

Eve Moros Ortega:
Art21 is a nonprofit art
and education organi-
zation with a mission
to make contempo-
rary art accessible to
broad audiences. That
is one of our official
mission statements,
but people don't talk
that way, you know.
The founder, Susan
Sollins, was a vision-
ary, who was—I'm
seeking the right word
for what she was—like
a saint in the world.

Susan Dowling:
She took Art21
to heights I never
dreamt of. She passed
away in October
2014. Just, really, it
was so shocking.

Eve Moros Ortega:
She just lived and
breathed love for
contemporary art, and
deeply, deeply, deeply
believed in why it was
important, and why
it should be shared
with everybody.

Susan Dowling:
It was a great bonus
that artists and collec-
tors loved *Art21*, but
we thought originally
that we wanted it to
be for all people. I still
think it's for all people.
I love that someone
way in the boondocks
somewhere, that it's
important to them,
whether they're a
teacher or an artist or
just a curious person.

Eve Moros Ortega:
We film the greatest
artists of our time,
to show them as role
models for creative
thinking and to re-
ally show why art
matters. Because it
really does, and it's not
given credit in many
places, especially in
American education.

Scott Stowell:
Susan Dowling worked
on a show in the 1980s
that I watched when I
was a pretentious high
school student, called
Alive from Off Center.
It was cool, you know?

Susan Dowling:
For *Art21*, what Susan
Sollins and I did was
think visually—like
the composition of a
painting, or a dance.

Eve Moros Ortega:
On a practical level,
Art21 was founded to
make a documentary
series about artists.
My role, when I was
initially hired, was
to figure out how to
make that happen.

The art21 symbol is made up of a circle of straight lines radiating from a center point. There are 16 lines, reflecting the specific structure of the program (four years/four programs, four programs/four segments).

The symbol's open structure projects a feeling of accessibility. The fact that it is made up of many parts reflects the diversity of the program. Its simple yet expressive form communicates exuberance, while its clean, abstract quality maintains the detached objectivity of a serious art institution.

Since art21 will be broadcast both on traditional broadcast television and on high-definition television, some unique demands are placed on how (and where) information can be placed on screen.

The grid at right was developed by combining the safety grids of both formats and dividing the resulting space into units.

Using this grid as a guide, information on screen is always in safety in both formats. The grid will never be visible on screen. It is simply a guide for the placement of other elements.

←
pages from
Open's first *Art21*
presentation book,
6 September 2000

Scott Stowell:
There are two things I'll never forget from that meeting. First, Susan Sollins hated what we presented that day. Second, she noticed—and pointed out—how all the window shades at Open were lined up, exactly halfway closed.

Susan Dowling:
PBS originally hated *Art21*.

Wesley Miller:
We had never made a documentary before our first season on PBS, nor did we know anything about motion graphics or creating an identity for a television show. Everything was possible, including the ability to make myriad and costly mistakes.

Eve Moros Ortega:
Susan Sollins, Susan Dowling, and I were like, *Who's going to design the graphics?* So we interviewed a lot of design firms like 2x4 and Trollbäck.

Scott Stowell:
I don't even know if we had a reel of stuff to show them.

Eve Moros Ortega:
Frankly, all of those firms are very talented. As with any creative decision, I think it was a combination of the aesthetic and the personality of the people you'd be working with. Presentation style matters. Budget matters a hell of a lot, you know? Those are practical considerations. Nonetheless, you have to get along with the people.

Scott Stowell:
For our first presentation, we wanted to treat *Art21* almost like a museum, with an identity that would have a logo. I had latched onto this idea of a logo—which looks just like what's now the MacOS progress icon. It kind of looked like a box of pastels, or a sun. But it was a symbol. A thing.

Eve Moros Ortega:
Rule number one was, *Don't overshadow the art and the artist*. This is not the *Scott Stowell Open Show*. This is the artists' show.

Scott Stowell:
Art21 didn't want a logo and a set of guidelines. They just wanted to know what their show could look like.

Eve Moros Ortega:
How do I have that moment where I can just sit back and look at something that's very beautiful and engaging, but not grabbing the part of my brain that's still processing that last artist I just learned about and is prepping for the next artist I'm about to learn about?

Scott Stowell:
They hated that logo, but they loved the typeface.

Scott Stowell:
I went to school with Tobias—he was two years behind me at RISD.

Tobias Frere-Jones:
At this bar in Providence called Steeple Street, we would meet up and pass bar napkins around, drawing letters. It was really through those sorts of type-nerd nights out that I got to know Scott in the first place.

Scott Stowell:
For projects like this, I would just call him up and be like, *Hey Toby, I'm doing this thing about art. Do you have like some typeface that would be good for that?*

Tobias Frere-Jones:
I had this idea that was spinning around about an approach for the design of letters for especially hostile conditions, like for very, very small sizes.

Scott Stowell:
His sketches were for a typeface to be printed at really small sizes in newspapers, but that's kind of the same principle as the low resolution of pre-HD tv.

Tobias Frere-Jones:
The greatest weakness that a typeface could present while appearing on an NTSC system is having a very thin horizontal feature. Because if it's just one scan line or falls in between two adjacent scan lines it would just be a blurry mess—or it just wouldn't be there at all. And the thinnest horizontal through-out a typeface will likely be the middle of the lowercase e.

Scott Stowell:
It's drawn to be more legible and readable and open and clear.

Tobias Frere-Jones:
I sent a test to Scott and he had someone put it on a VHS tape so I could look at how the letterforms were behaving on my tiny tv. I wanted to look at the most extreme case. I took photographs of the screen to see what was working, what was falling apart, and what changes we needed to make.

Scott Stowell:
It just looks unlike any other typeface.

Tobias Frere-Jones:
I got to crack this puzzle, figuring out the strengths and weaknesses of this particular medium.

Kate Davis Caldwell:
The font appears a bit outdated and some-what '90s to me.

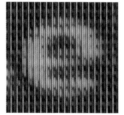

↑
Tobias' faxed draft of what was later called Retina Broadcast, 11 July 2000

←
a Retina e interacting with scan lines on a tv screen

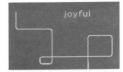

↓
storyboard pages
from the fourth
presentation book,
17 January 2001

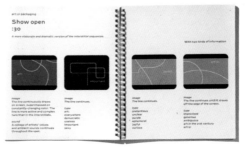

↑
three directions shown
in the second
presentation book,
3 October 2000

↑
three directions shown
in the third
presentation book,
31 October 2000

Scott Stowell:
The format of the show is that there's no narrator. The artists just talk and the narrative comes out of that.

Wesley Miller:
Creating a palate cleanser between the artist segments was our motivation.

Scott Stowell:
We didn't want to do anything that was representational, or looked like art.

Eve Moros Ortega:
How do you make something that is interesting and is beautiful, but doesn't steal the artists' thunder at all? It was a tough assignment.

Scott Stowell:
We decided that we would kind of be metaphorical about it. We had this idea of this 3D, *Tron*-like space of a museum. You would actually go into a room, and the color would change. But then we came to the idea of a line.

Eve Moros Ortega:
Why do lines matter? For one thing, they are foundational to art. The earliest art was lines on cave walls.

Scott Stowell:
The line could reference so many things, from Kandinsky to *Harold and the Purple Crayon*.

Wesley Miller:
I remember thinking Etch a Sketch.

Eve Moros Ortega:
So we went with the direction of just color and line and maybe some words.

Su Barber:
We talked about the interstitials as the sorbet course between segments. That metaphor stuck in my head for the length of the project and still rings true. They were meant to be small, bright, cleansing moments. That goal informed the shape and personality of the drawings.

Mo Caicedo:
It's a very simple concept, but when design is broken down to its simplest forms, it takes on a clarity of communication, which then makes it a thing of beauty.

Eve Moros Ortega:
We spent a lot of time trying to see if the lines could convey the theme of each show. How does a line convey the notion of *place* or *spirituality* or *consumption* or *identity*?

Cat Kirk:
The movement of the line actually has real purpose. If the episode is about, say, *triumph*, the line will have these big, triumphant angles.

→
Su's line drawing
for a "Spirituality"
interstitial,
November 2000

↓
season one
color palette study,
February 2001

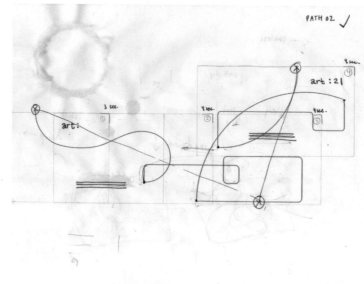

Su Barber:
I'd never done any-
thing quite like it, but
the process was pretty
intuitive. We made a
grid system based on
the 16x9 aspect ratio,
and I made a little
16x9 picture frame
that I'd move over my
drawings to map out
the camera moves.

Scott Stowell:
I was very involved
in the process, but
without Su Barber, it
would not exist. I mean
it's her, this project.

Su Barber:
When we designed
season one we didn't
actually know that
Art21 would become
an ongoing project.

**Scott Stowell
to Eve Moros Ortega:**
1 August 2002
*When you have any
news about season
two, let us know—we're
still very excited about
getting back into
art:21 at some point.*

**Eve Moros Ortega
to Susan Dowling:**
6 August 2002
*FYI, Scott emailed me
the other day to ask
what was happening.
Should we respond
for the moment?*

**Susan Dowling
to Eve Moros Ortega:**
6 August 2002
*If he presses you, I
guess you can say
we are interview-
ing others as well. I
know it is awkward
and I feel sorry but
that is life I'm afraid.*

**Scott Stowell
to Eve Moros Ortega:**
30 August 2002
*Just checking in
to see if you need
anything else from
us. Let me know the
status of things when
you have a chance.*

**Eve Moros Ortega
to Susan Dowling:**
4 September 2002
*At this point, I think
the consensus is to
stay with Scott.*

Su Barber:
Of course we were
pleased when they
asked us back for
season two.

Scott Stowell:
Every year we've
worked on it, things
have gotten looser
and bigger and more
expressive, and it's
still totally consistent.

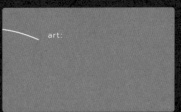

art:

everywhere

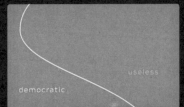

democratic   useless

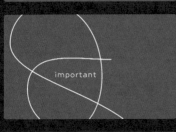

important

sexy

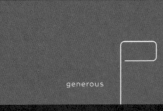

generous

unclear

ephemeral

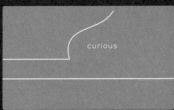

curious

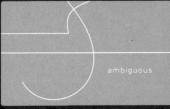

ambiguous

art in the twenty-first century

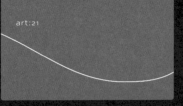

art:21

←
frames from
Art21 season one,
2001

Susan Dowling:
I still think the
season one line is
still a little too, I don't
want to say, *boring*.

Su Barber:
When I go back
and look at season
one now it looks
ridiculously simple.

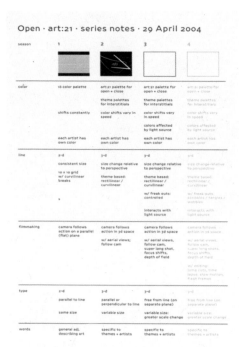

Open · art:21 · series notes · 29 April 2004

season	1	2	3	4
color	16 color palette	art:21 palette for open + close	art:21 palette for open + close	art:21 palette for open + close
		theme palettes for interstitials	theme palettes for interstitials	theme palettes for interstitials
	shifts constantly	color shifts vary in speed	color shifts vary in speed	color shifts vary in speed
			colors affected by light source	colors affected by light source
	each artist has own color	each artist has own color	each artist has own color	each artist has own color
line	2-d	3-d	3-d	3-d
	consistent size	size change relative to perspective	size change relative to perspective	size change relative to perspective
	10 x 10 grid w/ curvilinear breaks	theme based: rectilinear / curvilinear	theme based: rectilinear / curvilinear	theme based: rectilinear / curvilinear
			w/ freak outs: controlled	w/ freak outs: scribbles / tangles / wobbles
			interacts with light source	interacts with light source
filmmaking	camera follows action on a parallel (flat) plane	camera follows action in 3d space	camera follows action in 3d space	camera follows action in 3d space
		w/ aerial views; follow cam	w/ aerial views, follow cam, super long shot, focus shifts, depth of field	w/ aerial views, follow cam, super long shots, focus shifts, depth of field
				w/ editing: jump cuts, time lapse, slow motion, flash frames
type	2-d	3-d	3-d	3-d
	parallel to line	parallel or perpendicular to line	free from line (on separate plane)	free from line, separate plane
	same size	variable size	variable size: greater scale change	variable size: greater scale change
words	general adj. describing art	specific to themes + artists	specific to themes + artists	specific to themes + artists

↑
adjustments to
Open's four-year plan
after season two,
April 2004

Susan Dowling:
Each year, it would
take so much deci-
sion making. Then
to also be thinking
of the years ahead
was quite phenom-
enal, I thought.

Scott Stowell:
The show was going
to be every two years
for eight years. We
saw it as this big opus
project, so we decided
we were going to
make a design system
that would change
over the eight years.

Su Barber:
It was just so fun to
explore the narrative
possibilities of our sys-
tem. What else could
you do with color,
line, and language?

Scott Stowell:
Season one was
super flat, and the
background was a
flat color, and the
graphics were on a
flat surface, and the
type was all one size.

Eve Moros Ortega:
It was a nod to the his-
tory of film. You know,
we make films. And
we evolved with our
technology, how we
were making the films,
and going from tape to
digital, high def. There
were technical chang-
es, and still are, with
each passing season.

Bryan Keeling:
For season two, we
literally went from a
2D to 3D realm. That
was a pretty big jump.

Scott Stowell:
For season three,
there was lighting
and depth of field. So
things would go out of
focus when they were
farther away from or
closer to the camera.

Rich Scurry:
Utilizing things like
depth of field on
design-based graph-
ics really hadn't
been done before.
Borrowing from
much more advanced
techniques used in
feature films, we were
able to bring a style
that was unique.

Scott Stowell:
And then season four
had the idea of edit-
ing. Until that point, all
the graphics were one
Steadicam shot. And
then there were edits.

Mo Caicedo:
The biggest challenge
for me was getting the
camera movement to
work smoothly with
the edits and energy
of the words. I found
that since there was
no visual information
in the background,
editing from one
scene to the next
tended to be jarring.

Su Barber:
The seasons evolved
sort of naturally, devel-
opments in the soft-
ware we were using
allowed drawings
and the space they
inhabited to become
more complex. With
each season we shed
some constraints and
added new elements.

Scott Stowell:
We couldn't have
made season
four when we did
season one.

↓
frames from
Art21 season two,
2003

Christina Milan:
Why is the line so
erratic—straight,
curvy, swirly—is this
meant to personify
haphazard creative
thought? I prefer
straight lines.

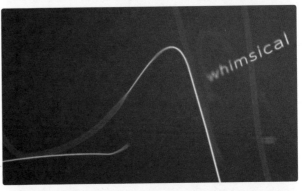

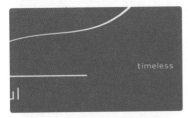

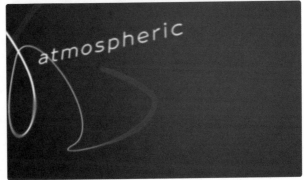

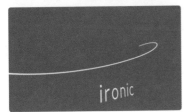

↑
frames from
Art21 season three,
2005

Kate Davis Caldwell:
I thought the graph-
ics were fluid and
subtle, and were not
aggressive or hitting
me over the head with
their message and
design. I am more
receptive to this kind
of communication!

art:

hybrid

ethereal

art:21

↓
word lists and
correspondence,
2001–2003

Scott Stowell:
We brought a layer
of meaning to the
graphics with words.

Susan Dowling:
I didn't like the words.

Jack Watson:
It's a bit like the wall
label text one might
see when entering a
gallery exhibition.

Susan Dowling:
Everyone was very ex-
cited about the words.
Sometimes we would
have pages of words.
It was just endless.

Scott Stowell:
We kept telling Art21
that all the words can't
be positive. Art can't
just be *beautiful* and
ethereal and *inspi-
rational*. It has to be
dumb, too. Because
some art is dumb.
Some art is awesome
and dumb. I mean Jeff
Koons' art is dumb,
but it's still cool art.

Jack Watson:
My students often
pay special attention
to the words. They
always get a chuckle
when something
like *weird* floats by.

Scott Stowell:
Art21 would just go on
and on questioning
the words and then
I'd say, *What about
the animation?* And
they'd say, *Oh. It's
fine*, because they
would just be dis-
tracted by the words.
Which is also a good
reason for designers
to do more writing.

Susan Dowling:
The other thing that was
difficult was the music.
But Peter Foley, the com-
poser, was fantastic.

Peter Foley:
Susan Sollins was ada-
mant that the music
not sound like the
Discovery Channel.
At the time I didn't
even get the Discovery
Channel, so I was safe.

Susan Dowling:
He had to do a lot
of work, fast.

Peter Foley:
We wanted energy,
atmosphere, but not
necessarily melody.
When I saw the
animation, I thought,
*Fantastic! I can just
compose music that
follows the line. The
line will be the theme
and the music will
support its journey
through space and
react to it, rather than
compete with it.*

Susan Dowling:
We didn't believe
in this wall-to-wall
music, which PBS has,
especially with art. It
really has a terrible
impact on the artwork.

Peter Foley:
There's virtually no
underscore now, ex-
cept during Open's
animation. This was
deeply disturbing to
some of the veteran
tv folks working on
the show. A composer
backing the idea of
less music! They
thought we were nuts.

↑
sketches for
Art21 season five,
October 2008

Eve Moros Ortega:
In the early days, *Art21* was meant to end after four seasons. So Open's original idea was a four-season idea. And that is why it was very challenging when in fact, it didn't end. Challenging and wonderful.

Scott Stowell:
Now what do we do? We finished it. You're going to keep going?

Zak Jensen:
So what more could the line actually do? The line could maybe start to have some depth of its own, like the weight of the line would change as it came closer to—or went farther from—the viewer. I got started on sketches on the computer for that, figuring out how the line could become a dimensional form itself, and then just suggesting colors and words that weren't used yet, that could potentially be used.

Scott Stowell:
Their budget was not adequate to do a whole new thing, so for seasons five and six, *Art21* has basically the same graphics as season four, but with some of the colors and type changed. Meanwhile, Art21 kept us busy with other things.

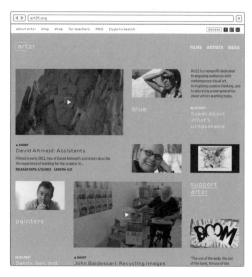

↑
art21.org
redesign concept,
2013

Jason Jude Chan:
We more or less designed their website, but it was never developed.

Jonathan Munar:
Our objectives for the redesign were to encourage exploration of Art21's massive library of video and related content, and to showcase the breadth of that library.

←
Art21 logo,
2011

Ryan Thacker:
They were moving past just the tv show. If you look at the logo, it's like half of a tv proportion rectangle with the name coming out of it.

Eve Moros Ortega:
Scott, Ryan, and Jason did a heroic job proposing wonderful and beautiful designs. We just didn't have the money to do it.

→
The Art21 Collection
DVD box set,.
2012

Christina Milan:
I loved *Art21* so
much I bought the
set as a graduation
gift for myself.

←
100 Artists
campaign,
2013

Cat Kirk:
After six seasons, *Art21*
realized they had fea-
tured 100 artists. Ryan
and Scott designed
these spots, and I
did the animation.

→
Art21 Creative
Chemistries
symposium identity,
2015

Cat Kirk:
We didn't have to
use the line. In the
end it looked really
Rauschenberg-
esque and I hadn't
really thought about
that. Art21 said,
*Oh, it really looks
like Rauschenberg.*
I thought, *Oh, no.
We're going to have
to change everything.*
They said, *The
Rauschenberg
Foundation is one of
our biggest sponsors,
so this is fantastic.*

↑
New York Close Up
web series,
2011–

Ryan Thacker:
New York Close Up
was cool. It wasn't
as slick as *Art21*. It
wasn't slick at all.

Jonathan Munar:
The creators of the
New York Close Up
series wanted to tell
stories about artists
who were in the early
stages of their career.

Ryan Thacker:
It was two of the
younger guys in the
organization's baby.
They were the
ones running it, as
opposed to Eve and
Susan Sollins.

Jonathan Munar:
In a sense, it is almost
a conceptual prequel.

Ryan Thacker:
The graphics are all
about type placed in
the environment in
some way that was
kind of unexpected.

Jonathan Munar:
The series has also
allowed the produc-
ers to experiment
with different styles—
narratives, filming
techniques, editing
approaches—some
of which make their
way into the flagship
broadcast series.
It is a lab of sorts.

Ryan Thacker:
Sometimes they do it
really well and some-
times I'm like, *Well, I
wouldn't have done it
that way, but yeah.*

Jonathan Munar:
The exercise of creat-
ing a sub-brand has
actually helped us bet-
ter define our overall
brand identity. Having
to consider different
use cases for our
identity lent itself to
better understanding
how the Art21 brand
might—and does—
exist. Our visual iden-
tity is the strongest
that it has ever been.

↑
frames from
Art21 season seven,
2014

Uroš Perišić:
We tracked the line into
the environment, show-
casing the art. It was
intercut with graphical,
gradient backgrounds
that were already
kind of established.

Eve Moros Ortega:
The concept in season
seven was this revisit-
ing of the past. I have
to say that I didn't like
it. I'll just say that.

Scott Stowell:
Art21 came to us and
said, *You know, we
want to do something
different, and we want
to change it up a little
bit, so could you come
up with some ideas
of what it might be?*

Eve Moros Ortega:
I think the brief was,
*We want to have it be
different, but we want
people to know that
they're related.* Like
they share blood-
lines or something.

Scott Stowell:
We were trying to
make it economical. To
create less animation
would be cheaper. We
came up with the idea
of using animation
from the six previous
seasons, plus a little
bit of new stuff, and
making this remix. It
worked really well.

Cat Kirk:
We had hours of foot-
age to sift through. For
something that has to
be 30 seconds, there
needs to be some
kind of story, even if
it's a really light one.

Scott Stowell:
So there's flat stuff,
3D stuff, focused
stuff, non-focused
stuff. The line creeps
out of the graphics
over the footage.

Cat Kirk:
Then we wanted the
line to also be even
more abstracted
where it could be a line
that the artist drew
or like a paintbrush
stroke. So the line was
evolving out of being
that little line that
we know and love.

Scott Stowell:
It just looks like
somebody took the
six seasons of ev-
erything we'd done
so far and put it in a
blender, which is basi-
cally what we did.

Uroš Perišić:
It took like two and
a half months.

Jason Jude Chan:
Cat was editing as
fast as she could
and Ollie Perišić was
delivering animation
with our direction, as
quickly as he could.

Cat Kirk:
I remember at some
point Eve emailed a
private message to
Scott. She wanted to
get on the phone and
have a conversation
about everything.
We thought, *Uh oh.
What is this about?*
She felt it still didn't
feel like *Art21.*

Eve Moros Ortega:
I just think it was
not the right
idea, basically.

Cat Kirk:
It came as a surprise
to me because they
had been approving
it the whole time.

Eve Moros Ortega:
It's very hard to find a balance with designers. They're working for you, and yet you're hiring them for their vision. The designer's vision versus the client's vision. The client often kind of has some vision. Sometimes you need that person to say, *You, the client, that idea you have, it's a bad idea. Trust me.* And other times you need to say you feel really strongly about that idea, and you say, *I can make it work.*

Susan Dowling:
Now, PBS realizes that everyone else in the world loves *Art21*.

Nikki Kalcevic:
I love using *Art21* videos in my classroom. It lets students know that artists don't have to be dead to be important!

Wesley Miller:
I hope that Art21 continues to be a home for artists who want to experiment with the documentary form as a vehicle for their art and ideas.

Susan Dowling:
It's become more and more exactly what I wanted. All the graphics are better. We ended up with great editors and great cameramen. Now, it will go to another whole, exciting new life.

Eve Moros Ortega:
Everything I do really honors the spirit of Susan Sollins. I feel humbled by the amount of work before us, but I feel confident that we will pull it off. Because we care and we're paying attention!

Kate Davis Caldwell:
I like the graphics for the show, although I do feel they could use some updating.

Linda Montanaro-Kramer:
When I see the graphics, I think about being in a museum, and it feels like the design district in Miami circa 2010. They are very clean and minimalist.

Susan Dowling:
I'm not as involved with Art21 now. I'm phasing out. My feeling right now is that whatever Eve is going to do is going to be great. But I don't know if they're going to use Open again.

Eve Moros Ortega to Scott Stowell:
30 July 2015
Hope the book is going great. Was that quote about "artists make you think" from me? If not, I wish it had been! I'm going away next week to France for a couple weeks but when I'm back, I'd love to chat with you about yes—season eight!

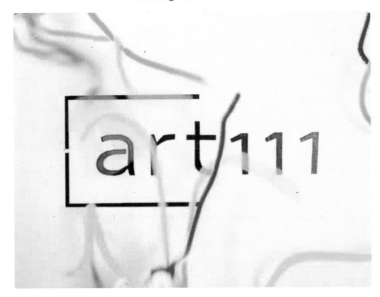

← *Art111* video by Don Ball's 12th-grade visual arts students at Cawthra Park Secondary School, 2014

Don Ball:
Last year, I had a stellar graduating class who had used *Art21*—the videos, the website, the books—extensively during their high school years in our class, room 111. They created a thank you video for me. It starts off with a terrific visual tribute to the *Art21* opening sequence, done lovingly with pipe cleaners and hands that occasionally can be seen in the frame.

Maira Kalman:
I'm an author/
illustrator and
the owner of
Toscanini's pants.

I don't have anything surprising
to tell you. And if I did, I don't
know if you would be pleasantly
surprised. You might say
about something that it is really
an unpleasant surprise. That
actually happens very often.
Even a surprise party is something that is not always enjoyed.
More often than not the birthday person says, *I told you not
to do that, because I hate
surprise parties.*

   In this world of fleeting time,
there are limited opportunities
to be surprised. I would think
that one of the nicest surprises
is to hear that someone likes
you a lot or loves you. Out of the
blue, someone tells you how
much they like you or love you.
And in that surprised glowing
state of benign well being, you
can start to think of other things.

I had been teaching at Yale for just a couple of years when one of my students recommended us for a project: signage for the Yale University Art Gallery—specifically, for a landmark building designed by one of my favorite architects. At the time, the building wasn't looking that great. Part of our job was to help it look like new. We had never worked on a signage project before, so this was also our chance to learn how to do it.

in order
of appearance

Scott Stowell:
Greetings.

Lesley Tucker Zurolo:
I was the director of graphic design for the Gallery.

Patrick Dugan:
I'm a creative director for an ad agency in Avon, Connecticut.

George Feese:
I'm an asset manager at BASF in Florham Park, New Jersey.

Jeffrey Yoshimine:
My title at the Yale University Art Gallery is deputy director for exhibition and collection management.

Anna Hammond:
My job at the Gallery was defined as deputy director for programs and external affairs.

Jena Sher:
I was technically assistant to the head designer at the Gallery.

Rob Di Ieso:
Scott brought me to Open to help out on this. I ended up being there for four years.

Jock Reynolds:
I'm the director of the Gallery.

Eric Cornwell:
My primary work has been as a theatrical lighting designer.

Su Barber:
I worked on this project at Open from the beginning.

Zak Jensen:
I was an Open summer intern. I helped figure out the Yale signage.

David Gibson:
I am the designer of the campus wayfinding system for Yale.

Kate Kittredge:
I was the studio manager at Open, which was also a project manager type of role.

Christopher Sleboda:
I've been the director of graphic design here at the Gallery since 2005.

Leslie Myers:
I was the renovation project manager.

Parvinder Heer:
I am a research assistant in the psychology department at Yale.

Jessica Svendsen:
I am a designer at Apple.

Alberto Noriega:
I'm a security supervisor at the Gallery.

Gary Fogelson:
I drew icons for Yale while I was at Open.

Joel Sanders:
I am the principal of Joel Sanders Architect.

Nicholas Benson:
I am a stone carver and the owner of the John Stevens Shop in Newport, Rhode Island.

Tobias Frere-Jones:
For this project, I was more of a commentator than anything else.

3.

↑
the Kahn building,
August 2004

Scott Stowell:
The building was in
disrepair, so they
had to restore it.

Lesley Tucker Zurolo:
Over time, due to the
need for office and
storage space behind
the Gallery walls, the
large expanses of
exterior window walls
had been covered
up. As a result, the
building lost its soul.

Patrick Dugan:
I had heard about the
Yale University Art
Gallery for years but
never had a chance
to check it out until
my agency decided
to plan a summer field
trip to the museum.

George Feese:
I invited people there
for a birthday party.

Jeffrey Yoshimine:
The museum is a
three-building com-
plex: the signature
1953 Louis Kahn build-
ing, the 1928 Old Yale
Art Gallery, and the
1866 Street Hall.

Anna Hammond:
I started working at
the Yale Art Gallery in
January of 2003, and
the Kahn building was
just being emptied
for the renovation.

Scott Stowell:
The thing is, the
building predated
any modern signage
requirements of any
kind, certainly ADA
and stuff like that.

Anna Hammond:
One of the greatest
graphic design depart-
ments in the world
is across the street
from the Gallery. We
had an intern at the
time, Jena, who was
a student of Scott's.
She recommended
him for the job.

Jena Sher:
Scott is very thought-
ful. Even if someone
came forward with
something that
was just not well-
conceived, he would
always find some ele-
ment in it and make
them go forward and
keep building on it.

Anna Hammond:
When Scott and his
team came in, they
had mined the mu-
seum. He and Su took
pictures, they did
research, they went
into the basement.
There are very cool
things in the building
from the time it was
built, and there was
a kind of reverence
for the handmade.

Upon entering the Gallery you would be greeted with a huge word projected on the elevator banks: LOOK. This is both an invitation to visitors and an introduction of the idea of **projected signage**, which we'd like to use for selected signs throughout the Gallery.

The projections are inspired by the graphic language of travel. A **map** on the stairway column highlights current exhibitions. An **arrow** on the floor leads to the elevators. And one lobby wall would be a giant screen, functioning as both **information center** and virtual exhibition space.

The lobby should be an **inviting, comfortable place** to relax, with simple, modular, contemporary furniture. This kind of friendly space signifies that the Gallery is a place for everyone.

We'd like to offer **reading material** in the lobby, allowing further study of the exhibitions' subjects. Books, magazines and newpapers could be available for browsing, as well as Gallery literature to take home.

The YALE UNIVERSITY ART GALLERY invites people from the world, New Haven and Yale to: LOOK at collections of historic and contemporary objects, EXPLORE what cultural artifacts reveal about their creators, REFLECT on aesthetic and intellectual traditions and UNDERSTAND how people communicate through art.

↑
concept presentation,
5 March 2004

Anna Hammond:
Open made a presentation to me which I thought was great, and then they gave it to the executive group. For the most part, everyone was very taken with the idea. You know, making sure the signage didn't interrupt the building.

Rob Di Ieso:
It was terrifying that it was a Louis Kahn building. *Are they gonna knock a wall down by accident?*

Jock Reynolds:
When we went to renovate the building, it almost looked like a war zone. People had been drilling through the walls for decades. We carefully patched thousands and thousands and thousands of bulk drill holes with matching mortar to bring those walls back. We decided we were never again going to drill into those walls or violate them. We were going to treat the building with respect, give it back its original life, and then not mess it up again.

Eric Cornwell:
The building was as significant as any of the art in its galleries. Signage could not be screwed to the walls, glued to the walls, printed on the walls, or painted on the floor.

Su Barber:
The design strategy we took was to have the lightest touch as possible. The point of contact between the sign and wall had to be as small as possible.

Scott Stowell:
Everything we did had to be reversible, so the building could be restored to its original state if necessary.

Zak Jensen:
I hadn't ever had a design job before.

Rob Di Ieso:
I think I had two years of experience working on environmental graphic design at that point. Scott was relying on me to be the consultant who knows what he's doing. So that was slightly alarming.

Zak Jensen:
I had come from college in Salt Lake City, and I had never even been to New York. So it was completely crazy to me, like, *Alright, I'm here, they're just letting me start working on this stuff.* I did a little bit of materials research, but I had never done anything like that.

David Gibson:
Scott was pretty green about wayfinding design. We had a freewheeling conversation. I think I was fairly open about sharing the steps in the process and I remember he was an eager student.

Zak Jensen:
I had no idea how appropriate what I was suggesting was. You know, *Is this totally stupid? Is this crazy? I don't know, these are the ideas I have. I don't know if I'm going to get fired.*

- WHAT MATERIALS WILL
  THE TRACK AND LETTERS
  BE? WOOD, METAL, PLASTIC?

- WHAT DIFFERENT WALLS
  (MATERIALS) WILL THE
  TRACK NEED TO BE ATTACHED TO?

- HOW WILL THE TRACK ATTACH?

- HOW IS BRAILLE PRINTED,
  WHAT ARE USABLE MATERIALS?

- HOW LARGE IS BRAILLE?

- WHERE WILL A SIGHT IMPAIRED
  VISITOR EXPECT TO FIND BRAILLE
  WHEN APPROACHING A DOOR?

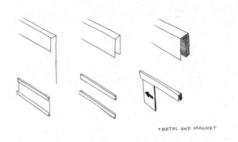

• METAL AND MAGNET

• PROBABLY METAL,
  MAYBE PLASTIC.

• PROBABLY WOOD, ALTHOUGH
  COULD BE PLASTIC OR METAL.

MOUNTING SEEMS LIKE A
QUESTION FOR LATER. I AM
NOT PARTICULARLY FAMILIAR
WITH THE HARDWARE, BUT
THE MORE I THINK ABOUT
IT, THE EASIER IT SEEMS.

CUT-OUT

METAL
HARDWARE

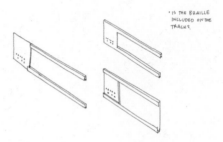

• IS THE BRAILLE
  INCLUDED ON THE
  TRACK?

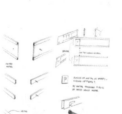

ROOM
41
IS NOW
BEING
USED AS [STORAGE]

ROOM 5 IS [STORAGE]

←↑
Zak's sketches,
July–August 2004

Zak Jensen:
The idea that I came
up with was kind of a
combination of letter
boards and marquees,
like with tiles or some-
thing like that, and
the order rail used in
restaurant kitchens.
Then you could kind
of slide in whatever
kind of signage you
needed, which would
hang underneath the
rail, and it would be
flexible, so that if like,
rooms were chang-
ing, you wouldn't
have anything perma-
nently affixed other
than the hardware
to hold the letters.

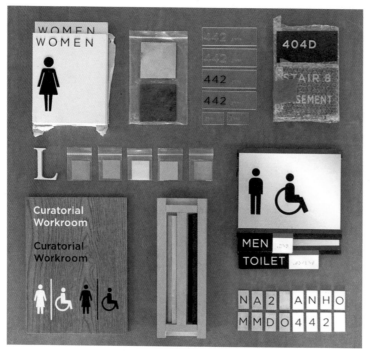

Christopher Sleboda:
I'd work with Open on all the day-to-day stuff and then, a lot of the time, give them the direction. And then once they'd send designs, I'd have to go to the Gallery side of it and present it to like 20 people and then correlate all that feedback.

Leslie Myers:
Decisions were made collectively by the entire curatorial department—more than a dozen individuals—with ancillary departments including exhibit installers, editorial, historians, conservators, and of course, senior leadership.

Rob Di Ieso:
I felt like sometimes Scott and I were like, *What's happening over there?*

Christopher Sleboda:
It was definitely very time consuming. Because we'd have a good design. And then we'd bring it to the bigger group and they'd be like, *Well, what if this? What if that?* So we'd have to constantly be rethinking.

Leslie Myers:
I was less a manager of designers, I was managing the decision makers. Group decision making is unmanageable. No, I take that back, it's outright impossible.

Christopher Sleboda:
If the overall conceptual design had three big phases, it went from more complicated, to sort of middle ground, to the absolute bare minimum.

Parvinder Heer:
Most of the signage always seems to be discreet and in keeping with the ambience of the Gallery. Whilst it isn't obvious and doesn't stand out, when you are looking for something in particular then it is very well signed.

↑
sign mockups
and samples

room sign versions,
August 2004–
December 2005

Kate Kittredge:
We wanted to find a fabricator who would extrude these letters out of metal, so that they could be installed in a museum. I was doing a lot of research on that end, trying to write to a fabricator, and doing a lot of samples of cut metals. To be honest with you, when we started the project, I did not even know what the word extrusion meant. By the end of it, I was the expert.

112

Christopher Sleboda:
Open came up with
this brilliant idea
of projecting the
wayfinding onto the
cinder block walls.

Lesley Tucker Zurolo:
When you stepped
off the elevator,
you knew exactly
where you were.

Eric Cornwell:
It sounded like a
simple solution, but
there was one big
problem: distortion.

Rob Di Ieso:
To make it happen
was, sort of, torture.
We originally went
to this guy that did
robotics for NASA
or something.

Scott Stowell:
He built scale models
of the space in their
office out of plywood.
I remember almost
pulling an all-nighter
in their office, with him
on a ladder, with a pro-
jector. Rob was there
with me and it was
like, *I want to get out of
here, this is ridiculous.*

Rob Di Ieso:
I started doing re-
search and I came
across a lighting con-
sultant for Broadway,
and it just so hap-
pened he was based in
New Haven. He had a
real simple technique
to figure out how you
distort the art so when
the light hits the wall,
the art is right, or true.

Eric Cornwell:
Without revealing
too many secrets, I'll
share that the testing
and tweaking involved
full-sized printouts
of sample signs, a
tape measure, a lad-
der, a digital camera,
a MacBook, Adobe
Illustrator, a box of
clear acetate sheets, a
printer, and scissors.

Christopher Sleboda:
Eric made the slides
for all our projected
signs for years.

Eric Cornwell:
The lights that had been purchased were intended for much less exacting applications, such as creating a soft square of light to feature a painting, or casting a pattern across a floor. They were not precision optical instruments, and we were pushing them beyond their limits. The text looked great from a distance, but up close it was a mess and there was no practical solution within the time and budget constraints. I steeled myself for Scott's trip to New Haven to view the results of many hours of testing and tweaking.

Scott Stowell:
I thought it looked great up close, too.

Eric Cornwell:
In that moment a proverbial lightbulb turned on in my head. The projected signage was not digital voodoo, but a simple synthesis of light, glass, and geometry sitting there for anyone to see. The rainbow artifacts were like an artist's brushstrokes or chisel marks—a natural part of the process that created the illusion.

Scott Stowell:
The way the light looked was just the way the light looked, you know?

Eric Cornwell:
The projections shared a sensibility with the exposed concrete of the honeycomb ceilings and raw cement block walls of the building, combining and arranging simple elements in an honest, obvious way to create something that was both practical and unexpectedly beautiful.

Jessica Svendsen:
Using projection was a brilliant idea. It preserves and illuminates the building's physical materials, but it's also a wonderful reference to Kahn's structured light within the building.

Jeffrey Yoshimine:
The signage was able to both announce itself and to blend into the background.

Alberto Noriega:
The projection on the wall draws the visitor and gives extra attention to the structure of the building, and the kids are eager to know from where or how the sign is placed on the wall.

Christopher Sleboda:
It's not quite apparent when you walk in, how that typography is being placed on a wall. That's really a thing that, even now, people talk about and take pictures of and are really amazed by.

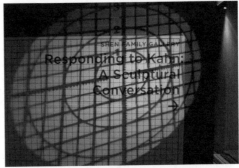

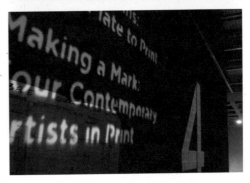

↑
projection tests,
2005–2006

Rob Di Ieso:
We knew we wanted projections in light. We just didn't know how to do it.

Gary Fogelson:
One thing we tried to do was suggest alternative signage for the men's and women's bathrooms. We made a ton of those different versions to try to get some humor into the project. We were drawing pizzas and the old version of the iPod. It's a beautiful space and the architecture is amazing, but I think we spent a lot of time trying to get some funny things to happen.

Anna Hammond:
That was when people started to think Open was a little bit too out there for the project.

↑
icon options,
18 March 2005

→
final icons

↓
icons silkscreened on a restroom door, February 2008

Scott Stowell:
There was a whole other part of the job. We thought we were going to be designing the lobby, too.

Anna Hammond:
We wanted to make the lobby a more lively place for students— a place for convening and thinking.

Scott Stowell:
I remember during one of our presentations, I realized that our drawing was at the wrong scale. We had drawn the lobby at like 200% compared to the chairs. And everyone was like, *Oh, a lot of chairs are going to fit in there.*

Anna Hammond:
It became clear that we really had to do much more— with an architect. That was when we brought in Joel.

Scott Stowell:
We didn't end up doing the lobby.

Joel Sanders:
These discussions evolved into the concept of broadening the scope to create a multipurpose space geared to students as well as visitors to the art museum that could consolidate a variety of functions—information, bookstore, new media, lectures, and events.

Christopher Sleboda:
They transformed the whole front area into a huge lobby with nice seats and couches and little things where you can browse the books that the Gallery published.

Joel Sanders:
I was very excited about the prospect of integrating Open's concept of projected signage into the lobby. This took the form of a translucent screen for the projection of museum information that was a reinterpretation of the modular pogo wall system Kahn had designed for the building.

Alberto Noriega:
Another important sign was the calendar on the first-floor lobby, with the day's event calendar. It helped the most shy visitors, those people who don't like to ask questions or directions.

Joel Sanders:
Unfortunately this award-winning design, which received quite a bit of attention, was dismantled during the second phase renovation in 2011 to make more room for crowds.

→
projected sign showing the daily event calendar, 11 February 2008

Scott Stowell:
The Gallery was already using Gotham as the typeface in its identity. That was no problem until we got to the front entrance sign.

Jock Reynolds:
That signage was really important for us.

Scott Stowell:
The old sign was not good looking. It was gold and it was ugly. I knew about the John Stevens Shop and wanted them to carve a new one.

Nicholas Benson:
I said, "Let's not think of this purely as a piece of signage. Let's think about this a little bit more in terms of a sculptural element."

Scott Stowell:
The thing is, hand-carved lettering is not done with typefaces. It's drawn by hand. We made a layout for the sign using Gotham for inspiration, but Yale sent it directly to Nick, like, *Please make this.*

Nicholas Benson:
The mechanical quality of Gotham was, to me, a little overbearing.

Scott Stowell:
I tried drawing Gotham as a Roman letter, like the Trajan Column had eaten Gotham. I sent it to Tobias, who designed Gotham, to ask, *Are you going to be mad if we do this?*

Tobias Frere-Jones:
I said, "OK, this is a very small needle to thread that you're describing, but sure, I'd go give it a shot, particularly if Nick Benson is going to be involved in this."

Scott Stowell:
Of course, Tobias was fascinated by it.

Tobias Frere-Jones:
I think for most other people I would say, *You know, you should not do that. It's really not going to add up the way you think it's going to.* But Scott had the sensitivity and the invention and the imagination to make these kinds of things work.

Scott Stowell:
I sent it to Nick. Then he went from there. He drew it and it's another step farther away, but the bones of Gotham made it into that.

Nicholas Benson to Scott Stowell:
23 August 2006
Here is where I'm headed. Again, it is an odd combination of styles, but I think it is meeting what we both would like to see. The carved letter will soften the sweep of the strokes, but it is a subtle enough approach to give the inscription the influence of the hand that those samples you sent in the PDF do. Whatdyarekon?

↑ the original entrance sign, circa 1953

Rob Di Ieso:
The inspiration came from the original sign that was there, and I believe there were painted panels underneath the sign. We wanted to replicate that in a way that was more modern and easier to change.

↑ the Port Authority Bus Terminal sign that inspired Gotham

↑ Scott's sketch, 18 August 2006

YALE   YALE

↑ *Yale* set in Gotham Medium

↑ Nicholas' drawing, 23 August 2006

↑ Nicholas' carved sample, August 2006

↑ carving the sign at the John Stevens Shop, November 2006

Tobias Frere-Jones:
What Nick did was, I thought, a good middle ground between these two formal ideas that you would think are nowhere close to overlapping. But we managed to find some tiny spot where they were overlapping, and made this whole inscription out of it.

Nicholas Benson:
I ended up working up a very modernist form, which was meant to go along with Kahn's building. It was very straightforward monoweight sans serif titling cap really. I drew it with the carving entirely in mind.

Rob Di Ieso:
He just did an amazing job.

Nicholas Benson:
For the Gallery, I thought it was important to have some sense of humanity in there.

Tobias Frere-Jones:
Like a chef can take two ingredients that don't really sound like they're supposed to go together but then they show up on the plate and you try it and you realize, *Oh they do actually kind of work with each other.* They have this sympathy for one another that you hadn't noticed before.

Scott Stowell:
We did the same thing by combining the stone with LED.

Gary Fogelson:
Scott was bummed out about the typeface choice that they had for the LED sign. I remember they had this beautiful lettering carved out of stone, and then there was no choice in customizing the typography that was in the ticker sign that was below it.

Scott Stowell:
It looks kind of junky, and it moves too slow. I always thought that that could be a place for artists to do things. They still don't do much with the LED.

↑
the final entrance sign with LED ticker and a detail of the carving, photographed in October 2015

Anna Hammond:
I just remember how the carving came to a point on the inside. It was just this most beautiful thing.

↑
brochure rack with
building map,
February 2008

→
floor number in
the Kahn stairwell,
February 2008

Lesley Tucker Zurolo:
As I recall, Scott told
us a story about asking
our elevator manu-
facturer about setting
type in Gotham and
sensing utter baffle-
ment on the other end
of the line. It was clear
that no one had ever
inquired about this
possibility. A long si-
lence was followed by
something like, *Uh...I
guess it's possible.*
And of course, it was.

Anna Hammond:
I encouraged Open to
take a nontraditional
approach to a very
traditional building.

Lesley Tucker Zurolo:
We needed the new
signage system to
somehow have a quiet
conversation with the
building instead of
screaming loudly and
drowning out its voice.

Kate Kittredge:
Until this project, I
never realized how
much thought would
go into signage, and
how important it is
to people. If it's not
there, you're screwed.
When it is there,
it's meant to be the
thing that's like—you
don't even notice it.

Gary Fogelson:
The level of think-
ing that went into
the Yale project was
something I had
never seen before.

Scott Stowell:
I used to describe
the project as "a col-
laboration with a dead
guy." I really respect
Louis Kahn and I didn't
want to do something
that would piss him
off. Luckily, Yale had
the money to pay for
really nice materials.

Rob Di Ieso:
I was glad when
that job was over
because I was like,
*Wow, I did it. I guess
Scott won't fire me.*

Su Barber:
We had included this grand finale in our first presentation, which was kind of the idea of a highway gas station sign.

Anna Hammond:
The Gallery sits on the edge of the campus but at the center of the city, and we thought about how people would see this place from a distance. So Scott and his team came up with this fabulous neon sign, coming up like a flagpole, that would just say ART.

Kate Kittredge:
For us, it would've been this masterpiece, a beautiful object in the world, that we designed.

Scott Stowell:
In my mind, they had approved it, but they needed to raise extra money to make it, and they couldn't, so it didn't happen.

Jock Reynolds:
It sort of went beyond where we needed or wanted to go.

Christopher Sleboda:
There's a lot of sensitivity towards some of the other cultural arts places on Chapel Street. You know, there's the Yale Center for British Art across the street. There's the Yale Rep theater. There's the architecture school, which has a gallery, and then there's the School of Art, which also has its own gallery space. So I feel like the people at the Gallery don't necessarily want to try to be one-upping any of those other places.

Anna Hammond:
It was just way too much for the staff to handle. There was a financial aspect to it, but there was some feeling the sign was too modern for the encyclopedic collection within the museum.

Gary Fogelson:
It's amazing that it was even on the table for as long as it was.

Scott Stowell:
That idea is still available, if someone has a museum in another city. We can license it.

A
R
T

Emily Pilloton:
I'm a builder, an
architect, a teacher,
a sister, and a daugh-
ter. I founded the
nonprofit Project H
Design to do auda-
cious work with young
people and to give
a creative voice to
the underestimated.

I learned about love and design
watching my grandmother make
jiaozi dumplings. With each
dumpling, each pinch and pleat
in the dough, she brought forth
millennia of ancestors to the
present moment, shaped her
unconditional love for her family
into a bite-sized unit, and taught
me and my sisters the importance of process. "Try it again,"
she would say, if a dumpling
didn't meet her standard.

In my own work as a designer,
I think of the care in her flour-
covered hands often. She taught
me to take pride in my work and
my voice, and to create beauty,
with care and intention, for the
benefit of others.

You've probably never heard of Trio. I hadn't either when they first called us. Trio was a tv network that had started in 1994 in Canada and had just been bought by NBC. They were looking for somebody to do a network redesign—to help figure out what Trio should look and sound like. At that time, we didn't have a lot of experience doing that kind of work. But it turned out that somebody without much experience was just what they were looking for.

4.

in order
of appearance

Lauren Zalaznick:
I was the president of Trio. I got there right at the beginning of 2002.

Linda Ong:
Originally I was brought in to assist in creating the Trio brand.

Jason Klarman:
I was head of marketing, digital, PR.

Chris Wilcha:
I was in between jobs. I was nervously trying to figure out my next move. I found myself lingering here and there around Scott's office. I was around. I would stop by a lot.

Anastasia Rose Hyden:
I'm a graduate student at Hollins University in Roanoke, Virginia.

Tyler Banks:
I'm a language arts teacher for an international school in Ho Chi Minh City.

Scott Stowell:
Hey.

Emily Oberman:
My design studio, Number 17, designed the Trio logo.

Gary David:
I live in Miami, Florida, and work in internet advertising.

Cara Brower:
I was actually an Open intern at the time that Trio was going on.

Tobias Frere-Jones:
Scott asked me to make a customized version of my typeface Gotham for the Trio pitch.

Simone Pillinger:
On Trio, I worked with Open as a producer.

Jane Olson:
I was the creative director for Trio. I was Open's main contact on a daily basis through the process.

Jason Fulford:
I was hired to photograph a list of subjects—basically a scavenger hunt.

Beth Urdang:
I was the music supervisor on this project.

Dave Stoy:
I was the lead animator on this project. This was my first opportunity to lead on a large project like this, which I was both excited and nervous about.

Ryan Thacker:
The Trio project was happening when I was at Open as an intern.

Su Barber:
I was a—very young—designer at Open. I didn't have a specific role on this project, but I did go to meetings when Scott needed a bigger-looking team.

Lauren Zalaznick:
Absolutely no one knew what Trio was going to be, but I did.

Linda Ong:
Trio was not on anybody's radar.

Lauren Zalaznick:
It was, sensibility-wise, what you might think of as part public arts channel—in search of an original voice.

Jason Klarman:
Lauren was ahead of the vision for what Trio was going to be and that vision was a modern celebration of culture. High and low.

Chris Wilcha:
Lauren and her team were doing their best to try to find their voice, to try to high-light and emphasize things that were most conceptual and witty.

Lauren Zalaznick:
When you want to reinvigorate a busi-ness, one doesn't start with the package and figure out what goes inside the box. One starts with the idea of what the busi-ness is going to be.

Jason Klarman:
Right before the re-brand we had a month called Uncensored Month. We had every-thing from *The History of Pornography* to *Last Tango in Paris*. But nobody had really cel-ebrated television the way that Trio did with *Brilliant but Cancelled*.

Anastasia Rose Hyden:
The thing about Trio that stood out for me was *Brilliant but Cancelled*, which showed some of my favorite series in-cluding *EZ Streets*, which is one of the greatest and under seen shows ever.

Jason Klarman:
We also did a month called Flops: The Great Failures. We had Amy Sedaris, Quentin Tarantino, and Joel Stein curating from our library. For Joel, we got *Battle of the Network Stars*. We had *Pink Lady...and Jeff* on. All of this was part of the vision that Lauren had, which was, *How do we find a place to talk about the culture and celebrate it?*

Tyler Banks:
Trio's reruns of *Late Night with David Letterman* were a godsend.

Lauren Zalaznick:
The wrapping on the box was still in line with the old business vision.

Scott Stowell:
When it came time to do the redesign, Trio had a pitch process. Now for me, this was a new thing. The only tv redesign experi-ence I had was the work we had done with Nick at Nite years before, but that was a project that we kind of got by accident.

↑
Trio logos,
1999–2002

Scott Stowell:
We didn't do the logo.

Jason Klarman:
The old Trio logo had sort of like a paintbrush feel.

Lauren Zalaznick:
We had no brand rec-ognition whatsoever.

Jason Klarman:
We straightened it. We put it in a circle. You'll see various iterations of it, but the real leap forward was with the rede-sign by Number 17.

Emily Oberman:
The idea was excite-ment and a spotlight.

Jason Klarman:
They came back with the circle with the upside-down exclamation point as the *i*. Again, turning culture on its head.

Emily Oberman:
If you look around, there are a lot of logos that have the letter *i* used as an exclamation point. But I don't mind a cliché if it works. I mean, clichés are clichés for a reason.

Gary David:
The logo looked dif-ferent from other networks. When I look back on it now, it appears to be ahead of its time.

→
Scott's notes,
December 2002

Scott Stowell:
I got the first call about
the Trio pitch while
I was in Germany on
a business trip. We
were doing a website
redesign for an auto
parts company. Let's
just say that project
won't be in this book.

TRIO NETWORK REDESIGN:

Pitching: OPEN
PSYOP
DIGITAL KITCHEN
CLICK 3X
SPONTANEOUS
GENERAL + SPECIFIC
IN-HOUSE

Why open?
Trio wants to be a maverick
High/Low
Mainstream redefined
complicity w/audience "wink"
pop culture
MTV 20 places
pitch $7500 (present week of Jan 13)
budget $300K (deliver end of March)

Ideas:
tv is only part of life
viewers are selective
network as curator
boutique, not supermarket
not everyone likes everything
viewers like that they are in the minority
I HATE TV and I LOVE TV
searching = selective
(sifting content, not watching uncritically)

Attributes:
enthusiastic
optimistic
critical/"meta"

Tone:
friendly, not bombastic
modest, not over-reaching
NOT IRONIC

VO:
- always talk about making
and marketing of shows,
not plot
- first person plural ("we")
viewers = part of a club

Tagline:
"Get it."
taglines: three words
(imbues name with meaning
but not in a rigid way)
"you, yourself and us"
"big, loud and funny"
"silly, stupid and smart"
contest for submissions?

Linda Ong:
I remember that
Lauren gave me a man-
date, which I thank her
for to this day. When
we started the project,
she said, "We don't
want to work with any
of the usual suspects.
I want us to discover
somebody and work
with somebody that
we can elevate just
the way we're cel-
ebrating the elevation
of television in pop
culture." Sometimes
when clients say that,
they don't mean it.

Lauren Zalaznick:
I think at the time, the
risk with Open was
that they were known
as a print company.

Scott Stowell:
Apparently they had
seen our Art21 work
and some other stuff.

Linda Ong:
While I didn't have
any problems with
the usual suspects,
the idea of going to
discover new ones
was both thrilling
and daunting.

Scott Stowell:
I didn't really know
how this kind of pitch
worked. They'll iden-
tify three, sometimes
five, 10, 15 studios, and
you get paid a little
bit to come up with
ideas to try to win the
job. It's not free work.

Linda Ong:
Someone referred me
to Scott and I can't
remember if I just
looked at the work or
I met with him first. But
I'd long had an affinity
for M&Co., so his
background spoke to
me immediately. I
think, unlike a lot of
the motion designers,
he really started with
concept first.

Lauren Zalaznick:
I did have that worry,
just over the list of
deliverables. I don't
think they had done
an on-air package.

Jason Klarman:
Maybe they had. I
don't think they had.

Lauren Zalaznick:
They had to learn liter-
ally that the network
logo in the lower
right is what's called
the bug. They had
to learn what lower
thirds have to do.
They had to learn the
difference between
a doughnut promo
and a topical promo.

Jason Klarman:
We certainly didn't
hire them because
they had such great
expertise in television.

Scott Stowell:
We were 100% the
dark horse. Like, never
going to win this job.
I thought, This is a
bet that we have to
win, so I'm just going
to bet everything.

↑
a scan of a copy
of a *New York Times
Magazine* article
about *meta*,
17 November 2002

↓ →
Scott's early notes
and sketches from
meetings with Chris,
January 2003

Scott Stowell:
You want to make
yourself different,
which is probably one
of the reasons we
doubled down on all
the conceptual stuff.
The other studios
pitching were more
visually fancy. We
could never compete
with them.

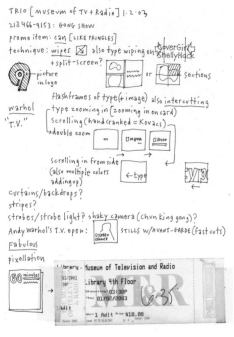

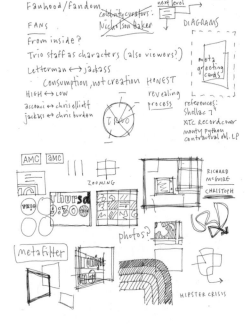

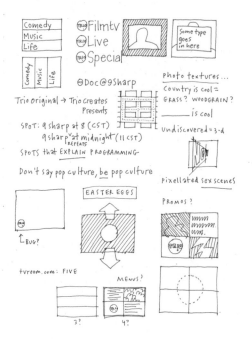

Cara Brower:
It was just a really small group of people working on the pitch. It might have only been me, Scott, and Chris.

Chris Wilcha:
I just camped out at the studio. We were lobbing ideas back and forth all day long. We kept trying to one-up each other.

Scott Stowell:
The iPod was a year old. And DVRs and these community things like MetaFilter were happening. It was this moment of mashups in music and stuff bumping up against each other. The tools of curation were being democratized.

Chris Wilcha:
You could take pop culture seriously. You could approach it with a conceptual appreciation, and you could also just love it and enjoy it.

Scott Stowell:
So the idea of a tv network as a curator—or even just the idea of curation or selection—seemed really interesting.

Chris Wilcha:
Also, the obsession of the network at that time was pop-culture minutia.

Scott Stowell:
There was no such thing as YouTube, so Chris and I would go to the Museum of Television and Radio and ask them to load up the VHS tapes of *Pink Lady...and Jeff*. We watched *Laugh-In*, old Letterman, and stuff like that. *The Ernie Kovacs Show*, *Monty Python*—stuff that acknowledged that *I'm in a box called your tv.*

Chris Wilcha:
Words and ideas and commenting on things became this engine that drove everything.

Scott Stowell:
It was this moment of meta in the culture. *Adaptation* came out then. Dave Eggers became a big deal then. Things about themselves.

Chris Wilcha:
Self-deprecating, too. Things that could make fun of themselves.

Scott Stowell:
We were just like, *We have to spend all this time on this. They're not paying us enough so the only way to make this work is to win the job. So we're going to win the job.*

Cara Brower:
I remember going in early every day and then leaving to go home no earlier than 11. It must have been one or two in the morning some nights.

Late Night with David Letterman

Sessions at West 54th

MediaTV

The Secret Life of Us

Leonard Bernstein's Young People's Concerts

TV Out of the Box

The Score

Rowan & Martin's Laugh-In

TV's Most Censored Moments

The Perfect Pitch

Face Time with Kurt Andersen

Brilliant but Cancelled

↑
Trio shows set in Trio Gotham, a custom typeface made for the pitch

Scott Stowell:
Number 17's Trio logo had a dot. A round dot. If you look at Gotham, all the dots and punctuation are square.

Linda Ong:
Scott was the first designer I ever saw use Gotham. It wasn't the new Helvetica then.

Tobias Frere-Jones:
Scott called up and asked if it would be possible to get a version where all of those dot-like things are changed from squares to circles.

Scott Stowell:
And that became Trio Gotham.

Tobias Frere-Jones:
There are so many people who want a custom thing simply because they would like some custom thing, and there's no problem to solve. They just like the idea of having a custom typeface. When I saw the Trio identity, which comes back to this circular form over and over again, it was obvious why Scott wanted this sort of micro detail of the shape of the period or the shape of the dot over the *i* to reflect the theme of circles.

↓
Trio pitch book
version one,
14 January 2003

Simone Pillinger:
It was a big, beautiful
book—so smart, so
well prepared. It was
very enjoyable to
pitch it. Everybody
in the room was ask-
ing great questions.

This book is full
of ideas that
Open came
up with for **Trio**.
We hope you
like them.

Scott Stowell:
For years, I had been
inspired by Paul Rand,
who would do these
presentation books.
Part of the reason
for doing a book is
that you don't know
if the people who
are really making the
decision are sitting in
the room with you.

Chris Wilcha:
There was a panicked
sprint to print them
and cut them and it
was all hands on deck.
Then there was that
nervous question of
cab versus subway,
like, *Subway could get
us there in like nine
minutes,* but you kind
of have that cab mo-
ment where you're
thinking, *Do we cab it?*
We took the subway.

Scott Stowell:
We had one hour
in a conference
room at 30 Rock.

Jane Olson:
It was probably at 75
Rock, which is the
building that has the
Atlas in front of it.

Chris Wilcha:
The room decor was
pretty grim. You got
the feeling that Trio
was scrappy and
trying to prove itself.

Scott Stowell:
The books all went
into these cute sealed
envelopes that said
each person's name,
which I just wrote
with a Sharpie, so
everybody felt like,
Oh, this is mine.

Jason Klarman:
Everybody else had
come in with, I don't
know, slide presenta-
tions, and video, and
PowerPoint, or whatev-
er. Scott came in with
a book. A little wire-
bound book that liter-
ally introduces itself. At
the end, it says good-
bye and thank you.

Chris Wilcha:
Scott was so thor-
ough in his presenta-
tion. It was carried
through every part
of the process.

Jason Klarman:
I still have that
book somewhere.
It's still good.

 sights,
sounds,
tv.

 art,
design,
tv.

 heart,
soul,
tv.

 fact,
fiction,
tv.

 comedy,
drama,
tv.

 obsession,
compulsion,
tv.

 actions,
words,
tv.

 dance,
theater,
tv.

 agony,
defeat,
tv.

 rock,
roll,
tv.

 heroes,
villains,
tv.

 stars,
co-stars,
tv.

 old school,
new school,
tv.

 setbacks,
triumphs,
tv.

 best boy,
key grip,
tv.

 songs,
stories,
tv.

 war,
peace,
tv.

 **pop,
culture,
tv.**

 artists,
models,
tv.

 reading,
writing,
tv.

 audio,
video,
tv.

 lights,
camera,
tv.

 irony,
sarcasm,
tv.

 vhs,
dvd,
tv.

 gossip,
scandal,
tv.

 coffee,
donuts,
tv.

 cable,
satellite,
tv.

Lauren Zalaznick:
Other companies were very, very snooty about having to inherit a logo.

Emily Oberman:
Sometimes you have to do something great with a logo you don't like and sometimes you have to design a logo and then someone else does something you don't like with it.

Lauren Zalaznick:
I remember Scott and team being much less ego driven about the logo part of the process and willing to say, *I understand you're giving me this object and I'm going to design around it and I don't feel limited by that.*

Emily Oberman:
I knew that Scott and his team at Open would do right by the logo and they did.

Scott Stowell:
In the briefing meeting I was like, *Trio, that's a catchy name. What does that mean? Three what?*

Jane Olson:
I believe there was a trio of content. I'm not exactly sure, but I believe that it was music, art, and journalism, or something like that.

Scott Stowell:
There were maybe 10 people in the meeting. They all looked at us with blank looks, like, *What do you mean, "What does it mean?"* That was part of the inspiration for us even thinking this way.

Chris Wilcha:
I remember one big breakthrough was the idea that a logo and its tagline could constantly change and accommodate anything it needed to do.

Scott Stowell:
We wanted to talk in this friendly and enthusiastic way about the idea of curation. So we had this idea that Trio would always have these three nouns stacked up against it. It was always three things, to validate the name. And the third thing was always *tv.*

Jason Klarman:
Nobody knows what Trio is if you don't put *tv* on it. They're going to think it's dessert topping or a floor wax. You just have to say it's *tv.*

Chris Wilcha:
It could be *pop, culture, tv,* or it could also be *no shirt, no shoes, tv.*

Scott Stowell:
In the entire time that we worked for Trio, we never repeated a tagline.

↑
design development, April 2003

Linda Ong:
One of Lauren's ways is to play through every valuable option. She had us go through probably hundreds of iterations of commas, semicolons, colons, periods, different weights, different fonts, different arrangements.

Lauren Zalaznick:
We must have gone 90 rounds on comma comma period.

Linda Ong:
It was great that Scott and team didn't push back. And they embraced it, too.

Scott Stowell:
I taught for a week in Philadelphia right around that time. Trio wanted a period after *tv* and I was like, *No! It's not a sentence!* I spent three all-nighters, after teaching all day, making presentations to rationalize why there shouldn't be a period. I remember walking down the street talking to my girlfriend on my cellphone, saying, "I have to quit! This is an outrage!" Of course in the end it's got a period on it. Who cares? It's fine.

↓
pitch book
intro spreads,
14 January 2003

Scott Stowell:
We started the pitch with a few basic ideas, and then showed a kind of kit of parts. I think this might have been the first time we did this, but now we always do it.

Chris Wilcha:
There's a certain percentage of bluffing and making promises that you don't know you can necessarily keep, but I remember being proud that we had a couple of really solid, anchoring ideas. I felt like we had done something that had coherence and clarity.

Scott Stowell:
We had this whole section in the back of the book saying, *No really, we can do this job. We have people who know what they're doing. Here are their bios.* And I remember Lauren being like, *If you get it we're sure you'll figure it out. You don't have to say this.* It was almost a little embarrassing.

Jane Olson:
I know all the groups presented a lot of interesting work, but I think Open's was the most—it was just very fresh.

Lauren Zalaznick:
I agonized over the decision because it feels like you're leaving great work and great people behind. I really liked some of the work from some of the other companies.

Scott Stowell:
To this day I remember the Trio pitch as the most intense, perfect meeting ever. It was like Don Draper before Don Draper ever existed, like, *This is this moment and I'm in it.*

Lauren Zalaznick:
It's never a perfect pitch, as much as any graphic design group wants it to be.

Jason Klarman:
Open was my favorite from the get-go. I thought they had absolutely nailed it.

Lauren Zalaznick:
Its beauty was its two-dimensionality. It wasn't asteroids being blown through space, and amazing explosions in 3D. It was an accessible, consumer-friendly, bold, clean idea.

Linda Ong:
We had some other folks in the process who did really admirable jobs, but I think in the end Scott's team came back with a concept, not just an execution. They came up with a clever concept that could be executed in a million ways, rather than a clever execution that had a limited shelf-life. It was a very flexible idea and system, which I think really appealed to Jason and Jane because they saw that from a marketing perspective.

Trio is smart

Trio is complex

Trio is meta

← rerun, language, and violence disclaimers, June 2003

Scott Stowell:
We wanted to just say what everything was. *This is a rerun.* Or, *FYI: This show has nudity in it.* Then we hired Jason Fulford to shoot photos that were kind of puns.

Jason Fulford:
Things were shot in their natural locations with available light. Digital cameras were a lot cruder at that point. I was using a point-and-shoot that Olympus had given me to experiment with.

Scott Stowell:
One of the things we thought about was that the tv screen you were looking at was like the interface of the channel. So we thought Trio was like the friendly computer. The voice of it was your friend, but it was almost like this assistant—your buddy the computer telling you about all these shows.

Chris Wilcha:
I think we were trying to find that voice and clean it up and make it a conceptual little commentary engine.

Jason Klarman:
Everybody overuses the word brand now and they think if you pick a color and use it all the time, that's a brand, but it isn't. When Scott talks about voice, it's really a brand. The voice is the brand. The brand is the voice. The voice is the essence of it. It's the soul of it. It's the thing that people need to connect to.

Beth Urdang:
It was important to us that the music had references within it. We didn't use a ton of—or any—samples *per se*, but there was a feeling of sampling. Most of all, it sounded fun.

Anastasia Rose Hyden:
I found Trio's tone to be arty and smart without being snobbish.

Scott Stowell:
Our point to Trio was, *Can we do something that thinks people are smart?* We wanted it to feel like the voice of the network was your friend and it'd be like, *Hey, this is a movie. We think it's pretty good.* Not like, *This is the special event of the century.*

Gary David:
I would describe the tone as one that is fun, genuine, and informative. Kind of like a very good upper-level college course.

Chris Wilcha:
In a way, the whole aesthetic and logic of the design was going to pull all that together, sharpen it.

Scott Stowell:
The idea that we are a tv network and we're talking about the fact that we are a tv network was this know-ingness that nobody else did. Everyone else was this big 3D glass, metal type flying around that said *Movie of the Week*. We didn't know how to make big 3D stuff flying around. But we knew how to write and use flat colors and make jokes.

A **TRIO** Presentation

triotv.com

Sessions

TRIC ads, programs, tv.

triotv.com

TRIC

A **TRIO** Original Production

TRIC

Classic Dav

RIC

TRIC fans, fanatics, tv.

A **TRIO** Live Presentat

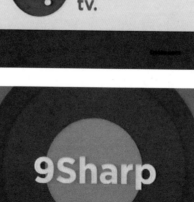

9Sharp

TRIC

Linda Ong:
The extreme nature of the deadline and working with Open for the first time, and working with a team that hadn't done a full-on on-air package, was part of the other challenge of discovering someone: that they don't have the full experience. We knew that. We knew that what Scott made up for in his intellect and his talent was going to far surpass the pain and suffering we'd have to go through on the production end.

Dave Stoy:
Previously I would go into a place and they would know what was going on and if I had questions, they would know how to answer them. Sometimes Scott or others there would be like, *Uh, we're going to have to figure that one out.*

Ryan Thacker:
I was there until like 10 at night every night just watching like, *Whoa, I've never seen anyone do motion graphics or anything related to tv before.*

Su Barber:
I learned how small type can be if you want it to be legible on a crappy old tv.

Scott Stowell:
We were inspired by all kinds of old graphics and stuff, but we also didn't want it to be retro. I just love big, fat, chunky, sans serif type with bright colors.

Su Barber:
It was a great challenge for Scott to translate the rigor and precision of his print-based knowledge into a time-based medium. And the resulting tension between that rigid system and the spontaneity and play of the motion was incredibly fresh and a joy to watch.

Simone Pillinger:
I think the reality of articulating a still design into a moving design was a frustrating process sometimes.

Dave Stoy:
I generally will slap on too much motion and effects and all that to see how far I can push it and then I start whittling it away and get to a medium, happy spot. Scott is definitely one who likes minimal design, little effects, just focus on the elements that are there. That was something I learned a lot, too, just to restrain myself and let the elements speak for themselves.

Simone Pillinger:
Motion is loved in the world of motion, if you know what I mean.

↑
search-based menus, July 2003

Chris Wilcha:
Searching was also new—the novelty of searching in search engines and sifting through all this information and texture and culture.

Scott Stowell:
Our idea was that if you could list the shows on tonight, why not list shows based on a keyword search? It was a way to let people know what was on, no matter what time it was on.

Scott Stowell:
We got to make a
tv network. It was
the channel I would
want. It still is. I still
think about it.

Jane Olson:
At the time, cable
channels tended to be
pretty easily defined.
*You are a movie chan-
nel. You are a channel
for women.* Trio was
really trying to do
something different.

Tyler Banks:
Trio seemed to rec-
ognize that even the
most disposable piece
of entertainment had
the ability to reach,
connect with, and
influence its viewer,
transforming it into
legit, capital C Culture.

Scott Stowell:
They would show
like weird Japanese
game shows, and then
like some show with
Susan Sontag. People
watch tv like that all
the time now. I literally
go home and watch a
Hell's Kitchen and then
Mr. Robot. Who cares
about a channel now?
Every channel shows
everything now. Every
channel has a few real-
ity shows, a couple
of original dramas, a
bunch of old movies.

Jason Klarman:
Everything is so the
same. Everything
is so the same. I'm
so bored. Oh my
God! Everything
is so the same.

Scott Stowell:
The meta idea was
the crux of Trio. It's
language; it's selec-
tion; it's voice; it's
writing. If they had
said, *We love all this
but we don't like that
idea,* our whole system
would've fallen apart.
It would've just been a
font and some colors.

Jason Klarman:
I loved Trio. We put
a lot of energy and
passion into what
we thought was a
stellar product.

Lauren Zalaznick:
Trio was a digital
idea before its time.
I think that there was
a movement that it
anticipated towards
Google-like simplic-
ity in typography
and color. We were a
television-first com-
pany. But Trio was a
UX/UI-first design be-
fore those terms could
really be applied.

Chris Wilcha:
When you're doing
something that is so
you and you know it,
it's a beautiful thing
to behold. Trio was
the logical conclusion
of everything Scott
had been doing up
to that point. It was a
perfect summary of
a lot of his instincts,
a lot of his aesthetic,
and his experience.
But Bravo was the mo-
ment where his busi-
ness was born. It was
a messy, painful birth.

Thanks for coming to Open's **TRIO redesign party** on October 15, 2003 · www.notclosed.com

↑
Trio redesign
launch party at
Good World Bar
and Grill,
15 October 2003
(top: Dave Stoy and
Tobias Frere-Jones,
Simone Pillinger; bot-
tom: Jason Klarman,
Beth Urdang)

↑
launch party name tag

Ryan Thacker:
I went to the party
and that was really
fun. I can remember
talking to Tobias and
these legends in our
world and being drunk
enough to think that
they would care about
what I had to say.

↓
technical difficulties
disclaimer,
November 2003

Scott Stowell:
Trio stayed on the air
until the beginning
of 2006, when it got
replaced by a network
called Sleuth. That
whole time, this thing
never aired once.

triotv.com

pop,
culture,
tv.
TRIO

We're sorry, but there seems to be a problem.

Chip Wass:
I draw pictures,
design characters,
write stories,
and stay up late.

Why the long face? Work feeling
dull, lifeless? Maybe what's
missing is your sense of humor.
Play is crucial to creativity.
Humor is not a luxury.

A good joke is often a
problem resolved in a new way—
as is good design. And like joke-
telling, where the biggest laugh
sometimes springs from a
raised eyebrow instead of a spit
take, the most effective formal
wit is often subtle: a pattern
disrupted, a clever juxtaposition,
an image upside down.

The playful detail makes plain
its creation was not a chore.
Behold: fun was had! And if that
doesn't work for you, we could
still get a drink, tell some jokes.
So this horse walks into a bar...

Coming up with ideas is easy.
Getting people to understand
and approve and then help
make them is hard. When we
got the chance to do redesign
of the Bravo tv network, it was a
lot like our Trio project. We were
supposed to design almost
everything on Bravo that wasn't
a show or a commercial (and we
got to do the logo, too). But this
time there was a lot more work,
a lot more money, a lot less
time—and a lot more at stake.

5.

in order
of appearance

Chris Wilcha:
I was hovering. I was
an ambient presence.

Linda Ong:
I was the brand strate-
gist and sort of the
creative consultant
on the relaunch.

Jason Klarman:
I was Bravo's head of
marketing and digital.

Scott Stowell:
Well, this was quite
an experience.

Jane Olson:
I was the creative
director of Bravo.

Rob Di Ieso:
I was an all-around
designer at Open.

Lauren Zalaznick:
I was the president
of Bravo and thus the
leader of the business
as well as the brand.

William Morrisey:
Su Barber and I were
co-leading aspects of
this project at Open.

Gary Fogelson:
I started at Open as a
freelancer on Bravo.

Simone Pillinger:
I was Bravo's producer.

Su Barber:
This was my first
experience as an
art director.

Frankie Salati:
I'm an assistant
in a hair salon.

Tobias Frere-Jones:
Open hired me to
draw the word Bravo.

Corinne Vizzacchero:
I was at Open, help-
ing build Bravo's new
identity. We were gen-
erating lots of stuff.

Rob Carmichael:
Open was knee-deep in
work. I got a call asking
if I was available to help.

Chip Wass:
I was a sounding board
for ideas and I made
some drawings.

Beth Urdang:
Just like on Trio, my role
was music supervisor.

Christoph Niemann:
I got a list of adjectives
and had to draw them.

Jesse Crawford:
I am a corporate visual
merchandising man-
ager residing in the
suburbs of Manhattan.

Chappell Ellison:
I'm a design writer and
editor in New York City.

Dave Tecson:
My company, Edgeworx,
provided design execu-
tion, much like how a
contractor builds what
an architect designs.

Chris Kairalla:
I was animating
at Edgeworx.

Kate Kittredge:
At Open, I was like
a project manager.

Greg Hahn:
I'm the owner of Gretel,
a creative studio.

Amy Troiano:
I'm senior vice president
of creative and brand
strategy for Bravo.

← Bravo, circa 2004

→ Scott's notes for Open's first Bravo presentation, October 2004

Chris Wilcha:
It was all fun and games with Trio, but with Bravo, the stakes got higher and the tension ratcheted up.

Linda Ong:
The biggest challenge was to not just repeat ourselves. We were so proud of Trio and I think we all wanted to surprise ourselves and that was the hardest part. I think we did it, but it was hard.

Jason Klarman:
Well, NBC bought Universal Cable so they got USA, SciFi, Trio, and NWI—which became Current and is now Al Jazeera America.

Scott Stowell:
NBC had bought Bravo first, so they ended up with two weird little arts networks. Trio was in 20 million households and Bravo was in 80 million households. Trio, I remember to this day, was channel 102, and I think Bravo was like 17 or something. It was really low down on the dial, which is probably not as important now, but at the time it was huge.

Jane Olson:
Lauren had become president of Bravo and she brought a bunch of Trio people over.

Scott Stowell:
They said, *Yeah, so we thought we might do a pitch or we might just hire you guys to do it without a pitch.* And I was like, "I'd go for Plan B, maybe."

Rob Di Ieso:
Open got the Bravo job and basically shit hit the fan.

Linda Ong:
We had to get the relaunch of Bravo on the air in three months. I think we almost killed a couple people in the process.

Rob Di Ieso:
Scott used every resource we had on that job.

Scott Stowell to Chris Wilcha:
16 September 2004 *Trio just called. They want to do a redesign of Bravo and they want Open to do it. No pitch. They're handing it straight to us. It will be confirmed next week but it looks like it's going to happen. Are you on board Mr. Creative Consultant?*

Chris Wilcha:
There was a sense of, *We did it once and they want us to do it again. Holy shit!* It went from playful to stressful.

Scott Stowell:
Thinking about it now, we would have been better off doing a pitch.

↑
frames from
the first Bravo
presentation,
21 October 2004

Scott Stowell:
We had three direc-
tions: *Bravo is about
buzz* was all enthusi-
astic, *Bravo is a point
of view* used the idea
of a magazine as a
metaphor, and *Bravo
is an experience* was
more decorative.

Linda Ong:
Bravo had been
launched in 1980
as—and sort of re-
mained—a very polite,
as I called it, arts and
entertainment net-
work, where you could
see opera, and ballet,
and *Cirque du Soleil*,
and James Lipton.

Lauren Zalaznick:
Bravo was bought by
NBC and then just a
year or so later, this
gigantic acquisition of
Universal happened.
Bravo barely had a
chance to get on its
feet. Except that they
had one huge show,
called *Queer Eye for
the Straight Guy*. At
the time, *Queer Eye*
was on everyone's
list. Bravo wasn't a
big cable network
but it was getting a
tremendous amount
of ink from this show.

Jason Klarman:
Lauren kept saying to
me, "I don't want us
to be the *Queer Eye*
network," because
that's what people
were starting to call
Bravo and we needed
to be something else.

Linda Ong:
With Trio it was differ-
ent. We knew what the
programming was. We
could say it was pop,
we could say it was
culture, we could say it
was tv. With Bravo we
had no idea what they
were going to develop
at that early stage.

Lauren Zalaznick:
Open was still really,
really small and you
really do get this fear
that a big company is
going to "call it in." I
needed bespoke at-
tention on this very
fragile brand that had
one huge hit that was
about to be, if it wasn't
already, defined by
that one hit. I needed
design work that could
take it into the next
decade. And it did.

Jason Klarman:
We said, "Give us three
ideas," versus hiring
three companies that
each give us an idea.

Scott Stowell:
Before we were sup-
posed to present to
Lauren, we showed
Jane, Jason, and Linda
the three directions.
I said, *How about we
take the logo from this
one and the structure
from this one and
this part of this one
and just make one
thing and show that
to Lauren?* And they
were like, *No. You have
to show three differ-
ent things. Keep it the
way it is.* And when we
presented to her the
very next day, I'm not
making this up. She lit-
erally said, *I think this
logo is really good and
the structure of this
one is good and this
aspect is really good.
Do you guys think it's
possible to put these
three things together?*
And I was like, *I guess!*

William Morrisey:
The notion of Bravo being a magazine was what moved forward. We used certain parts of the other two directions to bolster it.

Scott Stowell:
Project Runway was going to launch with our Bravo redesign. *Top Chef* I think was soon after. Then there was *Celebrity Poker Showdown*, which was hosted by Dave Foley from *The Kids in the Hall*. It was this total hodgepodge. What is the thing that ties this all together? Eventually we got to magazines because basically, a magazine is full of all kinds of weird stuff.

Jason Klarman:
It's about the voice, and it's the pictures, and it's a magazine, and the promos had headlines. It was so smart.

Scott Stowell:
We took all the elements of a magazine— the slug, the caption, the photo, the illustration, the folios, the everything—and just exploded them into this animated world.

William Morrisey:
I think that a lot of the great work that Open had done prior to this, with Trio, had to do with rethinking things at an editorial level so that there's a lot of content imbued in the entire piece.

Scott Stowell:
The headlines were written the way you would for a magazine, stupid puns and all. But we weren't making a magazine. We were making a thing about being a magazine.

Gary Fogelson:
When you have an idea that's that strong, it becomes like a puzzle you're solving. It made it really easy as a designer to do that because you could tell if something was right or wrong. Like if it didn't fit that concept but it looked cool, that wasn't enough. It had to actually relate to this idea.

Scott Stowell:
The client's eyes would kind of glaze over when we talked about the magazine too much, but for us, that was our way of making stuff.

Simone Pillinger:
The redesign completely reframed the way you looked at all the stuff that had aired.

Linda Ong:
I think the design, and the library of imagery, ideas, and words that Open put together enabled us to have a very flexible system that could encompass all these different things that were changing and evolving as the content did. And yet, still say something, right?

↑
a (fictional) page of Bravo as a magazine, made to show the design concept

→
magazine sections versus Bravo on-air content

Scott Stowell:
The idea for the work, like, *It's a magazine, and it's exploded and it's a word balloon and it has drawings and photos and whatever,* that was all developed by Chris and me in a day. The rest of the project was people running around not knowing what the hell was going on.

Actin
Impu
=

Scott Stowell:
The colors, whenever they would overlap, would mix together. So if you had yellow on top of black, the yellow would disappear. If you had blue on top of red, it would make purple. That reveals layers, that reveals process, and that can make elements that are super simple turn into something more complicated, just automatically. It would force the design to look a certain way. So enforcing that rule ended up kind of dictating what the whole network would look like.

ard

ears and 100
es **Lipton** has
some of the
ors.

Scott Stowell:
Bravo in Canada is
a separate network.
Their logo was the
name Bravo with an
exclamation point. So
I was like, *Then ours
has to be a word bal-
loon.* Obviously there's
a million logos that
have word balloons
already, but Bravo
could own it, because
Bravo is a word that
you say. It's not like
ESPN or something.

Rob Di Ieso:
We had an idea for
the logo, which was
a speech bubble that
just had *Bravo* in it.
But they were all weird
about it, like, *It's too
generic. We need a
shape we can own.*

Su Barber:
One weekend we as-
sembled a crew of de-
signers and executed
literally hundreds of
variations in defense
of the speech bubble.

Rob Di Ieso:
We just dumped every
resource and every-
body we had on that,
like, *Let's just make
a bunch of logos!*

William Morrisey:
And that is not some-
thing that would be
deeply characteristic
of Open, *per se.*

Scott Stowell:
Already at that
point, the process
was starting to slip
out of my control.

Lauren Zalaznick:
Some things are
actually better than
others and matter
and some things
don't. It's important
to see if something
speaks differently
than something else
because of a minute
detail. It's absolutely
not indecisiveness.

Scott Stowell:
Bravo held focus
groups, like, *What
do you think about
this logo?* Somebody
said, "I think you don't
pay your graphics
department enough."
And I said to the
client, "I think this
guy's got a point."

Lauren Zalaznick:
The detail—you can
argue whether it was
worth it or not, but
I'd say whatever it
was that we picked,
it really worked for
that brand. We really
enjoyed the process
of the process.

Scott Stowell:
I don't really like the
final logo. It looks
like a weird hair-
dryer, but Lauren was
right—she wanted it
to be a unique shape,
like their word bal-
loon, not just a word
balloon. That, from
a strategic stand-
point, is very smart.

Frankie Salati:
The logo is cute
and clever! A little
turquoise makes ev-
eryone feel good.

↑
the Bravo logo,
before and after (with
type redrawn by
Tobias Frere-Jones,
December 2004)

Tobias Frere-Jones:
If you look at the old
logo, it looks like the
r is punching the *a*
in the face. So Scott
called up and sent me
this thing, the exist-
ing logo, and asked
what could be done
to improve this clearly
awkward and not suc-
cessful arrangement
of shapes. After *Art21*,
I was very familiar with
the sorts of things
that would work or
not work at a small
size on a screen.

Lauren Zalaznick:
For my going-away
party from NBC
Universal, they made
a tape that's liter-
ally 11 minutes long
of Jane Olson leafing
through every single
version of every single
talk bubble. Three
rounded corners,
one square, two and
two, one and three,
all square, all round,
450 shades of blue.

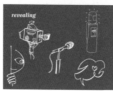

↑
illustrations by Noah Butkus, Marcellus Hall, Scott Lenhardt, Tucker Nichols, Christoph Niemann, Antonio Paiva, Brian Rea, Laurie Rosenwald, and Chip Wass, November–December 2004

Scott Stowell:
We said, *Here are nine things that Bravo is:* inventive, enthusiastic, dynamic, idiosyncratic, accessible, iconic, evocative, revealing, *and* glamorous.

Scott Stowell:
If Trio is all words, Bravo is all pictures. If Trio is all slick typography, Bravo would have a ton of handmade stuff and color. If Trio was flat, Bravo would be 3D.

Jane Olson:
There was something in Open's Bravo rede-sign about discovery, for sure, especially with the illustrations. And then there was this notion of layers that you could peel away or not peel away.

Corinne Vizzacchero:
Formally, my favorite elements of the Bravo identity were the hand-drawn doodles we did, and the mix-and-match-ness of the overall system.

Rob Carmichael:
The Bravo redesign was a pretty modular thing—a couple dif-ferent type styles, a bunch of textural images and whatnot to choose from.

Scott Stowell:
We hired all these great illustrators and we gave them each some words. I didn't care what they drew. So for like, *inventive*, we got a weird joystick tape recorder. The only rule was that it had to represent this word and it had to be a line drawing. That's how I love to commis-sion illustration—it's basically like a game.

Chip Wass:
Scott sort of makes a boundary for where there's going to be looseness and almost anything can happen within that space.

Beth Urdang:
We approached the music as music. We weren't scoring in-dividual bumpers or promos, as much as producing lots of music that just felt like the design and then finding places for those individual ditties.

Christoph Niemann:
Usually my work is totally idea driven. What was so interest-ing about the thing for Bravo, was that I really tried to sit down and come up with a style that somehow seemed much more open. It was a great exercise and I was really happy.

Gary Fogelson:
At one point the client asked for a graphic way to call attention to things. I remember thinking, *Well how do you do that in a maga-zine? As a reader you would underline things or circle things. So that's what we should do.* Once that idea got in their hands it was like everything was underlined and circled and arrows were going everywhere.

←

Project Runway promo with headline, May 2005

Beth Urdang:
Bravo did have a very quirky feel that was both immediate and sort of quirky and naive, that felt very specific and special.

Frankie Salati:
Bravo to me always looked like a little bit of a higher-end reality channel—more stylish, if you will!

Jesse Crawford:
Not to mention, they were so bold in being very liberal and open with their programming.

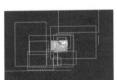

←

Inside the Actors Studio promo sketch, After Effects setup, and final frame, 2004–2005

Scott Stowell:
The way we kept some rigor in the 3D animation was that no element ever moves, they're just placed in space and the camera moves through them. *Art21* was the same way—the line doesn't move. It's just being drawn on, following an invisible structure that's already there. The camera moves, but the line doesn't move.

↑

Hidden Howie promo

Chris Wilcha:
There'd be graphic elements but it would be happening around James Lipton or the *Queer Eye* guys or Howie Mandel. Bravo wanted these graphic elements to exist alongside their talent.

Chappell Ellison:
It felt like a tangible world that I could somehow be a part of.

Jason Klarman:
I had fun working with Heidi Klum. She was pregnant most of the time.

Scott Stowell:
We had hundreds and hundreds of elements to make.

Gary Fogelson:
I was surprised that a small graphic design studio was responsible for so much stuff that I didn't think of as design back then: directing shoots, taking photos, writing copy.

Rob Di Ieso:
I had zero experience in broadcast design, and basically Scott would say, "Do some storyboards," and I would say, "OK." *I guess I'll figure it out.*

Beth Urdang:
We produced an enormous amount of music.

Dave Tecson:
Scott had started by bringing freelancers to Open to explore and test ideas. We would pick up design style and direction from his studio, progressively adding to the team as design aspects got locked down. Well, in theory at least.

Chris Wilcha:
At a certain point, there was nothing conceptual about what was going on. It was about bulk production of design furniture. It was way less about coming up with the look of it or the theory of it and way more about just pure execution and delivery.

Su Barber:
There were lots of tiers of approvals, which can be maddening. Also everyone important was in California, so we mostly interacted via conference call.

Lauren Zalaznick:
That's the process and the sheer volume, the speed, the approvals, the details.

Dave Tecson:
Well, Open was getting overpowered by their client.

Scott Stowell:
I basically couldn't even see straight. I had no idea what was going on. And suddenly everything spiraled out of control.

Dave Tecson:
My team was being tasked to work well past midnight and then show up at 8 am to tackle the next set of notes.

Chris Kairalla:
I remember there being tiny little things like a color blue would not be the exact RGB value of the color blue that was in some design document. We're talking about a document that would be printed versus a screen. I'm sorry but that blue isn't going to be that blue anyway. I remember thinking, *Here we are staying up until midnight. Is this really the battle we're going to fight?*

↑
behind the scenes at Open and Edgeworx, November–December 2004

Kate Kittredge:
The stakes and production value were quite high: celebrities, green screens, telecines, and highly technical animation techniques.

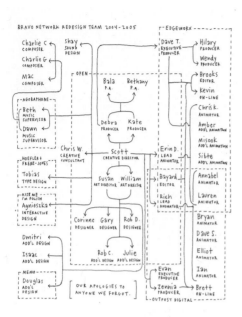

BRAVO NETWORK REDESIGN TEAM 2004-2005

←
Bravo network
redesign team,
2004–2005

Rob Di Ieso:
At one point I think
Scott drew a flow-
chart of every person
that was involved in
that job. It was basi-
cally impossible
to keep track of.

Chris Wilcha:
There was this sense
of like, Scott all of a
sudden had to run
a design studio as
much as he had to
be a designer.

Kate Kittredge:
It was so large and so
fast paced, and took
all of our attention, all
the time, which was
not the way we were
accustomed to work-
ing with our many
clients and projects.

Lauren Zalaznick:
The technology never
makes it easier. You
have to make all the
stuff. It doesn't come
off the factory line
any more efficiently.
You still have to
make every single
element perfectly.

Linda Ong:
I think we missed
some deadlines.

Su Barber:
The studio environ-
ment was a little nutty.
Lots of optimistic
mornings and dire
late nights. Scott was
bleary at times, like the
rest of us. When I think
of him during this time
I see him hunched
over a tiny laptop,
holding it together.

Chip Wass:
If anything I was more
of a therapist during
that period of time.
It was causing Scott
a lot of anxiety.

Dave Tecson:
It was not a pretty call
to Scott when I told
him to rein in his pro-
ducer and stop making
these time demands.

Chris Wilcha:
I was there to do some
brainstorming or sit
over lunch and come
up with some ideas,
but I wasn't a designer.
I remember feeling
bad that I couldn't
jump on a computer
and help make stuff.

Rob Di Ieso:
I don't know how
Scott kept his sanity.
I don't actually think
he did keep his sanity.

Kate Kittredge:
There were so many
late nights, so much
delivery dinner, and
some whiskey.

Su Barber:
I spent all my waking
hours at effects
houses, eating three
meals a day out of take-
out containers around
their glass conference
room tables, napping
on their leather sofas.
We routinely sent tapes
to LA via hand courier
because we'd missed
the FedEx cutoff. I
got migraines for the
first time in my life.

Simone Pillinger:
Every tape cost
$180 and don't even
ask me how many
were needed.

Rob Di Ieso:
I found it highly enter-
taining, just because
sometimes I think
it's funny and amus-
ing when people are
stressed and tired. It
can be funny, even
though I feel bad for
them. It's also funny.

Chris Wilcha:
Scott's business
was being born in
the sense that he
needed to ramp up
his studio to actually
produce this stuff, but
also I don't think he
was in his aesthetic
comfort zone.

Feel free to leave your **cellphone** turned on.

you're watching

as seen on tv

Hidden Agenda

as seen on tv

Film Score

bravotx.com

brought to you by

Bravo **watch what happens**

CALIF.

you're watching

brought to you by

as seen on tv

Panic Attack

Jimmy Carter

CALIF.

you're watching

as seen on tv

Everything's Wild

bravotx.com

Hair Honcho

bravotx.com

Bravo **watch what happens**

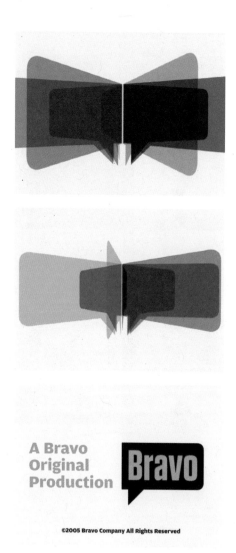

A Bravo
Original
Production   **Bravo**

↑
Bravo Original
Production tag,
May 2005

Chappell Ellison:
I grew up in a small, sheltered town in the South, and then here comes this channel that gave me a glimpse into other ways of life. Chefs mixing chocolate and ghost peppers! Real gay couples who weren't out of a *Will & Grace* script!

Dave Tecson:
In the end, things improved. Scott and his team did make adjustments, Bravo settled into their new design, my team got to go home at night, and the final work was delivered cleanly with a minimum of fuss. Then we all took a brief rest and moved on to the next job.

Su Barber:
The work we made was beautiful, complex, cohesive, and at the time, unique in its landscape. Pushing those ideas through was, at times, like pushing a huge boulder up a huge mountain.

Scott Stowell:
Our stuff stayed on the air for four years, which is a really long time for a redesign to last. When Bravo wanted studios to pitch for the next redesign, we kind of both agreed that we wouldn't participate. Bravo ended up hiring one studio that worked on it for a long time. That didn't work out, and then they gave the job to another studio called Gretel.

Greg Hahn:
I loved what Open had done to bring a handmade feel to a network brand. We tried to keep elements of that. But Bravo was very demanding. We ended up doing tons and tons of iterations.

Amy Troiano:
When we did our last redesign, we changed from a mostly white background with accent colors to a colorful background with other accents, but it still had some of the spirit of Scott's original design.

Greg Hahn:
Let's just say it was a very challenging job. All things considered, I was satisfied with the package, but it's not really my taste.

Scott Stowell:
What Gretel did, I really liked. It looks like our stuff dipped in the Apple iTunes store.

Greg Hahn:
If you look at our website, you won't see Bravo. It's not in our portfolio.

Rob Di Ieso:
After the Bravo job was dying down, I think the first thing I did was just email Scott and say, *Heyyy, this has been really fun! I'd like to stay here if you need me.* Yeah, that's the main thing I really remember after Bravo: fear of losing my job.

Lauren Zalaznick:
The thing that made all of the design and programming and business work pay off for me is when people said, *I don't know how you do it. There's 80 channels that I flip through but I know immediately when I flip by that channel.*

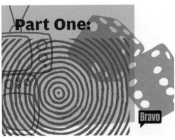

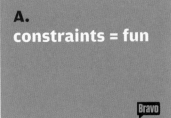

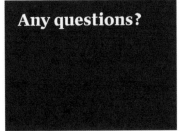

→
slides from Scott's
presentation to
the Bravo design
team in LA,
June 2005

Scott Stowell:
This kind of hit the
reset button on the
whole project for me.
Bravo asked me to go
out to LA for a day and
do a workshop with
their whole design
department about how
to use the redesign.
I was able to do then
what I'd had no time
to do in the begin-
ning: to reconfigure
everything we did
back into a narrative
that made sense.

Amy Troiano:
I really do look back
fondly on that rede-
sign and that day that
Scott came in and
talked to my team.
Creatives can be really
cynical, and for them
to be excited was fun.

Alisa Grifo:
I am a partner in Kiosk,
a project devoted
to showing things.

My grandmother's name was
Joy. As a child, I never really
understood what that meant.
I wondered, *Why would she be
named after a feeling?* It was only
after I felt it that it became clear
why it was her given name.
The reality is, joy can be found
in everything. Look deeply at
anything for long enough and
you'll see it. Turn the thing over.
Change the view. Everything
holds both the highest high and
the lowest low. It's you who
creates the parameter and the
frame. When you see it, bring it
in and then let it out. Never get
tired of our big, beautiful marble
filled with all its nuts, little
jumping dogs, cotton candy,
and electric cherry trees.

When Jazz at Lincoln Center (everybody there just calls it Jazz) moved into their new building, they decided to build a hall of fame to celebrate some of the most important people in the history of jazz. Each of those people would be the star of their own movie, to be shown exclusively in that hall of fame. Jazz hired us to make all those movies. We didn't know that much about jazz, and our clients weren't design experts. But we had a few things in common, so we improvised.

6.

in order
of appearance

Nyala Wright Nolen:
I was manager of programming for Frederick P. Rose Hall, part of the education program at Jazz.

Michael Fischer:
I'm senior associate at Rockwell Group. I was in charge of this.

Bobby Martin:
I was the design director of Jazz.

David Rockwell:
I'm the founder of the Rockwell Group. We were the interior architects for the Ertegun Jazz Hall of Fame.

Laura Johnson:
I was vice president for education at Jazz.

Rachel Abrams:
I'm a design strategist and critic.

Scott Stowell:
How are you today?

Daryl Long:
My title was probably assistant director of marketing for Jazz. I was the creative guy who knew the music.

Rob Di Ieso:
I was just a designer at Open on this job.

Su Barber:
I was a designer and art director at Open.

Cara Brower:
When I was at Open, Su and I were the designers. Scott let me run this project.

Samantha Samuels:
I was in the education department at Jazz.

Geoffrey C. Ward:
I was asked to write the very, very terse words that had to go into those very, very brief videos.

LaFrae Sci:
I am a music composer, drummer, and educator, who teaches at Jazz.

Eli Yamin:
I'm head of instruction for Jazz's Middle School Jazz Academy.

Darrell Smith:
I am an assistant instructor in the Middle School Jazz Academy.

Gary Fogelson:
I designed a few of these videos, but not in the first year.

Zak Jensen:
I worked on Jazz after being an Open intern for a month or two.

Şerifcan Özcan:
I worked on two or three of the videos while I was at Open.

Dave Stoy:
I was an animator.

Uroš Perišić:
I came in as a freelance animator on the Jazz videos.

Bryan Keeling:
I was more like a secondary character.

Rich Scurry:
I worked as an animator on some of these videos.

Nyala Wright Nolen:
Under the direction
of artistic director
Wynton Marsalis, we
were tasked to find
new ways in which
to communicate the
sound and feeling
of jazz to the public
at large, as lofty as
all that sounds.

Michael Fischer:
Ahmet Ertegun, who
was on the Jazz at
Lincoln Center board,
had wanted to do
a jazz hall of fame
and dedicate it to
his brother Nesuhi.
Ahmet was sort of
deep in the recording
industry on the rock 'n'
roll side. Nesuhi had
been a seminal per-
son on the jazz side.

Bobby Martin:
Wynton had a very
strong point of view
on how jazz needed
to be portrayed and
how the building
needed to feel. It
was all about being
warm. It was about
being soulful. It was
about being welcom-
ing. It was not cold.

David Rockwell:
I was interested in
Wynton's description
of creating some-
thing with the spirit
of improvisation. Part
of the goal, as he de-
scribed it, and I love
this quote, was "high
minded but down
home." We wanted it
to be open and acces-
sible to everyone.

Michael Fischer:
Jazz at Lincoln Center
gave us the charge
to create a hall of
fame in a space that
wasn't being used.

Laura Johnson:
It felt like the heart of
the entire complex.

David Rockwell:
The goal was to cre-
ate a flexible exhibi-
tion space that would
convey a long, rich
history of jazz for ca-
sual listeners and jazz
aficionados. Central
to that idea was that it
had to be a total sen-
sory experience that's
only 1,200 square feet.

↑
the Ertegun
Jazz Hall of Fame at
Jazz at Lincoln Center,
photographed in
December 2005

Michael Fischer:
There's one long
bench that's opposite
the screen, that has
this kind of soft curve
to it, which sort of
feels like a guitar.

Rachel Abrams:
The environment was
plush, like historic
uptown joints—the
revamped Minton's,
the Lenox Lounge in
its heyday—all sump-
tuous, busy textiles
in muted colors, and
lit for a permanent
state of after hours.

Michael Fischer:
The centerpiece was this large screen, which we imagined could be used in multiple ways, but in its default mode would have a continuous loop of some kind of visualization for each of the people who had been inducted into the Hall of Fame.

David Rockwell:
Part of what I wanted to do was to create a space that was about storytelling. Someone who could help do that from a not-obvious angle or point of view, seemed like the right choice.

Michael Fischer:
That's where Scott's office came into play as somebody who could work with the music, and try to understand who each of these individuals were, and come up with some sort of unique way to visualize that.

Nyala Wright Nolen:
The idea was that inductees would be done on an annual basis, but for the first two years we should induct a very robust class, so that there was a lot of content for the Hall of Fame.

Scott Stowell:
The first year we had to make 14 videos. The second year there were 12. We did fewer in years after that.

Daryl Long:
The notion was to take the iconic song of a jazz legend, and visualize it—make it—so that it could be seen and apprehended with the eyes as well as the ears.

Michael Fischer:
There's this really wonderful film from the late 1940s by Norman McLaren. It was a collaboration between McLaren and Evelyn Lambart, set to music by the Oscar Peterson Trio, called *Begone Dull Care*. McLaren took this 35-millimeter film and, frame by frame, was just scratching into it, choreographing visualizations in time to the music. I think it's a seven-minute piece.

Scott Stowell:
Michael sent me *Begone Dull Care* as inspiration.

Michael Fischer:
It became a goal for us collectively: to achieve something using non-figural and abstract imagery. That's where we started with Scott: *OK, here's one version but now you have to come up with 14 unique ones.*

← Rockwell Group's DVD of *Begone Dull Care*

↓ photo research and storyboard sketches, May–July 2004

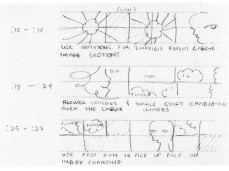

Scott Stowell:
The video wall was 21 by 3 feet, something like that.

Michael Fischer:
That was with the technology that we had. The hall was kind of long and we wanted the screen to be as big as it could possibly be. We were constrained by the available sizes of things, so we did have to make it out of smaller screens.

Scott Stowell:
I think we'd signed the contract without knowing that it was that crazy shape. I was like, *Can you guys change that?* They said no, of course.

Michael Fischer:
It created a bit of a hardship for Open because of the aspect ratio. The screen is so much wider than the proportions of normal film. They had to work within a pretty unconventional set of boundaries.

Scott Stowell:
That constraint became an engine for so much of the work, because jazz on a base level is really about playing and improvising within a structure.

Su Barber:
The odd shape of the screen inspired us to mix the multiple elements we wanted to present simultaneously.

Scott Stowell:
The thing I wanted them to change ended up being a total gift because it would just kind of tell you what to do.

Rob Di Ieso:
The grid was advantageous. *We can't ignore it, so let's use it.*

↓
research and sketches,
May–August 2004

Scott Stowell:
We did a lot of research. We rented all these movies—*Grand Prix*, *The Thomas Crown Affair*, Ang Lee's version of *The Hulk*—that do split screen or multiple panels.

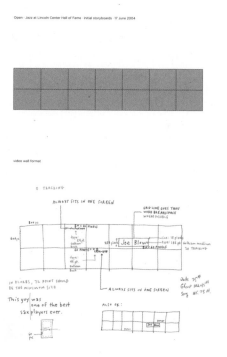

Open · Jazz at Lincoln Center Hall of Fame · initial storyboards · 17 June 2004

video wall format

Open · Jazz at Lincoln Center · Hall of Fame video · creative research · 3 June 2004

Charlie Parker

Open · Jazz at Lincoln Center Hall of Fame · Style Frames · 8 July 2004

Charlie Parker

Open · Jazz at Lincoln Center Hall of Fame · Revised/Final Style Frames · 15 July 2004

Charlie Parker · original/revised

↑
creative research,
3 June 2004

style frames,
8 July 2004

revised/final
style frames,
15 July 2004

Scott Stowell:
Some of them were
pretty straightforward.
For Charlie Parker
we showed tons of
Jackson Pollock,
because Charlie
Parker in our analysis
served exactly the
same purpose as
Jackson Pollock.

Scott Stowell:
Wynton Marsalis is the
artistic director of Jazz
at Lincoln Center. He's
the boss. I remember
he came to our first
meeting and asked,
"What kind of videos
do you want to make?"
And I replied, "I want
to make videos for
people who hate jazz."

Laura Johnson:
We wanted to give
people an impression
that wasn't pedantic.

Scott Stowell:
We try to think about
this with a lot of proj-
ects. Our point was to
get more people into
jazz. Obviously that's
their agenda, too.

Bobby Martin:
With videos and try-
ing to visually and
experientially tell the
story—the life—of
these jazz musicians,
each person, in some
ways, has a differ-
ent point of view on
what that should be.

Scott Stowell:
A lot of designers
use mood boards to
present the feeling
of a thing before they
present the real thing.
Most of the time it's
kind of bullshit. What
we did, we called art
boards. Using fine
art, painting, photog-
raphy, sculpture, ar-
chitecture, whatever,
that, to us, embodied
the spirit of what that
musician felt like.

Cara Brower:
For each musician,
we tried to learn their
history and then find
a visual aesthetic that
would represent them.

Daryl Long:
It was fairly ab-
stract, but it was a
good exercise.

Su Barber:
It's so difficult to agree
on words to describe a
visual metaphor for
how something sounds.
The art boards were a
meeting place that ev-
eryone could access.

Nyala Wright Nolen:
It was up to me to
go to Wynton and
get his approval,
get his feedback.

Samantha Samuels:
I don't remember
Wynton being in those
meetings all the time
but he was omnipres-
ent in our thinking.

Nyala Wright Nolen:
He found the process
to be quite difficult
because he was work-
ing with me, the ad-
ministrator, over the
content and the bud-
get, and his primary
concern was the cre-
ative. The music. The
way in which the artist
was being conveyed.
He'd be like, *You know,
Nyala, you're always
telling me if I don't ap-
prove this now, we're
not gonna get it done,
and I'm more con-
cerned about how we
are not treating Duke
Ellington correctly.*

↑
Cara's notes
on John Coltrane,
May 2004

Cara Brower:
That project was so
great because I
really got to learn a
lot about music.

→
a phone message
about the John
Coltrane video from
Daryl Long and
Keith Henry Brown,
August 2004

IMPORTANT MESSAGE

FOR _Scott_
DATE _____ TIME _3:20_ A.M. / P.M.
M _Daryl + Keith_
OF _____
PHONE _We are calling them at_
☐ FAX _10 am tomorrow to_
☐ MOBILE _get input — @ 15 min._

TELEPHONED		PLEASE CALL	
CAME TO SEE YOU		WILL CALL AGAIN	
WANTS TO SEE YOU		RUSH	
RETURNED YOUR CALL		SPECIAL ATTENTION	

MESSAGE
on coltrane:
"The horizons linger a
little too long before
it becomes fucking
brilliant"

SIGNED
Tops. FORM 3002P
MADE IN U.S.A.

Cara Brower:
We went to one meeting and for some reason, I don't know why, we thought it would be a good idea to put a little blurb, like a little summary about each person.

Scott Stowell:
Of course Jazz at Lincoln Center was in charge of copy in the end, but we were just showing that we were getting into it.

Samantha Samuels:
We had Phil Schaap in our meetings, and he has this amazing photographic memory.

Scott Stowell:
He is like the jazz nerd to end all jazz nerds.

Cara Brower:
I got one or two really detailed facts, like you might find on Wikipedia, wrong. Like, *So-and-so's mother died of polio in 1968*, when she really died in 1967, or something like that.

Scott Stowell:
Phil was just shuffling papers and grumbling.

Cara Brower:
He wasn't paying attention to the visuals or the design that we were presenting.

Scott Stowell:
The meeting ended with Phil standing up and muttering, "This is an abomination."

Cara Brower:
Those were the first meetings that I'd been to, and that's the first time I'd ever seen it go terribly wrong.

Scott Stowell:
Cara broke into tears.

Cara Brower:
Then I offered up, "I did it. I'm the one who got that wrong." That made it even worse.

Scott Stowell:
I have this rule at Open where we never say *I*, we always say *we*. We share the credit and the blame. I didn't want her to hang herself out to dry, and I also didn't want them to think I didn't have anything to do with it.

Cara Brower:
We left the meeting and I just felt so terrible. Really terrible.

Scott Stowell:
It was terrifying, and I was like, *This is over.*

Cara Brower:
After that a woman from Jazz, who was lovely, called and apologized. The presentation was actually about the visuals, and our job was not to write a history.

Scott Stowell:
Our next meeting, Cara and I went and just met with Phil. The two of us were like, *We're so sorry. Tell us everything you know. You're the expert.*

"When you begin to see the possibilities of music, you desire to do something really good for people. I want to speak to their souls."

trane

1926–1967

BLUE TRAIN   blue note 1577

spent a lifetime in pursuit of

His devotion to jazz resonates

John Coltrane Quartet
"A Love Supreme"

December 9, 1964

Su Barber:
Jazz at Lincoln Center wanted to include information about each musician, a quote, and some photos.

Daryl Long:
There were those who were thinking Ken Burns. They're wanting to see facts, and images, and lots of Ken Burns effects.

Geoffrey C. Ward:
You couldn't give the musicians' full biographies. There wasn't time for anything elaborate.

Samantha Samuels:
They were like little poems.

Su Barber:
Our graphics functioned as the glue that held the rest together.

Geoffrey C. Ward:
It's a challenge to see if you could actually convey something about someone in very few words.

Daryl Long:
Even though these videos were supposed to be very serious, they were inherently whimsical. Tying all of these characteristics to this music that you think is heavy—that was kind of the purpose.

Laura Johnson:
Until the first time that Open actually showed us a draft video, I think we hadn't really understood what they could do and what they were going to do.

Scott Stowell:
Obviously there's this huge world of visual stuff about jazz. If anybody knows any graphic design related to jazz, it's Blue Note album covers. And if not, they're used to that stuff: blue boxes, guys smoking cigarettes or whatever.

Bobby Martin:
A lot of the way that jazz was communicated, especially in New York City, was by showing a Miles Davis picture, or John Coltrane, or some type of black-and-white or duotone photograph of somebody who was probably not even alive anymore.

Scott Stowell:
We didn't want to make stuff like that.

Daryl Long:
Even when Open was referencing things that were historical, they did it with a freshness of somebody not burdened by that well-worn and trite visual language of jazz.

Scott Stowell:
We started by adding more restrictions. We couldn't do anything that couldn't have been done on an animation stand in the 1950s. By imposing that restriction, that added this aesthetic thing to it—stuff I like: flat colors, hard edges, not weird glowy gradients or kooky stuff.

↑
Billie Holiday,
2004

Samantha Samuels:
Billie Holiday had these beautiful leaves floating. Those were probably the most abstract interpretations of the artist and their sound.

Cara Brower:
I think that putting images to music draws a lot out of somebody, just being intuitive, just knowing what's right and what's not right.

Bobby Martin:
When you walked into the space, you could hear it on the speakers. You could see it in very big scale, and it was something that you could experience with other people. It was definitely a multi-sensory experience.

Scott Stowell:
It was rear projection, not LCD, which is actually kind of beautiful.

Rachel Abrams:
If Jazz at Lincoln Center was a cathedral to jazz, here were the stained glass windows.

Laura Johnson:
It looked fabulous. Also the sound system wiring was such that you could hear it like it was surrounding you. It was really like an inner sanctum.

LaFrae Sci:
I thought it was magical.

Eli Yamin:
It was great to just sit there and quietly visit with the artist.

Darrell Smith:
I spent time alone in the space several times and my experience was always in awe of the great musicians that came before me. Seeing all of the history in the short videos was really exciting to me.

Daryl Long:
The music is inherently fun. Sit back and just kind of loosen up a bit. You'll have fun and you'll go on these journeys.

Samantha Samuels:
I remember after an inductee ceremony, going to sit in that room, in the Hall of Fame. There were only a few of us who had come back to watch the videos. It felt like a shrine.

↑
Max Roach,
2005

Gary Fogelson:
I remember going from Bravo to this project, and being like, *I get to come in and just spend eight hours thinking about art and listening to music?*

Scott Stowell:
Cara couldn't design them all, so I did a couple, other people did a couple. Over the years we would have other designers come in and we would say, *Here's the kit of parts.* Often, my role was a lot like air traffic controller in the studio.

Cara Brower:
Scott was amazing at finding what you were really good at as an individual and as a designer. Then really encouraging you and pulling that out of you.

Gary Fogelson:
Every year we would get a new batch of inductees.

Scott Stowell:
And the videos ended up a reflection of not just the system that we set up, or the personality of the jazz musician, but then the personality of the designer that got paired with the jazz musician.

Zak Jensen:
We heard a lot of jazz in the studio for a while. Everyone was getting pretty good at mouth trumpet.

Nyala Wright Nolen:
I was standing next to Sonny Rollins in the Hall of Fame. He saw his video and he's like, "Oh, that's pretty cool," but he sees the Max Roach video and he was just like, you know, tears in his eyes, "That's amazing."

Daryl Long:
As one geek to another, they were geeking out.

Rob Di Ieso:
You develop a new respect for the art form and the artists themselves, that you hadn't had before. That goes along with any project, not just Jazz.

Nyala Wright Nolen:
The people at Open were very visual people and you're getting something very visual. The question was always whether it told the story of that song. I have to say, when it was right and it was really, really strong, it was an easy process.

Gary Fogelson:
You knew that you had a really tough crowd that you were gonna have to present to. The jazz nerds, that's like a tough crowd.

Samantha Samuels:
You don't start working at Jazz at Lincoln Center if you don't care about jazz.

Scott Stowell:
A few of the people that we did these videos about were still alive. We didn't really have approval from any of them before. Like the video was a gift to them. We didn't have to run it by them or anything. But there was a special kind of pressure, like, *This dude's gonna watch it.*

↑
Scott and Şerifcan
on the way to the
2008 ceremony

Şerifcan Özcan:
None of our laptops
were good enough
to play for the pre-
sentation. So I had
to take my massive
iMac to the venue
on the 1 train.

↑
Şerifcan with
Ornette Coleman at
the Ertegun Jazz Hall
of Fame Induction
Ceremony Luncheon,
20 November 2008

Dave Stoy:
Rendering these files
took a ridiculous
amount of time. They
easily took over 12
hours to complete
for a movie with a
duration of anywhere
from one and a half
to three minutes.

Scott Stowell:
HDTV dimensions in
terms of pixels is 1920
x 1080. Back then,
normal, standard
definition tv was like
720 x 540. The files
we had to deliver for
this wall were 5600
x 1400. *What did we
get ourselves into?*

Dave Stoy:
Because of these tech-
nical constraints, it
was hard to know what
you were animating.
We were working at
the smallest file size,
so a lot of times your
type and the elements
you're working with
would be pixelated.
You'd render out a
pass to see what hap-
pens and be like, *Oh,
God, this isn't what
I expected at all.*

Uroš Perišić:
There was very little
room for error.

Dave Stoy:
I believe it's safe to
say that this was my
most technically chal-
lenging set of videos
to animate ever.

Scott Stowell:
We took months and
months to make these
and Wynton would see
them at very specific
times. I remember in
the first year, about a
week before the Hall
of Fame was opening,
we were really in the
fine-tuning and final
renders, and Wynton
looked at the Charlie
Parker video and was
like, *You know what,
I don't think Charlie
Parker is Pollock, I
think he's Mondrian.
Can you change that?* I
basically had to say no.

Dave Stoy:
I had to take a long
vacation after my first
year on this project.

↑
Ornette Coleman,
2008

Şerifcan Özcan:
Ornette Coleman was
probably like, *Who
are these people?* It
was all very abstract.
I don't think he under-
stood why we were
there or what we did.

Scott Stowell:
Ornette Coleman
was a man of very
few words.

↓
Charlie Parker,
2004

Scott Stowell:
We put footage of him
laughing and lighting
a cigarette in during
a break in his solo.
You get so much of
his personality.

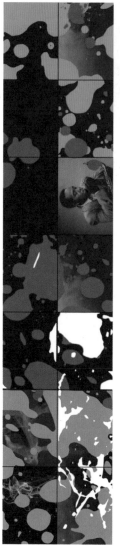

↑
Clifford Brown,
2007

Daryl Long:
We sat down and
we put on some
Clifford Brown and
it's like, *Listen to
that*. There was a
warmth in the music.
There was a round-
ness to the music.

↓
Thelonious Monk,
2004

Scott Stowell:
For Monk we wanted
to use handmade
shapes. We looked at
Saul Bass, *The Man with
the Golden Arm*. We
couldn't get it right.
Finally I said, *Let's just
copy Bass' shapes*.

with soul

taught the world to swing

↑
Louis Armstrong,
2004

Laura Johnson:
The fact that Open
chose to feature
scenic landscapes
for him was kind of
an oxymoronic choice,
but it worked.

↓
Lester Young,
2004

↑
Charlie Christian,
2007

Scott Stowell:
After a while our
own work became
reference material
for our work.

Zak Jensen:
We were trying to learn
as much as we could.

Scott Stowell:
Lester Young was
known as a really
sharp dresser, so we
did all these stripes.
Charlie Christian was
influenced by Lester
Young, but in a less
buttoned-up way,
both in terms of cloth-
ing and in music.

Scott Stowell:
The most important
thing isn't what's on
the screen, but the
timing of it. You could
have nothing on the
screen, and at the
right time have one
thing pop up. *Shit,
that's amazing. That
cut feels so powerful.*

Daryl Long:
The core ethos of jazz
is the unexpected.
It's an improvisa-
tional music.

Rob Di Ieso:
Once the storyboard
was complete, we
started working with
the animators.

Bryan Keeling:
There was a lot for
animators to sink
their teeth into.

Rich Scurry:
The first inclination
was to have the anima-
tion be totally synchro-
nized, note for note
with music. But that
overshadowed the
music. What we need-
ed to do was support
the music and, in a
way, play along with it.

Scott Stowell:
The idea of mak-
ing something out
of intelligence that
had a visceral feel-
ing to it—that's what
I learned about jazz.
Jazz isn't just a bunch
of guys smoking pot
and freaking out, it's
a super intelligent
system that results
in things that are so
joyful and emotional.

Rich Scurry:
Once we figured this
out it became much
less technical and
more soulful. We
would dive into each
song, breaking down
its structure, trying to
get at the essence of
the artist. It was like
we got to really know
and play with some
of the greatest jazz
musicians of all time.

Scott Stowell:
The process was kind
of musical in its own
way. We would do a
thing, then Jazz at
Lincoln Center would
riff off of it, and then
we'd come back to it.

Daryl Long:
None of this stuff was
dictated by Open.
Everything was a
conversation.

Scott Stowell:
Graphic design and
music have so much
in common. There are
structures, and there is
playing with the struc-
ture. We would set up
our own rules, play
with them, and then
try and break them, or
stretch them as much
as possible. Because
of that, this became
one of the most exu-
berant, visual things
we've ever done.

Earl Hines, 2005

Charles Mingus, 2005

Bix Beiderbecke, 2004

Duke Ellington, 2004

Roy Eldridge, 2005

Gil Evans, 2008

Fats Waller, 2005

Ella Fitzgerald, 2005

Count Basie, 2005

Jelly Roll Morton, 2004

Mary Lou Williams, 2008

Benny Goodman, 2005

Art Tatum, 2004

Coleman Hawkins, 2004

Sonny Rollins, 2005

King Oliver, 2005

Bobby Martin:
I think the Jazz Hall of Fame isn't there anymore, so a lot has changed. And I think that's a little sad because I think it is one of the more experimental graphic expressions they did at Jazz at Lincoln Center.

Daryl Long:
The Hall of Fame project as a whole was very conceptual. I think the videos were the most successful thing about it, hands down.

Bobby Martin:
Those were definitely not your typical Hall of Fame videos. They were not your typical way of expressing gratitude for an award winner. It was so unique and so special, and it's a shame to not have that be a continual part of who Jazz at Lincoln Center is.

Nyala Wright Nolen:
It was a rare occasion to be in a multimillion-dollar facility and see these African Americans honored for their talent and for their artistry.

Scott Stowell:
My understanding is a few years ago they were looking into refitting the wall because they had outgrown the technology.

Daryl Long:
The whole thing is not open to the public.

Nyala Wright Nolen:
One of the funny things about doing things that are technologically advanced— and futuristic at the time—is that very quickly those truths become untrue. Not really anything with the content, but literally things like keeping the lightbulbs in stock and replacing the parts became difficult.

Bobby Martin:
I want to make sure Jazz at Lincoln Center still has the ability to do something that's a little bit off the wall and unprecedented.

Nyala Wright Nolen:
That's what the Hall of Fame was there to do: to make jazz look even better than it really is. And not in an inauthentic way, but in a way that says, *This is important, and we care enough about this to put everything we have into making it look great, because it's worthy of that.*

David Rockwell:
There was never anything like this before and that was part of what made it so thrilling.

Scott Stowell:
I wanted to do hundreds of these. I would still do them today. But you know, clients change. Budgets change. Formats change. You can't see the videos anymore.

↑
Olivia Long with her parents, Daryl and Samantha, 11 November 2008

Scott Stowell:
One of the cool bonus products of this project was a human being. Daryl and Samantha were both working at Jazz, but they had never worked together until this project.

Daryl Long:
I was saying something in a meeting that I was really convinced was massively insightful, and that nobody else could possibly apprehend or contradict; and she did both.

Samantha Samuels:
He was holding court about how Coltrane's music, later in his career, became more avant-garde. They were talking about the idea of using cosmic imagery, which we ended up using in that video. I was like, *I don't know about that. He's from North Carolina. Space images seem like a little bit of a stretch.*

Daryl Long:
I was like, *Ah, oh. Wow. She's right. God, that was sexy. I think I'm going to invite her to go down to Open.*

Samantha Samuels:
That was kind of our first date.

Wynton Marsalis:
I am the artistic and
managing director of
Jazz at Lincoln Center.

Everyone loves to hear a good
story. Storytellers take us into
worlds wondrous and unknown.
They tell us how life is, was, and
perhaps will be. Whether a story
is ancient or new, scary, sad, or
funny, it's even better when spoken out loud—yes, much better.

Music makers have their own
ways of telling a story. They use
melody, rhythm, and the sounds
made by different instruments
to bring out parts of a story
that are sometimes hidden in
the telling. Music helps us feel,
understand, and remember
what the storyteller is saying.

It's like ketchup on some
french fries: They're still french
fries, but that ketchup makes us
feel a different way about them.

I went to school in Providence, Rhode Island, next door to Brown University, so I got to know the Brown campus pretty well. Things have changed a lot since then, but for a long time one thing stayed the same: their Sciences Library building. Architecture Research Office (ARO) was hired to redesign the bottom three floors of the building into something called the Friedman Study Center. They hired us to design some signage, but we came up with a bunch of other ideas.

7.

in order of appearance

Scott Stowell:
Hello there.

Stephen Cassell:
Our firm, Architecture Research Office (ARO), was hired to do the Study Center. I'm a partner here. Kim was a project architect.

Kim Yao:
That's right!

Joanna Saltonstall:
I was the project manager for Brown, which meant I ran the project from a design, schedule, and budget standpoint.

Gabbie Corvese:
I graduated in May 2015 from Brown University with a degree in public health.

Jason Hu:
I graduated from Brown in May 2015 as a computer science major.

Krishan Aghi:
I am a 2015 graduate of Brown University. Now I am pursuing my PhD in neuroscience at the University of California, Berkeley.

Matthew Lee:
I graduated from Brown in 2015. I'm a student in the Program in Liberal Medical Education.

Reem Rayef:
I am a Brown 2015 graduate working in communications consulting in New York. At Brown, I double concentrated in international relations and anthropology.

Nguyen Le:
I am Nguyen, a rising senior at Brown. I study chemical engineering.

Elizabeth Goodspeed:
I am in my fifth year of the Brown-RISD dual degree program, studying graphic design and cognitive science. I am also a twice-former intern at Open.

Rob Di Ieso:
At Open, Brown was like, my baby. It was my project.

Barbara Schulz:
I am the head of library facilities and building safety at Brown University.

Lukas WinklerPrins:
I'm a mathematician wrapping up my undergraduate degree in applied mathematics at Brown University.

Steven Lavallee:
I manage the Friedman Study Center in Brown University's Science Library, where I supervise the library's service desk.

Scott Stowell:
Every college
campus has one.

Stephen Cassell:
You can't miss it.

Kim Yao:
It's a Brutalist, kind
of 1970s, concrete
building.

Scott Stowell:
The whole college is
like beautiful brick
ivy-covered buildings
and then there's this
cast concrete space-
ship that landed in
1972, where everybody
shoots their student
sci-fi films. It's what
the future looked
like in the past.

Joanna Saltonstall:
Well, OK, so it's our
Sciences Library.

Scott Stowell:
They call it the SciLi.

Gabbie Corvese:
I describe it to people
who didn't attend
Brown as "that re-
ally tall, ugly building
on Thayer Street."

Jason Hu:
I'm aggressively neu-
tral about the SciLi.
After taking Modern
Architecture with
Professor Neumann,
who explained a lot of
the ethos and motiva-
tions of Brutalist build-
ings, I've been trying
really hard to appreci-
ate the SciLi and how it
represents a particular
moment in culture and
history. But I can't.

Krishan Aghi:
I also have some
rather caustic
thoughts regarding
the SciLi exterior.

Matthew Lee:
The exterior of
the SciLi portends
doom and despair.
The boiled, brutal-
ist concrete is not
kind. Perhaps murals
would help a bit.

Reem Rayef:
It must have been an
architectural trend in
the '60s, because I see
identical buildings on
nine out of 10 universi-
ty campuses. I am glad
it's not pink though,
which I heard was part
of the original plan.

Nguyen Le:
In my freshman year,
I used to come to
the SciLi to study
because I got sexiled
frequently. I ended
up loving the place.
The SciLi on a quiet
day, like Thanksgiving
or the time before
school starts after
Christmas break, is
just as wonderful as
any other place on
campus can be.

Gabbie Corvese:
I've always believed
there was a strong
sense of camaraderie
among anyone who
spent time in the SciLi.
We don't really know
whether we like this
strange building or
not, but we're here,
and we're going to
make the most of it.

↑
the Sciences Library,
June 2005

Stephen Cassell:
Open designed a little logo for the building that became part of the signage—that was really brilliant. It's a series of horizontal bars. It's really an abstraction of the floors of the building, of where the Study Center is in relation to the library.

SCIENCES
LIBRARY

FRIEDMAN
STUDY
CENTER

↑
the basement of the
Sciences Library,
November 2005

Kim Yao:
I think it was one of the
first vertical libraries
at a university in the
United States, so as a
building type for a li-
brary, it's really unusu-
al because it's a tower.

Stephen Cassell:
At the University, they
didn't like the build-
ing at all. We thought
some parts were actu-
ally pretty amazing.

Elizabeth Goodspeed:
I think the SciLi is a
building that regu-
lar people hate, but
designers love.

Stephen Cassell:
The building was actu-
ally really unloved.

Joanna Saltonstall:
It's a big concrete
building, so it needed
some personality.

Kim Yao:
But as architects,
we like it.

Joanna Saltonstall:
The project encom-
passed what we call
Level A. It's under-
ground. That was
20,000 square feet,
and then it encom-
passed the ground
floor, which is about
5,000 square feet, and
a little bit of the mez-
zanine, which is about
3,000 square feet.

Stephen Cassell:
The brief was,
"Create a 24-hour
study center."

Joanna Saltonstall:
We had an RFP pro-
cess and hired ARO
out of New York.

Kim Yao:
There was a longish
qualifications and
proposal and inter-
view process. The
team we put together
included Open and
Scott, from the outset.

Stephen Cassell:
When you read
Brown's mission state-
ment and how they
think about educa-
tion, it seemed like the
way Scott and Open
approach projects.

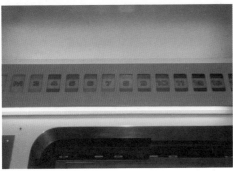

↑
existing signage,
November 2005

Kim Yao:
Even though it was in the Sciences Library, the Friedman Study Center had to become a place that really was a hub of activity for students from different disciplines. In building the team, we felt like there was a great opportunity to engage Scott's intellect in devising a strategy related to that, that could probably engage both the administration at the University and also the students.

Stephen Cassell:
You always want to work with someone who's going to come up with something that you wouldn't think of at all, because then it's like you push what you're doing further as well.

Scott Stowell:
It was the second signage project we'd ever done.

Stephen Cassell:
We had to think strategically.

Kim Yao:
It was a very tight-budget project. But basically, the dollar could go further in graphics than it would in architecture.

Stephen Cassell:
When you looked at some of the original photos of the building—I think it was finished in 1970—it had these amazing graphics. There were pieces of that left.

Rob Di Ieso:
The typography was strange.

Scott Stowell:
It was straight up 1980s movie era of *Star Trek* signage, like *warp core two levels down*.

Kim Yao:
We all agreed that we loved the existing graphic identity of the building, so it was a great direction to latch onto that, in a way, and embrace it, rather than trying to replace it. The character of that building was partially the architecture and partially the existing graphics system that was there, and Scott responded to both in his work.

Rob Di Ieso:
The great thing was like, obviously we couldn't do something like that on the Yale job because it was a Louis Kahn building and they were like, *You do not mess up any of the surfaces in any way or we will murder you all.* So, with the Brown job, they were like, *Yeah, we don't care! Do whatever you want!*

Stephen Cassell:
What does a study center mean? And what does it mean at Brown? A lot of it really had to do with talking to enough students—both grad students and under-grads—and librarians and administration, to try to frame what the project was and how to approach it. One of the key things that came out early on is the University just needed students to go study. How do you make a place where students want to hang out and study and engage in as many different ways possible?

Reem Rayef:
I built a complicated romance with the Friedman Center when I was a student. I spent a huge chunk of my time there—I worked at the circulation desk, and did most of my late-night studying there, although pretty much all my studying was late-night studying.

Stephen Cassell:
There was actually a really tough kind of wayfinding component to the project, just sort of old-fashioned graphic wayfinding, because it was both the Sciences Library and the Study Center.

Scott Stowell:
There's a scene in _2001_ that's the only real joke in the movie. This dude is taking a space-ship to the moon, which just basically feels like a jet plane, and he gets up and goes to the bathroom. There's this shot of him pondering the instructions for about 30 seconds silently and it's got like 500 words of instructions for the zero-gravity toilet, set in the same typeface we found in the SciLi. So for the basic ADA room signage, which was really the only requirement of this project, we just thought, _Let's go with that._

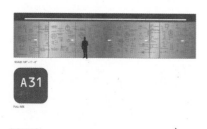

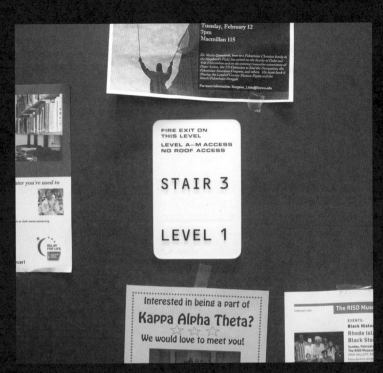

←↓
final signage,
photographed in
February 2008

→ sound level sign,
photographed in
February 2008

presentation of the
original concept,
10 April 2006

Scott Stowell:
Colleges want to
have more amenities
and fancier places
for students to hang
out. So the Friedman
Study Center was
the idea. You're al-
lowed to go there 24
hours a day. You can
eat there. You can
get a pizza delivered
there. You can pull an
all-nighter there with
friends and then fall
asleep under a desk.

Gabbie Corvese:
The basement is one of
the best places to feel
that hardcore SciLi
studying camaraderie.
I feel like the space
was designed to simul-
taneously be social
and academic. One
minute you're working,
and the next minute
you're going into your
friends' study room
because they have an
extra muffin to share.

Stephen Cassell:
They made a library
space where it's
OK to talk and have
food, so that was sort
of a radical idea.

Kim Yao:
The floor is organized
with quiet individual
spaces on one side,
and group and collab-
orative, louder spaces
on the other. The
concept of trying to
find those sound levels
with visible graphics
kind of evolved from
that organization.

Scott Stowell:
We made these
big signs that say,
00 DECIBELS, 25
DECIBELS, and so
on. It's such a weird,
dorky science joke.

Stephen Cassell:
When I talk to librar-
ians and students who
work there, they're all
like, *This has become
this really important
thing. Also, it's cool.*
I didn't predict, actu-
ally, how seriously they
would take the decibel
signs—how it actually
became like a social
contract in a way.

Barbara Schulz:
Students actually
point out the signs to
people who are talk-
ing too loud in the 00
DECIBELS level area.

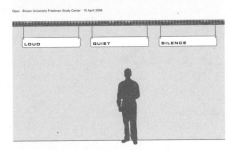

← rejected proposal
for existing signs

Scott Stowell:
We're always trying
to save the layers of
things. So we asked,
*You still can't smoke
here, but now you can
eat, right?* We wanted
to just paint a black
line over the *no.*

**Rob Di Ieso
to Scott Stowell:**
7 November 2005
*I was checking out
synonyms for the word
study and "brown
study" came up as
an option. I was like
what the fuck. Seems
like a great name for
the study center.*

Scott Stowell:
*Brown study means a
state of deep thought.*

Stephen Cassell:
The discovery
of what *brown study*
meant started to help
frame how we thought
about the pursuit
of knowledge, but
with a playfulness.

Scott Stowell:
This idea kind of
stuck in our heads.

Rob Di Ieso:
We pulled a bunch
of images from the
library stacks at Brown
and we silkscreened
them onto the walls
throughout the Study
Center. Attached to
each one was a card
catalog number and
a page number that it
could be found on.

Scott Stowell:
Basically the experi-
ence of the library was
somehow manifesting
itself in the space.

Rob Di Ieso:
The way I came up
with that idea was re-
ally weird. It was on a
train ride. I'm originally
from upstate New York
and I was coming back
down to the city.

Scott Stowell:
One of the things we
talked about a lot is
the stuff printed on
beer bottles, like, isn't
it Rolling Rock that
has that "33" on the
back or something?

Rob Di Ieso:
I started to think about
when people quote
things from the Bible.
They'll say the pas-
sage, then say, *John
3:16,* or whatever it is.
I thought that was an
interesting concept
and was like, *Well,
how can I apply that
to the library?* And it's
funny because I'm
not religious in any
way, shape, or form.

Scott Stowell:
All the walls are cast
concrete with no
varnish on them or
anything. We didn't
want to print on plastic
and then stick that on
the wall—we wanted
to print right on the
wall. So the only way
to do that and not have
it look crappy was to
have it silkscreened
directly on the wall.

Joanna Saltonstall:
I mean, they weren't
literally—were
they printed on
the wall? I thought
they were decals.

Scott Stowell:
The guys that worked
for the sign company
were incredible. If
you know anything
about silkscreen, you
know they had one
chance to get it right.

↑
notclosed.com/josiah,
the website set up to
solicit ideas for the
Study Center graphics

silkscreening a
picture of a Slinky
under the stairs,
February 2007

Scott Stowell:
We sent out an email
to Brown students,
alumni, staff, faculty—
anybody that had
anything to do with
Brown, including the
librarians. We said,
*If there are words or
pictures in the library
collections that are
significant to you, just
tell us, and we'll stick
them on the wall.* This
way we didn't need
a rationale for which
stuff to put on the
wall. Our rationale
became, *This is the
stuff that people told
us to put on the wall.*

Joanna Saltonstall:
We actually didn't
get a lot of submis-
sions, but we tried.

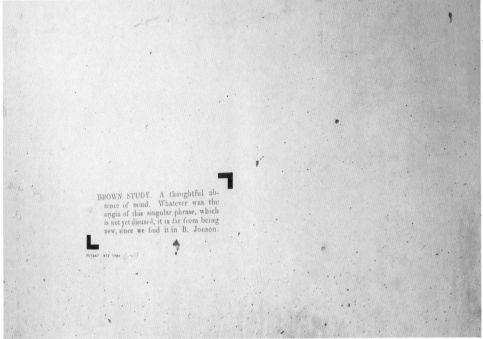

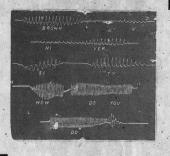

Figure 3.7. *Horse.* (From Bodenheimer 1935 pl. xm.)

MACARONI CHEESE

4 oz. macaroni (Naples macaroni is best)
3 oz. grated cheese
made mustard (French or English), 1 small teaspoonful
½ pint Bechamel or tomato sauce
salt
cayenne ⎫
lemon-juice (a drop or two) ⎭ to flavour

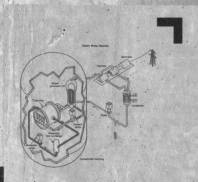

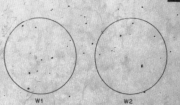

Fig. 45. Totally disconnected worlds. An event in W_1 is not connected to any event in W_2 by a timelike, lightlike, or spacelike curve.

12. Violations

There are none!

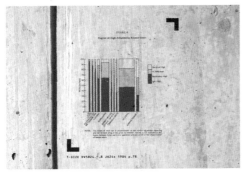

←
a chart from *Drugs and American High School Students 1975–1983* by Lloyd D. Johnston, Patrick M. O'Malley, and Jerald G. Bachman

downstairs at the Study Center, 16 November 2015

Scott Stowell:
There's this bar chart from a study of high school students in the 1970s, where they asked them, "Which drugs do you take and how high do you get?" So this is printed on the wall, in the middle of this library at Brown University. More than once I've gone there and I've seen, directly under this bar chart, a big bean bag chair with a kid just snoring.

Gabbie Corvese:
At first I thought they were some sort of guerilla stencil art by some student, but then I realized they were too cohesive and methodically placed to be a random tag.

Jason Hu:
I always appreciated them as small Easter eggs, something that rewards exploring the space and looking up from my books.

Lukas WinklerPrins:
They make you believe there is some kind of hidden treasure hunt in the space. I am both confused and delighted by them.

Scott Stowell:
We started having extra fun with it. Besides printing things on the wall, we identified objects.

Stephen Cassell:
I can't remember if it's the men's or women's room, but there's a little bracket and call number at the mirror, that ties in with Lacan and psychoanalysis and mirror theory.

Rob Di Ieso:
One of the bathrooms had brackets on the inside of the stall door. The title of the book that was referenced was *Retreat to Solitude.*

Scott Stowell:
These are jokes that maybe no one has ever even discovered, much less laughed at.

Reem Rayef:
Were some of them humorous, or am I making that up?

Matthew Lee:
They seemed almost occult, like a secret message was hidden in them and their associated books.

Rob Di Ieso:
We hoped that years from now, someone might move a chair, or a desk, or a bookshelf or something, and find one of these behind there and be like, *What the hell is this?*

Stephen Cassell:
It's like three in the morning and you're working on a paper and you fall asleep and then you open your eyes and turn your head and there's this weird thing on the wall, and what is it?

Joanna Saltonstall:
I think it definitely reinforced what we were trying to do. It gave the numbers to go find books and things, that these images were of, so that it referenced back to the library, which was the old use of the space. It just reinforced the whole conversion into a new type of space.

Rob Di Ieso:
I've done a lot of boring signage projects. Like hospitals or schools, where it's like, nothing fun. But for Brown, we got to propose purely conceptual signage that serves no purpose other than being cool or fun or whatever.

Stephen Cassell:
We just kept laying down the ideas of what we were thinking, knowing that Scott could absorb what the issues were and come back to us, like, *I have this sort of idea*. He always presents things in such a matter-of-fact and logical way.

Kim Yao:
It makes them seem sort of inevitable, which is a good technique on his part.

Stephen Cassell:
I remember Scott really just sitting down in one of our meetings with the client, just talking through how he thought this could add another layer of meaning and richness, and an important one, to the project.

Rob Di Ieso:
Scott is the best salesman I've ever met in my entire life. And that means a lot—I used to sell cars for a living at one point in my life.

Scott Stowell:
The people that I thought would be super annoyed by it—the librarians— were totally on board. Like they were super nice about it. They were super helpful during the process.

Rob Di Ieso:
They kind of let us do anything we wanted as long as they had the budget for it.

Kim Yao:
I think that what we did in that project is reinvent the building with a really simple palette. By making it a better place to occupy, it became an extraordinarily popular destination on campus.

Steven Lavallee:
The redesign led to a dramatic and sustained increase in building use by students, as well as renewed interest in the building by university administration.

Reem Rayef:
The SciLi is the first place I take people when they are visiting Brown for the first time.

Stephen Cassell:
Sometimes architecture just needs to get out of the way, and color and furniture and graphics and all these other things can do a better job at making a great place.

↑
unused Friedman Study Center Brown Study Collection guide, February 2007

Scott Stowell:
Rob designed a little brochure that you could get at the desk, that was like an interpretive tour or whatever. In the end they were like *Nah, that's OK. We don't need that. People will just find them.*

Rob Di Ieso:
Even if people weren't motivated enough to go find out what the graphics were, they're just like a cool thing that gives the space character.

Amina Huda:
I'm a policy advisor with the City of New York. I envision myself as an advocate and a policymaker, making sure that every person has access to opportunities that allow them to be empowered citizens.

I was curious as a child. There was enough wonder to keep me asking and enough people to answer—if not my parents and family, then my teachers, my mailman, my librarian. The whole community raised me and fed my insatiable curiosity with an endless stream of answers.

As adults, we seek answers from our experts, journalists, and our government. But the answers government provides are not just to quench the thirst of curiosity. These answers carry more weight. Answers lead to knowledge and can empower even the smallest of citizens. Government, especially local government, has the responsibility to raise communities by giving information, resources, and opportunities.

Now when I am asked a question, I pause. I think. And I answer.

When the ad agency Wieden + Kennedy asked us to make a logo and identity for their client, the National Multiple Sclerosis Society, we didn't know much of anything about MS or the Society at all. But we had to come up with a solution that would work for all the people who did. Almost every project starts with somebody who knows (or cares) more about something than we do. That's why they need help spreading the word. It's our job to catch up with them as fast as we can.

8.

in order
of appearance

Kim Phillips:
I am an ambassador for the National Multiple Sclerosis (MS) Society. That's my primary mission in life.

Scott Stowell:
Welcome.

Şerifcan Özcan:
We never had titles at Open. I was a designer and I worked on everything, pretty much.

Graham McReynolds:
I am the chief marketing and development officer of the National MS Society.

Todd Waterbury:
I was the co-executive creative director of Wieden + Kennedy New York. My partner Kevin and I were responsible for all of the creative work that came out of that office.

Buz Sawyer:
As managing director at Wieden + Kennedy in New York, I was essentially the senior account guy on this project.

Lu Chekowsky:
I was the copywriter on the project, with my partner, Bekah.

Kevin Proudfoot:
I'm a writer. At the time of this project, I was co-executive creative director of Wieden + Kennedy New York.

Rob Di Ieso:
I think I was a senior designer at Open then. Şerifcan did a lot of the work on this one.

Bekah Sirrine:
I was the art director.

Nicholas Rock:
I was in grad school at Yale and asked Scott if I could have a summer job at Open. I was really just learning about design.

Jon Varriano:
I am a senior graphic designer at *Food & Wine* magazine.

Dan Wieden:
I cofounded Wieden + Kennedy in 1982.

Mark Serratoni:
I am the director of creative services at the National MS Society.

Sherri Giger:
I serve as the executive vice president of marketing, and am responsible for the Society's brand and reputation, along with marketing and communications.

Daralee Champion:
I am a teacher—I teach deaf and hard of hearing pre-k and kindergarten students.

Kate Morse:
I am a wife, mom, and athlete living with MS.

Christie Germans:
I am a number-crunching photographer who loves riding my bicycle really, really fast and I happen to live with multiple sclerosis.

↑
the National MS
Society's old logo

Kim Phillips:
That was it. It just
stood alone. It said,
National MS Society,
without a lot of mean-
ing other than just
being pretty buttoned
up and pretty corpo-
rate and blah. That's a
technical term: *blah*.

Scott Stowell:
Every charity that
fights a disease is the
same. *AIDS is bad.
We're going to stop it.
Cancer is bad. We're
going to stop it.*

Şerifcan Özcan:
When you do some-
thing for an organiza-
tion like this, it kind of
feels like you're pro
that thing. But it's a
disease you don't re-
ally want to highlight.

Graham McReynolds:
You are for people with
MS—and against MS—
and want to express
both those things,
but with the emphasis
being on the people.

Scott Stowell:
We got a call from
Todd Waterbury, a guy
I've worked with for
many years. I think the
MS Society was a pro
bono client for them.

Todd Waterbury:
I will say there was
a real connection to
the Society's vision
and mission. Dan
Wieden's daughter
has MS, as did the
sister and mother of
the managing direc-
tor of our New York
office, Buz Sawyer.

Buz Sawyer:
I'm the one who
basically, as I like
to say, volunteered
the agency to help
out on the project.
It was very near and
dear to my heart.

Scott Stowell:
The Society was a pro
bono client for Wieden
+ Kennedy, but not for
us. It was our job to do
the identity. Wieden +
Kennedy would do the
advertising and strat-
egy. Actually, I don't
know who paid Open.

Buz Sawyer:
The Society was still
operating—for lack
of a better descrip-
tion—in an old-school
way. The president,
along with Graham,
was interested in
repositioning the
Society. And I don't
mean just the identity
but the overall feel
of the organization.

Graham McReynolds:
Buz and I met for lunch
and we discovered
that we each had a
sister living with MS.
We didn't talk about
work. We talked about
how you move through
this with people you
love so much.

Buz Sawyer:
What was happening
within the Society
was that people didn't
want to be taken care
of. They wanted to be
empowered—given
the tools to take care
of their own life.

Graham McReynolds:
We describe our mis-
sion this way: so that
each person can live
their very best life
while we work to stop
MS in its tracks, re-
store what's been lost,
and end MS forever.

WHEN YOU HAVE MS YOU
MIGHT NOT SEE TOMORROW.

YOU OPEN YOUR EYES. YOU CAN HARDLY SEE. AND YOU REALIZE IT'S HAPPENED AGAIN. YOU'RE
BLIND. THAT'S HOW MULTIPLE SCLEROSIS WORKS. IT'S UNPREDICTABLE. MS RANDOMLY ATTACKS
YOUR NERVOUS SYSTEM AND CAN BLIND OR PARALYZE YOU AT ANY TIME. THE FIRST SIGNS ARE
USUALLY SEEN BETWEEN THE AGES OF 20 AND 40 BUT THE NOT KNOWING ALWAYS STAYS WITH
YOU. THE NATIONAL MS SOCIETY IS THE LEADER IN RESEARCH AND SERVICES FOR PEOPLE WITH THE
DISEASE. CALL US AT 1-800-FIGHT-MS. WITH YOUR HELP, WE KNOW A CURE FOR MS ISN'T
ONE THING PEOPLE WITH MS CAN COUNT ON.   MS NATIONAL MULTIPLE SCLEROSIS SOCIETY

←
National MS Society
print ad,
1994

Lu Chekowsky:
There is this belief that
work of this nature
needs to be terrifying
or upsetting to inspire
people to want to
engage. Like, *Well if
you don't get people
upset, then how is
it going to work?*

Graham McReynolds:
People with MS are
not victims. They
are powerful. They
are in a place to take
charge of their life.
No matter what the
circumstance is, you
always have a choice
about how you're
going to live your life.

Scott Stowell:
The strategy that
Wieden + Kennedy
came up with
was brilliant.

Lu Chekowsky:
We worked for months
and months develop-
ing the strategy. Then
I wrote pages and
pages of stuff. I had the weight
of the world on me.

Scott Stowell:
Movement is essen-
tial to being human,
eating, drinking, and
having sex, but MS
hinders movement.
Rather than being like,
*We hate this disease
and we want to stop
it*, the Society would
become champions
of movement.

Lu Chekowsky:
We had a meeting to
go over some of the
writing and I overslept.

Kevin Proudfoot:
Lu probably overslept
because she'd been
up writing all night.

Lu Chekowsky:
Everyone is rolling
their eyes and it's
terrible. I don't have
the line yet. Then I
slide a piece of paper
across the table, and
Kevin, our creative
director, takes a pen
and he circles *Join
the Movement*, which
is buried in a para-
graph that I wrote.
And he says, "Why
are you freaking out?
That's the line."

Kevin Proudfoot:
If I look through a
bunch of writing and
can't remember any-
thing, I take that as a
bad sign. If something
feels right and it's the
only thing I remember,
then it might strike
people out in the
world in a similar way.

Graham McReynolds:
It's truly a movement.
It isn't about the or-
ganization, but about
fueling all the people
who care about MS to
find solutions. That
is so different than
branding an organi-
zation, because in a
movement, everyone
has to own it, and
everyone has respon-
sibility for its success.

Kevin Proudfoot:
At face value, *Join the
Movement* is about
as straightforward
a way as possible to
convey the invita-
tion the MS Society
is extending—to rally
around eliminating
MS. But because MS is
a disease that affects
one's ability to move,
the line also has a
layer of defiance to it.

Todd Waterbury:
There was an op-
portunity in my mind
to create something
that was memorable,
iconic, and indicative
of what we felt the mis-
sion for the MS society
was. I was intrigued
to see what Scott
and Open would do.

↑
preliminary sketches,
August 2006

Scott Stowell:
I didn't know anything
about the disease or
anybody with it or any-
thing. None of us did.

Graham McReynolds:
MS is a chronic condi-
tion where the myelin,
which is the coating
that surrounds all of
your nerves, starts to
wear away. For what-
ever reason something
is triggered where the
body attacks itself.
What that means is
nerve signals either
within the brain, or
between the brain
and the body, can
get interrupted.

Şerifcan Özcan:
We just started work-
ing on lots of ideas.

Graham McReynolds:
For some people, it
becomes issues of
mobility, for others it
can cause blurriness
or dizziness. For other
people it can be is-
sues of cognition. One
of the challenges of
MS is how it affects
people so differently.

Scott Stowell:
This was a result of a
few people working
all the time, and me,
day and night, being
like, *What the hell is
this going to be?*

Scott Stowell:
Is the logo about
nerves? Or the lay-
ers that encapsulate
the nerves? Or the
network of things
that have to work
together to make
things happen?

Todd Waterbury:
Open rarely starts with
a lot of assumptions.
They're starting with
almost nothing some-
times, but bringing
curiosity to the table.
Looking at it from the
most simple, most
human perspective.

Şerifcan Özcan:
I think Scott came
up with the idea in
the shower. He was
like, *I think I solved
it!* His explanation
was super long.

Scott Stowell:
I had this realization.
What does a move-
ment look like? You
have to move to make
a drawing, therefore
drawing is evidence
of movement. If you
have this thing called
MS, and you want to
fight it with a draw-
ing, the simplest way
is to just cross it out.

Şerifcan Özcan:
When you make your
mark across it, you
make the movement
against it, and also you
cross it off. Therefore
you really don't want
MS, and you'd rather
not have this organi-
zation at all. Which is
a really, really deep
thought, actually.

Graham McReynolds:
I remember Scott
saying, *If you look at
all the other organiza-
tions, they put the
disease in giant letters.
They're promoting
the very thing they're
trying to get rid of.*

Scott Stowell:
Let's say you didn't
know what cancer
was and you saw
*American Cancer
Society*. It sounds like
a group that thinks
that thing is awe-
some. Like what's the
difference between
that and American
Ballet Theater? We
must stop ballet?

Şerifcan Özcan:
It's weird that
no one had ever
pointed that out.

Lu Chekowsky:
Cancer! It's treated
so reverentially from
a design point of
view. Why would
you do that?

Rob Di Ieso:
The idea should be,
*We're against this,
we hate this, we
don't like this at all.*
The easiest way was
just to cross it out.

Scott Stowell:
The idea that we
proposed was that
every time you see
the logo, it's crossed
out with a different
gesture, made by
a different person,
with a different tool.

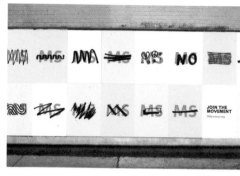

←↑
images from the
logo presentation,
September 2006

Bekah Sirrine:
I thought it was such a smart, simple, and meaningful solution—to create an open logo.

Nicholas Rock:
The whole idea of the gesture, and people actively striking out MS—when that happened, everybody was like, *Yes, absolutely. Of course it has to be this.*

Todd Waterbury:
When you actually studied the solution, you understood there was a lot of thinking that went into what most identities that are successful have, in that there is an utter simplicity to it.

Şerifcan Özcan:
When we first presented the idea we explained: *This is your typeface, this is your MS typography, this is your logo. But you can never use it like this. Let's say this logo is on a business card. When you're handing someone your business card, you find your pen, you cross out the logo, and then give it to them.*

Scott Stowell:
People would just have to carry around a pen. It reminds me of old school correspondence cards, where you put a line through your last name to say, *This is personal.*

Todd Waterbury:
In almost every case, an identity is this kind of unified, uniform, protected mark that has that safe space around it. This was quite radical because it flew in the face of conventional design thinking as it related to an identity.

Scott Stowell:
This was 2006, so I felt like it was a real moment of changeable identity systems.

Kevin Proudfoot:
It takes courage to embrace a logo that isn't complete until someone picks up a pen or marker and puts their own strike through the letters *MS*.

Todd Waterbury:
It left room for, or in many ways demanded, interaction between the individual and the Society.

Graham McReynolds:
No one had done anything like this, so it was shocking. To see something so different, an expression of where you could take an organization and build a movement with something so simple. It was incredibly emotional to me.

Lu Chekowsky:
Graham was in tears at the meeting.

Scott Stowell:
The logo presentation was received well, but then Graham was like, *Just in case*—because we only ever showed him this one logo—*if it isn't this what would it be? Could you show me that? I probably won't pick it*. We had to do our best to make another logo because it might get picked. Plus we didn't want to show them garbage.

Şerifcan Özcan:
It's really hard when you have a really good idea, trying to make a second one. That's the hardest thing to do. So I think we suffered for like, I don't know, a week or 10 days 'til the next meeting, trying to figure out a way of making a bad idea, so that we could sell the good idea.

Scott Stowell:
We ask our clients all the time to just take this leap of faith. *We showed you this one thing we think is awesome*. But for them that's insane! We ended up with something pretty nice for the alternate logo, I guess.

Graham McReynolds:
I remember that it was sort of blue and it had a burst of some sort.

Scott Stowell:
It looks like what such a thing should be. And it's totally fine.

Graham McReynolds:
It didn't tell a story. It looked like another identity. You could just throw it in a pile with all the other nonprofit, disease identities—it was just some variation of that.

Scott Stowell:
Graham looked at it and he was like, *Thank you, nope*. If he had picked it I would go around saying how awesome it is. But the other one changes my perception of what a logo is.

Graham McReynolds:
We had to go through that discipline.

Scott Stowell:
We had to do our best and keep our fingers crossed that the client would sort of appreciate this, but then realize why it was strategically wrong. I felt OK doing it, mostly because I trusted Graham. And I thought the original idea was so right that this other one would clearly not be right.

Todd Waterbury:
It's really evident to me now that the one that was produced was absolutely the right one. It possessed what I think the best ideas always have, which is equal parts inevitability and surprise.

↑
sketches for alternate logo, September 2006

↑
alternate logo as presented, September 2006

Scott Stowell:
This one just looks like, *Ask your doctor*, or something.

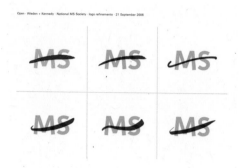

gestures

↑→
gesture studies and
final "hero" logo,
September 2006

Graham McReynolds:
We wanted to find the
right starting point.

MS

National
Multiple Sclerosis
Society

Scott Stowell:
We said the logo
would always change,
but the Society said,
*Sometimes we just
have to send artwork to
the baseball cap com-
pany. We can't change
the logo every time.*

Todd Waterbury:
There was a conversa-
tion around practical-
ity. Is there an "official"
version of the logo?
Which gesture do we
end up using as the
universal one? Does it
have the right spirit?

Rob Di Ieso:
We just grabbed pen-
cils and markers, any
kind of writing instru-
ment that we could
get our hands on, and
started making marks.

Scott Stowell:
This was just like
what happened with
Trio's punctuation,
or the shape of the
Bravo logo. It's like,
*We're cool with the
idea but let's beat
the crap out of it.*

Rob Di Ieso:
That was a pretty
lengthy process. I
made many tweaks.

Graham McReynolds:
We wanted to make
sure that we didn't
come across as
people who are mad.
We aren't mad. We're
optimistic and de-
termined. We went
through versions of
marks until we felt
that we had one that
expressed that.

Şerifcan Özcan:
I think anyone from the
outside, any person
<u>walking</u> into the office,
would be like, *What
the hell are you doing?*
Because you're talk-
ing about a tiny curve
of the brushstroke
and you'd be like, *Oh
that's not as good
or as inspirational.*

Scott Stowell:
The final gesture is
one that I don't really
like. Certain factions
within the Society
wanted a logo that was
really uplifting, so we
went with it because
otherwise it wouldn't
make it through. This
ended up being the
"hero" version of the
logo, as they call it.

Rob Di Ieso:
It was fine, but for me
personally I thought
that we had other
gestures that would
have been better.

Scott Stowell:
The ones that I like
are the ones that are
more like, *Fuck you
MS*, or they're done
with a big marker
instead of a brush.

Jon Varriano:
I like that it's at a
slightly upward angle,
sending a message
of hope and positivity
towards the future.

Scott Stowell:
It got launched at the Society's national conference in Florida.

Graham McReynolds:
We presented in a room with about 800 people—volunteers and staff from across the country—who come together at our leadership conference every year. People with MS, people who fundraise for us, people who sit on our boards, staff members.

Buz Sawyer:
We put on a huge, 10-screen show that basically launched the whole thing.

Lu Chekowsky:
Talk about nerve-racking. Presenting the work to people who are living with the disease and profoundly affected by it. Here you are trying to represent their story. It was terrifying.

Graham McReynolds:
They just immediately all leapt to their feet. It was a raucous standing ovation for 10 minutes.

Lu Chekowsky:
It was a big wow.

Scott Stowell:
They also made these big vinyl banners with the logo all over them, but not crossed out. Everyone got markers in their kits.

Graham McReynolds:
Inside of this giant ballroom we had the MS repeating over and over again on the walls. Four and five high and wrapping the whole room. Everyone could make their mark against MS.

Scott Stowell:
There were some people who had MS and couldn't move anymore, and they're telling their caregivers what mark to make.

Graham McReynolds:
You have to see all these people, people who are using scooters or wheelchairs or walkers all making their mark against MS.

Lu Chekowsky:
There's actual momentum in the mark—you can't help but feel it.

Graham McReynolds:
To walk around the room and see the hundreds of things people had to say. How they expressed that, how they were going to be in this movement.

Bekah Sirrine:
It was an incredible experience, beyond any that I've had, work-wise.

Kate Morse:
I love the logo. Seeing it the first time brought me to tears.

↑
participants at the National MS Society conference in Orlando, Florida, November 2006

Şerifcan Özcan:
People dedicate themselves to this organization. When they make that mark they really feel it.

Graham McReynolds:
It took some courage by our organization to do something that different.

Buz Sawyer:
I do remember taking the new identity into the CEO of the organization and she was scared to death of it. Literally sitting down with her and saying, "You know, this is gonna be OK. This is what you need. It's a very progressive and advanced way of doing things."

Todd Waterbury:
There were a number of things that were a part of the launch: tv advertising, outdoor advertising, print.

Kate Morse:
Join the Movement, to me, was a call to action. Living with a disease that impacts my mobility means that every day my body is working should not be wasted.

Kim Phillips:
I'm in a couple of ads. It was at the beginning of the relaunch of the brand, and that's when Graham was showing us ideas and asking us for our feedback and reactions.

Dan Wieden:
You're trying to create strong bonds, so that you understand what this issue is, deeply. Essentially, you have to say something in 30 seconds that will not only change people's ideas, but change their behavior.

Kim Phillips:
When I saw that slash, and I thought, metaphorically, about what that means to me, I thought, *This is perfect, because if I could, with my arms, with a weapon, I would eliminate MS.*

Mark Serratoni:
Moving to this mark was an 18-month process. Since the Society is a large organization with 48 chapters all across the country, it was daunting to switch this many business cards, stationery, lobby signs, etc.

Sherri Giger:
Like any branding change, it took planning, patience, and persistence. Our approach emphasized that this change would be a transition, and not a light switch that could be flipped.

Graham McReynolds:
When you're trying to create a movement you want some unifying features. You want it to tell a story. Then there are pieces where you just have to let it go.

↑
wristbands and lenticular clip, February 2007

Nicholas Rock:
I actually had done a lot of color research, which I think led to that orange-ish color that we picked.

Scott Stowell:
Actually, the orange got picked, funnily enough, because that was basically the only color of wristband available that no one else had claimed. You can't have a charity now and not have a rubber wristband. If purple had been available, it might have been purple.

Kim Phillips:
People say to me, *Oh my gosh, I love that bracelet. I love your orange bracelet.* It comes right off and I give it away. Spread the word.

Scott Stowell:
My favorite thing is this little clip we designed. There's a lenticular in there—a winky—so when you move it, you see the gesture come on and off.

Mark Serratoni:
We have inspired other MS organizations to adopt the color orange as the color of MS, which has expanded our movement to an international community.

↓
Make Your Mark
website
by BarkleyREI,
March 2007

Mark Serratoni:
One of the materials
we used in the begin-
ning was a website
built in Flash, which
invited people to
make their mark.

Sherri Giger:
More than 10,000
marks were created—
marks that still inspire
the MS movement
today—in various uses.

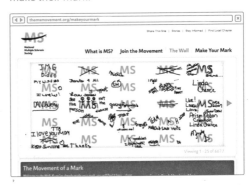

↑
full-page ad
in *USA Today*,
5 March 2007

Lu Chekowsky:
We even ran a full-
page print ad in *USA
Today*, showing the
MS logo with instruc-
tions on how to make
your mark through it.

Todd Waterbury:
That ad encouraged
people to mark out
the *MS* and then put
it up in their window
on a specific day.
Which was a lovely,
personal way to
use the medium.

examples

←
identity guidelines,
February 2007

Scott Stowell:
People would just
make their own stuff
and some of it the
headquarters just
never sees. I love
that we could give
people these tools
to get things done.

Scott Stowell:
That was all in like a six-month period. And then a year later they came back to us and they said, *Now we need identities for the walkathons and the bikeathons.*

Graham McReynolds:
Our Bike MS event is the largest cycling fundraising event in the world, generating over $80 million a year. It is sort of a signature event that we're known for. The same thing with our walk program, which is one of the largest events of its kind in America.

Kim Phillips:
It's the most exhilarating, positive thing I get to do all year.

Scott Stowell:
What I love about these events, especially with Wieden's strategy, is they are the thing that they are about. You're getting together to make a movement to fight the thing that's stopping you from moving.

Şerifcan Özcan:
It's not like, *Mini Golf for Leukemia.*

Scott Stowell:
I remember going to the meeting and just sitting there. I had no idea what we were going to do.

Şerifcan Özcan:
They started talking about walking and biking against MS, and I had an idea. It made so much sense. I got excited, but I held my breath and didn't say anything.

Scott Stowell:
In the elevator when we're leaving he's like *Oh yeah, I got it figured out. I'll show you back at the studio.*

Şerifcan Özcan:
You walk over the logo or bike over the logo just as you would cross out the logo. I was like, *This is the most obvious thing.* When you come up with the idea, you never think that it's amazing.

↓
Walk MS and Bike MS logos, August 2007

Daralee Champion:
I don't remember how I first learned about the MS Society, exactly, but it was probably soon after being diagnosed with MS in 2008. I do love the Bike MS logo, and proudly use it as my profile picture in the spring, during the time before the bike ride!

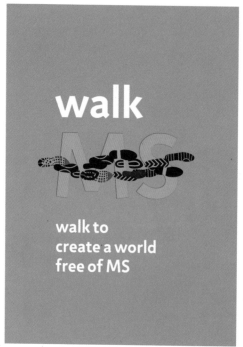

Graham McReynolds:
It just became so clear that this was the logical extension of where the identity should go.

Şerifcan Özcan:
Scott was just blown away. He was like, *You're right, best idea, no arguments, no other way.*

Scott Stowell:
I'm so happy he came up with the idea in the meeting and didn't say anything.

Şerifcan Özcan:
If you come up with the idea right at the meeting, it doesn't mean you came up with it right there. It's your whole way of problem solving leading up to that moment. But if you say it right then, it's not the best way of presenting the idea.

Scott Stowell:
Now you go to these events and you see these people doing this action, stomping something out, wearing a picture of stomping that thing out.

Kate Morse:
The logo is empowering. It's on my shirts, painted on my bike, and inspired my husband and I to co-found Team Strike Out MS. The name was inspired by the MS Society's logo.

Graham McReynolds:
There are 100 rides we do across the country, and they all looked different. Everybody had their own logo. The same thing with our walk program.

Şerifcan Özcan:
In Nashville you get a different one, in Brooklyn you get a different one. And all these events have separate sponsors, so how do these sponsors lock up?

Graham McReynolds:
People come in the door to the National MS Society through a bike event, through a walk event, and then they get to the concept of MS.

Şerifcan Özcan:
For bigger events we had lots of footprints. For local events, you use one step. Same thing with the bike events. That way just by looking at the logo you could see the size of the event.

Christie Germans:
I love how the bike tire tread strikes through the *MS* and the footprint stomps over the *MS* because it demonstrates why we join the events in the first place: to strike out, stomp over, and wipe out multiple sclerosis, so no one else has to hear the words, *You have MS.*

↑
Walk MS and Bike MS logo variations and sponsor logo systems,
August 2007

Şerifcan Özcan:
We made an amazing system that created a really nice balance of all the sponsors.

Todd Waterbury:
These sub-identities allowed events that had their own identity to be connected back to the overall MS idea.

Scott Stowell:
I was really proud of this. Because the sponsor logos were all different shapes, you couldn't say they had to be half the height of the MS or something. So we created this idea that there was a right triangle coming off of the logo and whatever sponsor logo had to fit within it.

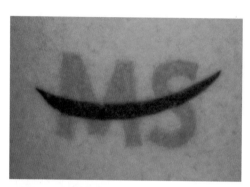

←↑
Kate Morse and
her MS logo tattoo,
2007

Graham McReynolds:
I can't even tell you
how many times
people are showing
me where they've
had this tattooed
on themselves.

Lu Chekowsky:
People felt owner-
ship over the mark
right away.

Şerifcan Özcan:
It was amazing to
meet people touched
by that logo, or see
people interacting with
it so much. You don't
really get that with
almost 99% of logos.

Todd Waterbury:
What I am really so
proud of is when I look
at this work today, it
still feels relevant. It
feels clear. There is
still that initial sense
of boldness. There is
a little bit of audac-
ity in it. That mix of
inevitable and unex-
pected is still there.

Mark Serratoni:
After nine years of
using the mark, it still
retains its power.

Kate Morse:
We have taken the logo
as a symbol of hope.

Lu Chekowsky:
I think it's actually
affected people's
lives, in a profound
and positive way.

Daralee Champion:
The message I think
the MS Society sends
is that they are there
and that they care.

Dan Wieden:
I've watched my
daughter, unfortunate-
ly, lose much of her
body's ability to work
as it used to. When
there are human beings
involved and you've
got a great client that
encourages you to
do the best work you
can—this kind of work,
it doesn't feel like work.

Graham McReynolds:
It is hard to overstate
how proud people are
of this identity, across
the organization.

Buz Sawyer:
I can honestly tell you
that in 37 years in the
advertising business,
this is the single most
meaningful thing that
I've ever done. It's a
very personal thing
for me. Three years
after the launch, my
daughter was diag-
nosed with MS, if you
can imagine that.

Lu Chekowsky:
Well, holy crap, I'm
getting emotional.
I'm going to start cry-
ing. Not like a lot, but
a little bit. It probably
is the most important
work I've ever con-
tributed to. Ever.

Scott Stowell:
Every project should
be like this. We learned
something, and
we helped people
do something.

Graham McReynolds:
Our dream is still prob-
ably what Scott's origi-
nal dream was. What
we hope to get to soon
is when you come to
our website, one of the
first things you would
do is make your own
mark against MS. Then
that becomes the logo
you would always see.
We want to make sure
people can participate
on their own terms—
we're ready now.

Willy Wong:
I'm a designer who
helps make places
more interesting,
organizations more
creative, and the lives
we lead within them
more meaningful.

My nephew Noah doesn't rock
ironic t-shirts or blog contrarian
about music—he drinks milk
because hunger. But at three,
he may be a budding designer
yet. He's full of relentless
curiosity (near Socratic in
asking, "Why? Why? Why? Why?
But why?"), resourceful
imagination (during visioning
sessions, aka playtime, he'll
generously offer me a seat
aboard his repurposed-
Amazon-box train caboose),
ambitious optimism (he eagerly
rebuilds his woodblock fort
over and over), and humor-
tinged humility (he smiles with
confidence as he paints outside
lines, onto walls, then himself).
Watching Noah reinforces my
commitment to design with
purpose and encourages me to
keep working towards a better
tomorrow for all.

The guys from *Good* magazine (and they actually were all guys, at least at first) came to us with a name and a logo and tons of enthusiasm. They wanted to change the world. They were looking for a studio to design their magazine. We were also looking for something: an opportunity. We wanted to work with words and pictures to make something new. And changing the world sounded good to us, too.

9.

in order
of appearance

Scott Stowell:
Here I am.

Casey Caplowe:
I'm one of the founders of *Good*. I took on the creative director role.

Ben Goldhirsh:
My title was founder and owner, and then CEO and cofounder.

Max Schorr:
When I got a title it was editor in chief and publisher, and then it became founding editor and publisher.

Zach Frechette:
I became the editor in chief after the second or third issue.

Joaquin Trujillo:
My title was photo director or photo editor.

Atley Kasky:
At *Good*, I was a junior designer and then a senior designer and then an art director.

Nicholas Rock:
I was an Open intern.

Dylan Reid:
I run Matter, a manufacturing company in Brooklyn, New York.

Rachel Bozek:
I'm a writer and editor. I copy edited *Design for People*.

Andréa Fernandes:
I'm a library assistant and freelance editor.

Morgan Clendaniel:
Deputy editor, I think they called me.

Bryn Smith:
I'm a graphic designer, writer, and critic. I still have every issue of *Good* that Open designed.

Siobhan O'Connor:
I was the *Good* features editor. I edited almost all the features.

Rob Di Ieso:
Good is the reason I have a career. When I worked on it at Open, I was like, *I want to be an editorial designer.*

Ryan Thacker:
I came back to Open to work on the *Good* media kit for two weeks. I ended up there for seven years.

Tom Manning:
I spent summer 2007 as an intern at Open.

Gary Fogelson:
I was at Open. A lot of what I did was as an art director.

Jorge Colombo:
I'm an illustrator, a photographer, and a graphic designer.

Maia Wojcik:
I live by the water in Greenpoint, Brooklyn. I am the cofounder of Fashion Tech Forum.

Alice Twemlow:
I'm a design writer and educator.

Şerifcan Özcan:
Good is the reason I was hired at Open.

Samir Husni:
I am the founder of the Magazine Innovation Center at the University of Mississippi.

THE NEW YORK TIMES, SUNDAY, SEPTEMBER 17, 2006

A Magazine for Earnest Young Things

By SHARON WAXMAN

LOS ANGELES

WE all want to change the world. But for the people at Good magazine it's going to take a lot of Red Bull.

It was 9 a.m. one morning last week, and a half-dozen staff members were drinking iced coffees on Sunset Boulevard, a few steps down the bleached California pavement from their tiny, worn offices on the strip.

At the center of the activity was Ben Goldhirsh, 26, the owner and a founder of Good, an unshaven bundle of enthusiasm wearing a Red Sox T-shirt and a pair of pale blue corduroys, held up by some clear twine from his car.

Not that he's poor. Mr. Goldhirsh is the multimillionaire financier of Good, the magazine he has just founded with friends from prep school (Phillips Academy Andover) and college (Brown). But he is perhaps a bit distracted, since Good's first issues hit the stands this week, and launch parties on both coasts are mere days away.

Still it doesn't take much to send Mr. Goldhirsh into full-throated evangelical pitch when asked, "Why in the world does anyone need another magazine?" (Yes! It's on real paper!)

"We wanted to bring valuable content to an audience that's not being respected," Mr. Goldhirsh explained. "You have The Economist, you have The New Yorker, with wonderful value, but they're not catering to the taste of a younger demographic."

Mr. Goldhirsh, the son of the founder of Inc. magazine, Bernie Goldhirsh, and heir to a fortune, doesn't read many magazines himself, nor do his friends. "I try to read The Economist every week, but it's almost like an assignment," he said. "It's an effort."

Nonetheless, he and his Andover buddy Max Schorr, now the publisher, decided that a new magazine was exactly what his generation needed most. "A free press for the critical idealist," as the inaugural issue proclaims.

In practice this means short features on subjects like a Los Angeles garage that converts cars to run on vegetable oil and an Austrian movie about processed food. The first issue has a distinctly unsexy cover, with a blank space for filling in a verb of the reader's choice, fol-

minded but financially unrigorous.

"This sounds a lot to me like vanity publishing, a bunch of kids sitting around with something they think is a really good idea, and one of them has a lot of money," said Chip Block, a retired magazine executive, publisher and consultant. "You can catch lightning in a bottle. But the odds are against them."

Other analysts said the magazine would face a challenge in finding enough advertisers to sustain revenues, besides those who may subscribe to its noble philosophy, like Timberland, which took an ad in the first issue. (It had 16 ad pages.)

"I was really surprised at how much I wanted to read it, and how good it looked on a first glance of a first issue," said Kurt Andersen, a former editor and founder of magazines, including Spy and Inside.Com. "First issues aren't necessarily

managing editor, Zach Frechette (from Brown, a year behind Mr. Goldhirsh), presided over a white laminate conference table and a whiteboard marked up with ideas for the second issue. Behind a bookcase, which serves as a divider, a refrigerator provided and stocked by Red Bull is largely depleted of that energy drink, while two half-empty half gallons of Cuervo Gold tequila suggest an alternative.

In the bookcase are The New York Times Manual of Style and Usage, "Basic Works of Aristotle," "Speak Truth to Power: Human Rights Defenders Who Are Changing Our World" by Kerry Kennedy and a stack of Men's Vogue. Yoga mats are neatly arranged in little cubbyholes next to the bar. The staff generally gathers for yoga classes out on the narrow balcony about three times a week.

The magazine's creative director, Casey Caplowe, Mr. Goldhirsh's roommate from Brown, displays mock-ups of early thoughts for the cover

NEW AGE, NEW MONEY The staff of Good, owned by Ben Goldhirsh, second from left and below.

Photograph by Axel Koester for The New York Times

←
The New York Times,
17 September 2006

↑
phone message slip,
27 April 2006

Scott Stowell:
I got a phone call out of the blue. I still have the pink message slip.

Casey Caplowe:
Good started with a name, and we figured it out from there.

Ben Goldhirsh:
There was this burgeoning conversation in society, which was certainly important in the lives of me and my friends, particularly Casey and Max. I called them up and said, "Let's start a magazine called *Good*, and try to rebrand good— give it an edge, and a pop, and a sex, and a pragmatism that fits with the way we see it."

Max Schorr:
This was 2005, when we started this. The political system felt pretty broken. It felt like a lot was going wrong in society, but more and more people wanted to do something in their own lives.

Casey Caplowe:
Good had been this soft, weak idea. Something people didn't want to be a part of, almost a pejorative, as Ben would say. Kind of like eating your vegetables.

Max Schorr:
We saw *Good* as sort of a reframing, and a reenergizing of being involved in society.

Casey Caplowe:
It wasn't about environmentalism, it wasn't about social justice, it wasn't about being a designer. It was about any and all of those things as they connected to using your interests and abilities to be part of something, to be part of pushing the world forward.

Zach Frechette:
This sounds more ambitious probably than it was, but they wanted to create a movement for our generation.

Joaquin Trujillo:
Good had so much potential from the beginning.

Max Schorr:
We were young, and it was definitely sort of an "anything is possible" vibe.

Scott Stowell:
Ben's dad was Bernie Goldhirsh, the guy who started *Inc.* magazine. After Bernie passed away, Ben inherited like a ton of money. But I think it was in a trust that said he should use it for things that are going to help the world.

Casey Caplowe:
The idea that something about doing good in the world should be well designed was fundamental to the whole idea.

Scott Stowell:
Things like this, when they come along, you're like, *Wait, this didn't already exist?* Because it seemed like such a good idea. *How is there not a magazine called* Good?

Casey Caplowe:
I saw in Scott's work a sensibility connection with mine. It was really about content, and always about ideas and meaning. But very, very simple, and really accessible.

Zach Frechette:
I think there's a history of participation that involves a lot of sacrifice and chaining oneself to trees and eating granola and wearing hair shirts that we were not excited about. We felt like that was a bad way to get people to want to be involved, so we tried to do it differently.

Scott Stowell:
It was my understanding that their goal—which is also my goal for pretty much everything—was to make every decision for the widest possible audience. And not in the sense of like, *We better dumb this down*, but basically to not exclude anyone.

Zach Frechette:
Like a lot of *Good*, we were making it up as we went along. No one had any official professional experience.

Scott Stowell:
We were hired to a do a prototype and then we ended up doing the first issue, and then the second issue. And then it was like, *Let's do it for a year*, then, *Let's do it for two years*. And we ended up doing 15 issues, which was three and a half years.

Zach Frechette:
Scott was not a utility designer. He had big ideas, and a vision, and integrity, and was really committed to all those things. Which is exactly what you want from someone who is helping you create a publication, but it also meant that things took time to do right. Compromises weren't always easily come to.

Scott Stowell:
We had thought of Trio being like a computer and Bravo like a magazine. I wanted *Good* to feel like a newspaper. When you'd look at a newspaper, you'd be reading about the situation in Gaza or something and next to it is an article about Nathan's Hot Dogs and you're like, *I'm going to read that.* That was an idea early on, of people being forced to see more than one thing at the same time.

Atley Kasky:
The way that Scott was able to make *Good's* aesthetic more human was appealing.

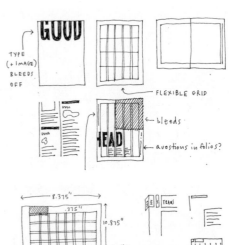

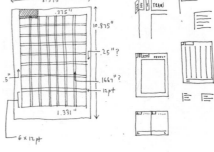

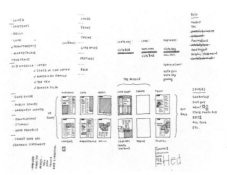

↑
Scott's sketches,
June–July 2006

Nicholas Rock:
I remember very clearly Scott's immaculate drawing of what the magazine could be, just still in sketchbook form, and then seeing that play out over the course of the summer.

Scott Stowell:
Everything in *Good* is on the baseline grid. There's not one piece of type ever on any page, in any issue, that's not on the grid. We set up this whole really complicated set of rules and played with it for over three years.

GOOD

A DO-IT-YOURSELF PERSONAL MANIFESTO:

(VERB)

*

LIKE YOU GIVE A DAMN.

Fill in the blank

FREE STICKERS INSIDE!

GOOD is for people that give a damn. It's an entertaining magazine about things that matter. Find out more: GOODMAGAZINE.COM

Issue 001
Sep/Oct 2006
$4.95 U.S. $5.95 Canada

0 74820 08311 1   1 0>

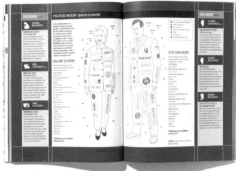

Joaquin Trujillo:
I wanted the magazine to be visually like when you haven't seen a friend or a family member, and you're about to go and give them a hug. I wanted it to be that moment before those two people actually connect—that space in the middle.

Dylan Reid:
It was cool, and colorful, and hard to pin down. It wasn't really a design magazine, or a political monthly. It covered technology, but not gadgets, lifestyle, but not fashion. It touched on social issues, but without a definitive political view.

Joaquin Trujillo:
Some magazines were definitely working on awareness, too, but I think they were so dry and almost institutional. We totally broke the mold. We totally wanted to be free. We wanted to show design and show color.

Rachel Bozek:
I was about 30 when I first saw Good on the newsstand. I remember thinking, I found my magazine. The only other time I've felt that way as an adult has been with Mental Floss.

Andréa Fernandes:
I read each issue, cover to cover, and usually found it all fascinating.

Morgan Clendaniel:
We would incessantly argue about various editorial decisions. People would often use the straw man, like, Does our audience want this? Whatever, people who are at this magazine don't like this! We would always come back to the fact that our North Star had to be that we were making decisions about a magazine that we would want to read, and the gamble was that there were other people like us.

Bryn Smith:
Good was the magazine I'd been waiting for.

↑
pages from
Good issue 001,
September/
October 2006

Scott Stowell:
The editorial staff was in LA for the most part. We were their art department.

Joaquin Trujillo:
At the beginning, we were working out of this house on Melrose.

Morgan Clendaniel:
For a long time, the New York office was just me in my house.

Siobhan O'Connor:
It was mostly dudes at the beginning, and it was all dudes at the top the whole time. In the New York office, where I worked, there were plenty of women, however. I think that was less the case in the LA office.

→
behind the scenes at Open and *Good*, 2007–2009

Ryan Thacker:
Processing the number of thoughts required to produce a more-than-100-page magazine in three or four days would pretty much turn my brain to mush by the end and I would need a day or two to recover.

Tom Manning:
I remember a few times I had an evening planned and then I'd be calling my wife, like, *I'm not going to be home at six. I'll make up for it.*

Max Schorr:
There were a lot of marathon sessions. I do think Open could kind of wait to the last minute and then some.

Rob Di Ieso:
The fact that they were all young—I mean they were fresh out of school—they would basically work around the clock.

Morgan Clendaniel:
We were all communicating on Basecamp, so we weren't even really talking that much. Being in two cities and two time zones at once was very frustrating at times, and not in a good way.

Scott Stowell:
They were three hours behind, so we would get in and have a few hours to work without them being around. And by the time they got in, we would be like, *OK, we're leaving now.* I think we pulled several all-nighters every issue..

Morgan Clendaniel:
We would wake up and expect there to be pages done. And they would never be done. Because, for all their genius, they did not work super quickly. We would all just be texting each other in the morning, furious that there were no pages done.

Rob Di Ieso:
I remember one night in particular, I finished *Good* and I closed all the files down, and then I opened up my Brown files and started working for the next day. So I was there for two full days straight.

Morgan Clendaniel:
We were up all night all the time because we wasted a lot of time because we were idiots, but we were having a lot of fun. We would always inexplicably start playing some shitty video game right before close. It wasn't until Issue 10 or 12 that we fully eliminated all-nighters from the schedule.

Rob Di Ieso:
Major magazines pay for and have these huge systems that manage text files linked to design files; it's more of a single process. With *Good*, we just had some InDesign files and we would email them, and they would edit those files and send them back so that we could check and make sure they didn't screw up any of the styling of the pages. It was a really slow process.

Gary Fogelson:
We had to treat it like a traditional magazine in a way, where different designers had different sections and they would just kind of run that.

Scott Stowell:
Marketplace was always my favorite section to lay out. It was fun to try to get everything to fit perfectly.

Rob Di Ieso:
I had a section called Look, and there was Portraits, and I often did the Good Guide in the back, which was always on some random topic. Like we had the Good Guide to North Korea, and the Good Guide to Buckminster Fuller. We all had our own sections that we had to take care of, then there was random stuff.

Scott Stowell:
Stimuli is basically the reviews: books, movies, whatever. We would hire the illustrators to do all three of them every time. We would give them the entire text and say, *You just have to pick out words and phrases from the text and illustrate those.* We didn't say which words or phrases to pick out.

Jorge Colombo:
Illustrators and photographers tend to be picky about having their art presented in as pure a form as it was received. But in the right hands, its deconstruction can be as stimulating as an extreme remix of a song.

Siobhan O'Connor:
Good's design was what drew a lot of us to it in the first place. It's also what made it stand out. There are a lot of new magazine launches every year, but the design elevated the magazine's profile, and made a concept that cynics might want to make fun of—*good*—feel edgy and kind of offbeat.

↑
pages from
Good issue 002,
January/February 2007
and *Good* issue 003,
March/April 2007

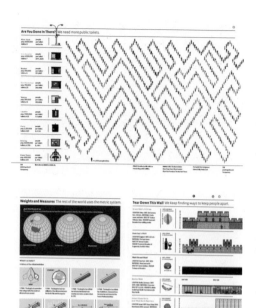

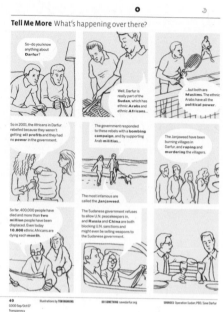

Scott Stowell:
There was a section called Transparency which was where all the infographics were.

Dylan Reid:
More than anything I remember the infographics, which *Good* was doing before anyone else was really publishing them.

Tom Manning:
There were a lot of times where Transparency was used as a wake-up call. A lot of them had a point around a social commentary—trying to get people to understand a complex issue, but also an agenda that was sometimes pretty naked.

Casey Caplowe:
We were going to these really great design studios around the world and asking them to take on this kind of meaty assignment of 12 pages of six different infographics. It wasn't just showing one visual style of information graphics, but a whole bunch of people doing really fresh and creative takes on them.

Morgan Clendaniel:
We often actively made them hard to read. We were like, *This should be more complicated.* Which is a crazy thing to do.

Tom Manning:
Infographics, in my mind, are made for people who are not design savvy. They're one of the most effective ways to remember information.

Casey Caplowe:
We wanted to help people understand the world better.

Scott Stowell:
I credit Casey with the entire renaissance of information graphics over the last 10 years—it's because of him.

Maia Wojcik:
We now see data graphics everywhere, but it wasn't the case then.

↑
some of Open's Transparency pages· from *Good* issue 006, September/ October 2007

Tom Manning:
Good wanted to do something on Darfur. We talked a lot about how no infographic is going to change people's minds or inform them any more than they've already been informed. Gary was like, *What if we do a comic?*

Casey Caplowe:
In retrospect, I really believe that was one of the strongest pieces of communication design and visual journalism that ever appeared in *Good*.

↑
Polling and Rolling, from *Good* issue 005, July/August 2007

Zach Frechette:
We created a board game—that was another fun insert. There were these little cardboard cutouts of all the candidates, we called it *Polling and Rolling*.

Morgan Clendaniel:
We got really obsessed with it actually being playable. So we spent days tinkering with the rules, never considering that no one was ever going to play the stupid election board game. We were like, *It must work properly.*

Zach Frechette:
I hold it up as a great example of us trying to be creative about how we communicate ideas and get people to pay attention to the things we want them to pay attention to. In this case, the election process.

Scott Stowell:
When we played Polling and Rolling in the studio, Hillary Clinton beat John McCain in the 2008 presidential election.

Morgan Clendaniel:
It always felt like Open was doing more than just designing it. Like, they were definitely a huge part of the creative process, beyond just the design. That was understood.

Gary Fogelson:
We had a certain amount of impact on content, and we tried hard to make it into a magazine we would want to read.

Scott Stowell:
I think that the intersection between words and pictures, or design and writing, had never been this integrated at Open before this point. I don't know if it got better, but I think that we got more brazen and comfortable doing it.

Ryan Thacker:
I mean it kind of just snowballed from, *Oh, we can get away with this?* To, *What else can we get away with?* Open doesn't really like dummy copy, so instead of putting *Big Headline Goes Here*, we'd try and write our own until they had a headline. Or they'd be like, *Sweet headline!* Sometimes they would rewrite stuff that we had written, and not always for the better. They had their reasons, but ours were usually funnier.

Morgan Clendaniel:
There were definitely times when I was like, *Why the fuck is Scott trying to change my headline?* It was very clear, even when we were annoyed at them, that they were incredible geniuses. So at the end of the day, it was like, *OK, this is good, it was helpful that you did this.*

Scott Stowell:
The amazing thing is we just kind of took it upon ourselves to do everything and their reaction 90% of the time was like, *Oh, thank God someone else did that because we have so much to do.* I can't even explain the level of empowerment we had from them. It was just basically like, *Oh, you guys are on it? Cool.*

Rob Di Ieso:
I don't think I've ever had as much editorial design freedom as we did on *Good.* Every publication I've ever worked on after that has totally been the editorial side driving the art side. I felt while we were with *Good,* in a lot of ways, the art was driving the editorial.

Scott Stowell:
All of this culminated in the sixth issue, which I think is the best. I was the guest editor, and both from a content standpoint and a design standpoint, I feel that it's the pinnacle of what we did.

Tom Manning:
This was the first time that we were going to do the whole issue, including the Transparency section. There was a lot of talk about design in this state of transition. All these large companies, like Google and GE, they were founding these design wings within large corporations.

Scott Stowell:
Alice Twemlow did the intro essay and the cover is there because of Alice. And to this day, her essay is one of my favorite things written on design for non-designers.

Alice Twemlow:
I simply took the title of the magazine and its founding premise—the concept of goodness—and considered its relationship to design.

Tom Manning:
Design was starting to emerge as this answer to a lot of things, but there was also a crossroads, a kind of questioning about it being this force for good.

Alice Twemlow:
The measure of *good design*, which has been used since the 1950s, has always seemed a bit phony to me, and so I just expanded it to ask, *Good for whom? And good for what?*

Scott Stowell:
She wrote this whole thing about the AK-47. It's just the perfect provocation because it's the most popular firearm of all time, and it's like beautiful as an object.

Alice Twemlow:
The AK-47 struck me as an example of everyday design that checked all the *good design* boxes like honesty to materials, form following function, pared-down aesthetic, no extraneous detail, and so on. And yet, if you questioned its purpose, the whole value system would start to fall apart.

Scott Stowell:
The design issue informs a lot of my thinking, including this book. The way I described that issue was that design is just about all these little choices you can make to make people's everyday lives a little bit better.

↑
the cover of *Good* issue 006, September/October 2007

Alice Twemlow:
It's a wonderful, hard-hitting cover: orange for warning and provocation. Then the singling out of the AK-47 from my article. That was Scott's idea, I'm sure. And then selecting an x-ray image of it, to reveal both the perfection and the organization of its working parts, as well as to underscore its deathly relationship to the skeleton.

Scott Stowell:
That issue ended up getting filed in the wrong part of the newsstand all the time. So you'd have like *Soldier of Fortune, Guns & Ammo,* and *Good.*

Casey Caplowe:
I think we knew it was the most provocative we'd ever been, and I think we liked that. And you know, it was one of the best-selling covers.

↑
the cover of
Good issue 008,
January/February 2008

→
scenes from *The Big
Idea with Danny DeVito*,
a documentary about
the cover shoot,
December 2007

Scott Stowell:
We had these giant
plywood letters that
were 10 feet tall. That's
two Danny DeVitos.
At the shoot, we real-
ized somebody had to
make sure they were
spaced properly. So I
stood across the street
yelling kerning instruc-
tions to some very
patient production
assistant-type guys.

Scott Stowell:
This cover started
as a joke because
they wanted to do
an issue called *Big
Ideas*. So we said,
*Let's just make the
word ideas really big.*

Ryan Thacker:
I remember it was
Gary Fogelson's idea.
It was like a sketch
of giant letters out in
the world, that said
IDEAS. And I think we
wanted David Cross or
something. We wanted
some cool celebrity.

Scott Stowell:
Someone at *Good*
knew Danny DeVito's
daughter. They were
like, *Danny DeVito is
really small. Let's get
him on the cover!*

Morgan Clendaniel:
He's not even
in the issue.

Scott Stowell:
And then they found
out that he owned
a Segway and was
super into it. That's
how it happened.

Ryan Thacker:
This was probably my
third or fourth week
at work, doing that
Danny DeVito cover
shoot. Coming from
a place like Philly, it
felt like I had arrived.

Morgan Clendaniel:
I thought it was re-
ally stupid at the time,
but Danny DeVito on
the Segway, that is
literally one of the
craziest things that
I have ever seen.

Şerifcan Özcan:
Danny DeVito is an
amazing Segway
rider. He was going
really fast all around
the place, weaving
in and out of traffic.

Ryan Thacker:
It wasn't his Segway
because of insurance
purposes. I'm pretty
sure I prepped the art
for the giant letters.

Morgan Clendaniel:
It was a great lesson
in letting creative
people be creative,
without putting too
many constraints on
them. I think the best
work we did was when
we just let ourselves
and the writers and
other designers be the
people they could be.

Siobhan O'Connor:
I still laugh when I
think about how weird
that Danny DeVito
cover—which made
no sense—was.

Morgan Clendaniel:
One of the saddest
things was when
we had to move to
a smaller New York
office because we
had no money. Those
giant IDEAS letters
wouldn't fit. So me
and one other guy
had to get rid of them
but they wouldn't fit
in the elevator. So we
had to break them all
in half to get them in
the elevator. It was
just this very sad,
literal metaphor.

Scott Stowell:
They had this subsection called the Good Guide, which we designed almost looking like a pullout. We designed it to kind of be the opposite of the magazine, like the grid is visible and there's a colored background.

Zach Frechette:
They were almost like magazines within the magazine.

Siobhan O'Connor:
Those were such a blast to put together— a true collaboration between design, edit, and data people. I edited a bunch of them.

Zach Frechette:
They were these little almost explainer-type sections that would dive into topics like North Korea or culture jamming. I think there was one about secret shadowy organizations.

Siobhan O'Connor:
The Good Guide to North Korea was especially awesome. I also loved The Good Guide to Slowing Down.

Zach Frechette:
It took a lot of effort to put them together, and I still think those are probably some of my favorite sections that we had in any of the magazines.

↑
The Good Guide to
North Korea in
Good issue 004,
May/June 2007

The Good Guide
to the Shadowy
Organizations that Rule
the World in
Good issue 011,
July/August 2008

→
concepts for
and the final version of
the cover of
Good issue.010,
May/June 2008

Scott Stowell:
Covers were always
contentious. Because
that's when they were
like, *We have to sell
some magazines.*

Morgan Clendaniel:
Open would be like,
*This just looks re-
ally beautiful*, and
we would be like, *No
one is gonna buy it.*
Which, no one did
anyway, but that
wasn't anyone's fault.

Ryan Thacker:
I remember Scott
almost quit over
one cover.

Scott Stowell:
The China issue cover
is the worst. It sucks.

Ryan Thacker:
He was so pissed. It
became about the
cover, but it was more
about them not trust-
ing us telling them that
it was a terrible cover.

Morgan Clendaniel:
The China cover was
really bad, and no
one's fault. Everyone
had their own opinion,
and thousands and
thousands of differ-
ent cover options. We
finally found that one.

Ryan Thacker:
It was like a red
Chinese flag with
black silhouettes
in the foreground,
like a stock photo.
Just exactly what
you would expect.

Scott Stowell:
They just wouldn't ap-
prove anything else.

Joaquin Trujillo:
China actually made
me really upset be-
cause we shot some
comps for it—these
fortune cookies,
which I thought were
really cool—then the
cover comes about
and it's the worst hor-
rible stock image.

Ryan Thacker:
The cover was sup-
posed to be this
fortune cookie. Now
that I'm saying this,
it also sounds cliché.
But it was definitely
more subtle.

Joaquin Trujillo:
We had people shoot-
ing internationally for
us, there's a lot of great
content inside, and then
that cover, totally, totally
ruined that whole issue.

Ryan Thacker:
That's definitely the
angriest I saw Scott
in seven years. Which
wasn't actually that
angry, it was just angrier
than you would usually
see your boss get.

Joaquin Trujillo:
When people see
the cover, they think,
*This is what the photo
editor chose?* I hate that
cover for that reason.

Ryan Thacker:
I don't remember how,
but everyone cooled off.

Ben Goldhirsh:
We almost went out of business. I think it's easy to blame the economy, but I think a truer account is that we didn't have our shit together.

Scott Stowell:
They were a start-up in every way. In the end when it fell in on itself it was like, *Oh, you mean they didn't know what they were doing?*

Morgan Clendaniel:
We were just gonna throw out some of these publishing orthodoxies, and then it turned out that some of them are like valuable and helpful.

Ben Goldhirsh:
We were constantly having to reinvent, tack left and right, and that's a really challenging thing.

Morgan Clendaniel:
I think everyone realized that we were investing too much of our souls at the beginning, so it became a little more of a job by the end.

Ben Goldhirsh:
In many ways, 2008 was the most important year for us, because it forced us to learn how to run a business. We laid off 40% of the staff that year. We had to cut our budget in half. We had to take the company and get it to break even. That was painful.

Morgan Clendaniel:
Open was a casualty— one of many casualties—of that bad time.

Zach Frechette:
I don't know that anyone would have ever accomplished the goal of galvanizing everyone and making the world a better, perfect place. But I think we had a great match between what we wanted to do and what we were trying to do, and there being an audience for that in the world.

Morgan Clendaniel:
When you look at the issues that we started doing without Open, that's when you can see what their influence was, and how important it was. There's a level of creativity that I don't think we hit. And not just in the design, but in our general ideas, because we had lost one of the key creative decision makers.

Scott Stowell:
I don't know that I will ever have a better experience than this. We had total buy-in from the client on every level and they were unabashedly enthusiastic about doing it. We stretched so far, but had so much fun.

↑
the cover of
Good issue 014,
January/February 2009

Scott Stowell:
Our last three issues were different. *Good* became this repository for stuff from their website. It was less interesting, even from a design standpoint.

Samir Husni:
I still get pleasure from those early issues of *Good* much, much more than from the present ones. The early *Good* issues are ones for the history books.

Alissa Walker:
I'm a writer who loves
cities, walking, and
gelato. Sometimes
all at the same time.

I have to be fastidious about organizing and interpreting information. But what I'm really doing is paying such good attention that I start to see relationships between concepts that other people don't.

I've taught myself to be more observant as I'm moving through my daily life because this is where all my best work happens, not sitting—or standing, or squatting, or hovering, or whatever we'll do next—at a desk. You can sit all day poking words into the internet, or you can walk a block, watch a blade of sunset slice between two buildings and realize your life is forever changed.

All the next great ideas are out there hiding in the shadows, stuck like gum to a sidewalk, waiting for you to put them together.

This story is about two projects we did with a company you probably already know about. Google first asked us to make a short movie. Then we got to make a whole ad campaign. I don't think that selling things is really our thing, but for Google we weren't really selling things— just ways for people to do their own thing. Of course, every project is an opportunity to do your own thing, if you can figure out how to do it.

in order
of appearance

Scott Stowell:
I hope you're enjoying the book.

Robert Wong:
I'm the executive creative director at Google Creative Labs.

Ryan Thacker:
At Open, I was involved with Google in the beginning and at the end, but not so much in the middle.

Şerifcan Özcan:
I wrote the script for the Google Chrome video. It was my last project at Open. And I think I had to end right before they started the production and shooting.

Lindsay Utz:
I was a producer in New York. I knew Scott through *Good*, where I ran the video department.

Lucia Vera:
I was the Open intern at the time of the Google Chrome project, meaning I was the unofficial photographer for the shoot, the backup hand model, the delivery specialist for liters of Starbucks coffee, and a fast learner.

Jason Jude Chan:
My midsection appeared in Open's Google Chrome video.

Anna Bishop Rehrig:
At that time, I was an associate product marketing manager on Google.org. I worked with a lot of different projects, but one big project during that time was to launch the Google for Nonprofits program.

Anna De Paula Hanika:
I was a product marketing manager at Google. My role in this project was basically building out a social media strategy for the launch of the Google for Nonprofits campaign.

Louise Ma:
My title at Open was, I think, just general designer. I was a freelancer at that point.

Chris Cheng:
I worked on Google for Nonprofits for four years as the product lead.

Shimmy Mehta:
I'm the CEO of Angelwish, a nonprofit that helps busy people grant holiday and birthday wishes to children with chronic illnesses.

10.

Scott Stowell:
This was when Chrome, the browser, first happened. Google was doing this launch campaign and they asked all these different designers and filmmakers to make little movies about Chrome. They called them Chrome Shorts.

Robert Wong:
This was one of those friends-and-family deals. We just reached out to people that we liked and whose work we admired—smart designers, or illustrators, or animators. I think Open had just done *Good* magazine, which I thought had a great aesthetic that seemed to really match the ethos and even the look and feel of Google.

Scott Stowell:
The budget was almost nothing. It was $10,000 to make a video. You know, because they're Google. They don't have a lot of money.

Robert Wong:
It's like beg, borrow, steal, get favors from friends who would want to do it just for the sake of the project. It was pretty scrappy.

Ryan Thacker:
It was like an insanely low budget. We spent it all on production.

Scott Stowell:
This was the whole brief: "What do you love about the web and being online? What about Chrome makes it better?"

Robert Wong:
We built Chrome to be faster, safer, and simpler. But it was never about Chrome. Chrome was just the thing that got people to the web.

Scott Stowell:
We didn't know what Chrome was, we didn't know why it made anything better, and we couldn't use it because it was only for Windows at the time—we all use Macs. What were we supposed to do?

Şerifcan Özcan:
We had a call with Google and they told us all about Chrome.

Scott Stowell:
They gave us a document with a list of features. We didn't understand that either.

Şerifcan Özcan:
Even the names, like *application shortcuts*, seemed unnecessary. If the application is there you click on it and open it. Why is the application shortcut a benefit that you need to talk about?

Scott Stowell:
I just really wanted to direct live action because I thought it would be fun.

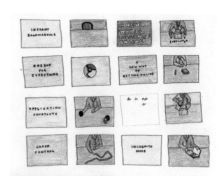

↑
Şerifcan's sketches and storyboards, February 2009

Şerifcan Özcan:
I thought it was hilarious, the things they gave us. A list of product details without images. I was just like, *We should just make fun of it.*

Lindsay Utz:
Open's idea was to find hyper-literal ways to illustrate its functionality.

Şerifcan Özcan:
I started making little drawings of those moments, of how I could interpret what they said. We actually ended up shooting it exactly the way I drew it.

Ryan Thacker:
It was shot in one day.

Scott Stowell:
We ended up working with the head of the video business at *Good*, Lindsay. She produced and edited it.

Lindsay Utz:
I hired the crew, rented the gear, and oversaw the production. And I kept Scott in check.

Lucia Vera:
It was the first shoot I had ever been in, and there was so much to take in.

Şerifcan Özcan:
We found an actual hand model who was really professional with making expressions with his hands, which is really a funny job.

Lucia Vera:
I don't think I made major contributions to ideas, but it felt as if I did.

Scott Stowell:
Jason makes a cameo in it, but he didn't work at Open at the time.

Jason Jude Chan:
I'm wearing a brown vest and a blue shirt and a tie—I think a red tie.

Scott Stowell:
The cast was basically friends of Lindsay's. Jorge Colombo and Gary Fogelson, too.

Lucia Vera:
We all couldn't stop thinking of ways to make it funnier, sillier, more goofily mechanical, and unexpected. It was like a collaborative joke that went on for...12 hours?

Robert Wong:
We must have launched at least eight or 10 of these videos. They were all so different. From style, to plot, to the way they were executed.

Scott Stowell:
We were so concerned with, *What is Chrome?* Obviously we were just making fun of it, but then we saw the rest of the movies, and none of them were about Chrome at all! Ironically, ours was the only one that actually talked about the benefits of the product.

Robert Wong:
The beauty was in the diversity. That's exactly how we hoped these would turn out. Which kind of mirrors the web—how different and wildly amazing it is.

Şerifcan Özcan:
We were like, *Who's going to download a completely new browser?* And now everyone is using it.

↑
Jorge Colombo with the Google Chrome logo in *Features List*, Open's Chrome Short, April 2009

Scott Stowell:
There were three mandatories. One, your Chrome Short is fun and awesome. Two, it starts with the Chrome logo. And three, if a web browser is in the short, make sure it's Chrome and not some other browser.

→

more scenes
from *Features List*,
April 2009

Jason Jude Chan:
Lindsay was like, *Hey,
do you want to be in
this Chrome video?*
And I'm like, *Do I have
to show my face?*

Lindsay Utz:
Safe browsing was
my favorite. It wasn't
easy to get, but in the
end our hand talent
delivered the perfor-
mance of a lifetime.

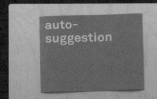 

Scott Stowell:
A year later, the people at Google.org, which is the philanthropic arm of Google, were making a program to make Google docs and Google apps more accessible to nonprofit users. They wanted to call it Google for Good.

Anna Bishop Rehrig:
What Google.org did was say, *How do we leverage the best of what Google has, that spirit of innovation, and really take that and do good in the world?*

Scott Stowell:
Robert recommended us again, to pitch ideas for a kind of ad campaign to launch the program.

Robert Wong:
Sometimes you play the role of matchmaker, finding the talented people from the creative design world and connecting them to those who could use some mojo. This was an easy match.

Anna Bishop Rehrig:
We came in with a scope of work, something like, *Help us create a visual identity for this program and help us create a tagline.*

Scott Stowell:
They contacted us and it was kind of a situation where somebody asks you to do this thing, and they don't mention money at all.

Ryan Thacker:
They wanted it to be like an advertising pitch, which means you have to show ideas for free.

Scott Stowell to Anita Yuen:
17 August 2010
It's typically unacceptable for design studios to develop work for no fee. That's speculative work, and the AIGA has a policy against it, which we support. Traditional ad agencies, on the other hand, pitch for free, and often pay studios like us to work on their pitches. Of course, the billings they compete for are often in the millions of dollars.

Ryan Thacker:
In the design world, small places can't afford to do that. Scott kind of told them off.

Scott Stowell:
They had like 10 agencies up for the job. If you wanted to do work for free, you could, but you didn't have to. We just showed some other projects. Google picked two finalists in that first round. Open was one of them. Then they asked, *How much should we pay for ideas? We have no idea.* I think I said, *I don't know, five grand?* They were like, *OK.* So they paid us to make some ideas. We won in the second round.

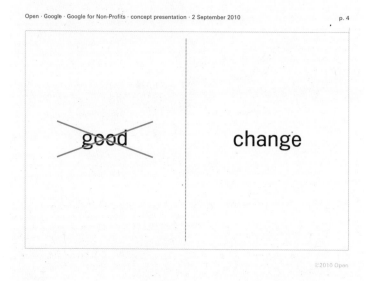

Open · Google · Google for Non-Profits · concept presentation · 2 September 2010   p. 4

©2010 Open

←
a concept image from Open's second-round pitch presentation, 2 September 2010

Scott Stowell:
Twice, I flew to Google and back the same day. I just didn't have time, so I would take a morning flight out there, arrive in San Francisco at like 10:30, take a cab out to Mountain View, have a meeting for like two hours, take a cab to San Francisco, meet a friend of mine for dinner, and then get on the red eye and come back and come to work. The first time, I was like, *This is cool. I feel like a spy or something.* The second time, I was like, *Never again.*

Ryan Thacker:
Our pitch basically told them they couldn't name their program what they had wanted to name it: Google for Good.

Scott Stowell:
One of the first questions I had was, "What are the requirements to be in the Google for Good program? Do you curate it?" My wife had tried to do a Kickstarter and they rejected her, because it was for a nonprofit project. Kickstarter was like, *We don't do that.* But they hadn't made that clear. So that was totally on my mind, this idea of like, *What are the criteria?*

Anna Bishop Rehrig:
I think it was pretty basic. It was a pretty simple online form. In the U.S., it would just require them to enter their 501(c)(3) nonprofit code. That was the prerequisite, and then we would vet for a few different criteria. In general, those who qualified would gain access.

Ryan Thacker:
Scott asked them if a neo-Nazi group or an organization that denies the existence of climate change could use the service, and when they said yes, he said, "Then you can't call it Google for Good," which they hadn't considered.

Scott Stowell:
Anybody who works for a nonprofit wants to change something. There are plenty of causes, and not everybody agrees that they're all good. So we ended up focusing on the idea of change.

Anna Bishop Rehrig:
You're changing the world. You've committed your life. You've probably sacrificed income and hours of sleep to be able to work on something that's so important to you and the world, but the reality is the day-to-day is often bogged down in bureaucracy or tools that don't work, rejected grant proposals, or various resourcing dilemmas. *How can we make this easier for them?*

Scott Stowell:
The Google for Nonprofits program— as it ended up being called—would give nonprofits a break on the corporate rate for Google Docs, a bunch of free Google ads, and stuff like that.

Anna De Paula Hanika:
How can technology really empower and amplify the efforts of nonprofit organizations?

Scott Stowell:
It's like, *We want to change the world, but first we have this crappy spreadsheet we need to deal with.*

↑
the three directions presented to Google, 2 September 2010

Scott Stowell:
We pitched three ideas. They liked pieces from each one, but they really liked the subverted infographics, which we can thank Louise for.

the fuzzy
feeling you
get from
changing
the world

donors reached

Google tools used

Google for nonprofits

reach more donors improve operations raise awareness
make a change: google.com/nonprofits

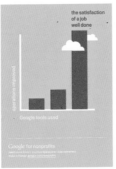

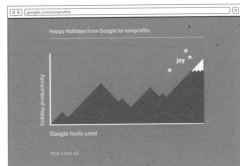

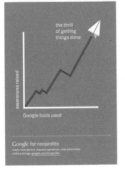

← infographic posters, September 2010

↑ Google for Nonprofits holiday "gift" microsite, December 2010

Scott Stowell:
From a design stand-point, Google's whole thing was pretty sim-plistic. Primary colors! Everything looked like preschool. I really loved using the prima-ry colors in a way that didn't look like regular Google primary colors.

Louise Ma:
For some reason I was sketching at home. I knew I had to turn in an idea but I didn't know what it was yet. I was just sitting on my couch, and I remem-ber I was very relaxed, and I was just like, *It's about nonprofits, and Google, and business for nonprofits*. So I just took these pieces and smashed them together. I remember thinking it'd be cute to make the graph line into a heart. So I did it, and it certainly was cute! Scott and Ryan were super stoked.

Anna Bishop Rehrig:
The infographics, I thought, were a really nice, irreverent way to touch on the fact that Google is known for using tech tools and innovation to help create progress, but at the end of the day, we're trying to reach people. We wanted to really touch on that human emotion.

Louise Ma:
And there were some bar charts with clouds around them, you know like very posi-tive, uplifting imagery. We weren't being cheeky or anything.

Scott Stowell:
Google saw these, and they were like, *OK, those are done.*

Anna Bishop Rehrig:
The campaign reso-nated with us almost immediately. I think ev-erything from the bold colors to the friendly language that seemed super relatable, to skirting this negative but dancing around it and becoming a posi-tive. *The fuzzy feeling you get from changing the world* on the x-axis versus *donors reached* on the y-axis, and then turning it into a heart—kind of a clever way of putting those two things together.

Louise Ma:
I feel like the idea, the whole concept, was driven by that first sketch. And everything else was just sort of riffing on that. So it was really kind of serendipitous. It really just sort of came to me. I wasn't pushing hard to come up with something. It was just one of those moments where it felt very effortless. So I guess the ideas were born of being very relaxed on my couch.

↓
print, video,
and web ads,
February–April 2011

Louise Ma:
I really fell in love with
the process because it
was so easy. The only
hard part about every-
thing was coordinat-
ing the colors across,
like, print and web.

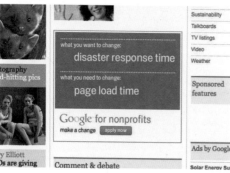

Anna Bishop Rehrig:
We had a discussion
around how to touch
on that sometimes-
frustrating element of
the day to day without
going to a negative
place: to take a mo-
ment and celebrate
the daily heroes
within organizations
and the sometimes-
unglamorous work
that they're doing.

Scott Stowell:
Our idea from the
beginning was that
Google doesn't
change the world,
they just help people
do their job, which
in this case happens
to be to change the
world. The print and
web ads we made
always tied *what you
want to change* to *what
you need to change.*

Anna Bishop Rehrig:
We would run ads
using Google AdWords
and YouTube to gen-
erate awareness of
the program, and
those drove direct
response to fill out
the application form
or learn more.

Scott Stowell:
We messed around
with the taglines. It
ended up being "Make
a change" which is
good because it was
a call to action.

Chris Cheng:
The Google for
Nonprofits campaign
was so inspirational.
It moved me and
others to action.

Shimmy Mehta:
I think it's a great pro-
gram for nonprofits.
It's one stop where
they can see how all
these pieces can in-
teract and be utilized,
and help support their
missions, and help
them to save money,
and time, and energy,
and effort, which is
a limited resource.

Scott Stowell:
At Open, we don't
make software. But
we are able to do this
campaign. And that
will help Google get
their software into the
hands of people who
need help doing their
job. And their job is
to save 100 sloths or
whatever. I see that
chain of events as a
totally ideal scenario.

Anna De Paula Hanika:
It takes a lot of people
a long time to get
Google, to balance
messaging and the
attempt at being
humble, while putting
other people forward
and letting other
people speak for us.
Scott and the team
really just got Google
and got the projects
really, really quickly.

Louise Ma:
And then it just be-
came churning out
stuff. And some of
that was really fun,
too—t-shirts and
water bottles.

↓ →
Google for Nonprofits
materials,
March 2011

Louise Ma:
I doctored many photos of t-shirts, sweatbands, and luxurious glass water bottles.

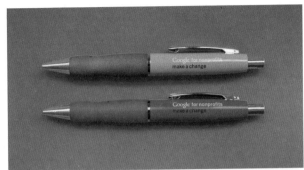

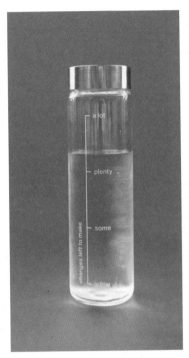

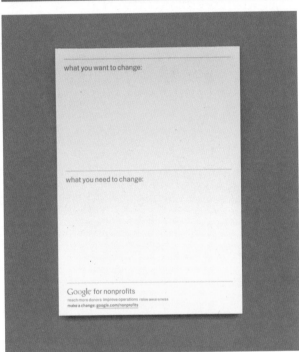

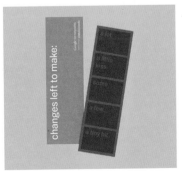

Scott Stowell:
We never got any of the candy bars.

Ryan Thacker:
That t-shirt is one of my prouder achievements as a designer, although I never got a sample.

Scott Stowell:
They didn't make those.

Anna Bishop Rehrig:
We did a Google blog post announcing the program. We did a number of events. The one that I remember most was a large conference in Washington, D.C.

Anna De Paula Hanika:
This was an example of how you can take a project or an effort that is normally treated with fairly dull, dry communication and really reinvent it through design.

Anna Bishop Rehrig:
The whole event presence was shaped by the campaign. That included everything from the booth space to swag. We had tote bags that were really well received, stickers that people could take with them, t-shirts. One thing that I really liked was the Make a Change wall.

Scott Stowell:
The booth we designed was just like the print and web ads we had written, but this time anybody could just walk up and write what they wanted to change themselves.

Robert Wong:
Think about Google. Most of our stuff is not really about our stuff, as much as what the stuff allows people to do on our stuff.

Anna Bishop Rehrig:
This was a huge wall across the entire booth space that was made of primary-colored panels. It was whiteboard material, and people could come and write the things they wanted to change on top—the mission that drove them—versus the things they needed to change—the daily work that just needs to get done.

Anna De Paula Hanika:
It was just such a great platform for everything else that we wanted to do. Open had really thought through all of the different components in advance, which is really rare. Normally you would have an uphill struggle to figure out how does this other thing that we want to do fit in with what we've already done?

Anna Bishop Rehrig:
At the end of the conference, we were able to look at this whole wall and say, *Wow, we touched people or reached people who are working on things as wide-ranging as the environment, women's rights, free speech, refugee rights*—everything that you can think of under the sun.

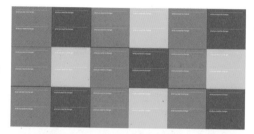

↑
the Make a Change wall in the Google for Nonprofits booth at the NTEN Nonprofit Technology Conference in Washington, D.C., 17–19 March 2011

Google for nonprofits

If you work for a nonprofit, it's your job to change the world.

What change did you make? Tell us your story.

Young reporters cover the Australian Election	Helped 122,648 survivors of sexual assault	We ended the abuse of sloth bears in India	Help developing communities via volunteering
Gavin Heaton from Vibewire Youth Inc	Maureen McNally from RAINN Rape Abuse and Incest National Network	Kartick Satyanarayan from Wildlife SOS	Alison B. Lowndes from AVIF ABLe Volunteers International Fund
We connect people to free volunteer projects!	Given over $46 million through 26,000 grants	Built web presence, 500 unique visits per day	Education to businesswomen in emerging mkts

Scott Stowell:
Make a Change was a microsite we designed as part of the campaign.

Louise Ma:
People would write in about their nonprofit and how they were using Google tools. The way the site worked was beautifully simple, understated. The only thing the microsite did was record people's experiences.

Anna De Paula Hanika:
Nonprofits could submit a story of what they changed and how they changed it.

Louise Ma:
With that project we were really on the cusp of doing something with social media.

Anna De Paula Hanika:
The other thing we were trying to do was build a community around sharing some best practices.

Louise Ma:
The DNA of Open is so populist. It's totally like Scott and Open to make any sort of marketing idea revolve around social, around what other people are doing, and have that come together to make an even stronger point about something.

Anna De Paula Hanika:
Our goal was to provide a platform to celebrate the work of other nonprofits, so that we could build up this really rich pool of case studies and examples for other nonprofits to look at and work from.

Chris Cheng:
If I was ever having a bad day, I could go visit the Make a Change page and see the entries up on the website. I connected with the campaign by knowing that I wasn't the only one out there wanting to do good in this world, and it was exciting to see technology play a central part in instigating positive change.

↑
the Make a Change microsite,
March 2011

Anna Bishop Rehrig:
Google was and is such a strong brand. It's iconic. It's become a verb in a lot of ways. How do you stretch the limits of the brand and help it evolve but stay really core to what it is? I think that's where design always comes in.

Scott Stowell:
More and more, we're trying to just break down that line between what's a writer and what's a designer. I kind of don't really see a difference in the end. The idea of thinking about the message, the form, and the content at the same time, both making it, and experiencing it, to me, is the best scenario. And we were lucky to be able to get this opportunity and it was kind of under the radar, maybe, so we were just able to do our thing.

Robert Wong:
Really good designers can put on any hat and do anything for any brand. When I look for designers for Google, I try to find people who at their core are already Googly—they have the same values and purpose as ours. The work inevitably comes out better, the designers are more satisfied, and it takes less management overhead. Open fit that bill.

Scott Stowell:
This is our ideal kind of project. Where we come up with the idea, we figure out where it's going to go, what it looks like—it's all one thing. It all fits together.

Louise Ma:
It felt like the nature of what we were doing was at once of tremendous importance and also of no consequence because of how fun it was.

Scott Stowell:
This was the first time that Open broke through to being the ad agency, not just the designers. The bonus of it being for both a huge, cool company, and for nonprofits at the same time? There's no possible better situation. And the people were pretty nice, too.

Chris Cheng:
I believed in the Google for Nonprofits mission so much that I would do the work for free. This kind of passion and zeal for nonprofit work is what drew me to the Google for Nonprofits space, and I am proud of the work we did as a team.

Louise Ma:
Yes, they were friendly and pleasant, even though they made us design a newsletter in Google Docs.

↑
Google for Nonprofits newsletter template, April 2011

Louise Ma:
Toward the end of the project, we had to design their newsletter—in Google Docs. It just got so ridiculously difficult. We had been working with this very minimal look, with these programs like Illustrator and InDesign and stuff, and it was just so funny, because then when we tried to pull this off on Google Docs, it was not working for us. At one point we even told them. We were like, *Your tool is weird.*

Charles Harrison:
I'm a retired industrial designer. For many years I was employed by Sears and Roebuck, and at the point of retirement, I was managing design for all of their consumer products.

I think it's absolutely imperative that a designer make the choice to be certain that whatever they do is not misunderstood. That means a lack of confusion: no trickery, cuteness, or anything where you have to dig in to discover what the intent of something is.

If you have something in your possession—whether it's a tool or a toy—if it's confusing, that's not a desirable feature.

Being original is, in my opinion, exciting and stimulating. However, to be able to use something comfortably when you want to and stop when you want to? I think that's more important.

Naked Pizza started with one small location in New Orleans, making healthy pizza that actually tasted good. When we heard from them, they already had a logo, but they needed lots of other things: menus, pizza boxes, signs, something called a "box topper," t-shirts, window graphics, and more. It sounded like fun. Plus, how complicated could it be? When they started opening locations in places like Dubai and Nairobi (and then closing them), we found out.

in order
of appearance

Robbie Vitrano:
I'm cofounder and headed design and brand for Naked Pizza.

Scott Stowell:
Pizza sounds pretty good right around now.

Randy Crochet:
I was one of the two original cofounders of the World's Healthiest Pizza—and of course, after the name change—Naked Pizza.

Vincent Vumbaco:
When I worked for Naked Pizza I was their in-house architectural designer. I put together the store book with all the furniture, fixtures, equipment, and branding information you would need to open a Naked Pizza location, and then project managed all the construction.

Zoë Scharf:
I was the intern at Open. I was really doing a little bit of everything.

**Reverend
Earl Williams:**
I am a minister and a community leader in the neighborhood of Hollygrove in New Orleans.

Ryan Thacker:
Aside from Scott, I was the main person on this project at Open.

Ian Ohan:
I opened the Dubai locations.

Ryan Page:
I started with Naked Pizza as their only graphic design hire at the time.

Hayon Shin:
I'm a senior at Rhode Island School of Design, studying graphic design.

Ian Cox:
I'm an American based in East Africa. I sell off-road vehicles across the continent of Africa, primarily to the humanitarian, security, and corporate sectors.

Ritesh Doshi:
I am a franchisee of Naked Pizza in Kenya, and the CEO of our business here.

Ralph Obure:
I'm a final-year medical student at the University of Nairobi in Kenya.

11.

←
the original
Naked Pizza, at
6307 South Miro Street
in New Orleans,
24 April 2009

Robbie Vitrano:
Naked Pizza was a
product of the post-
Katrina New Orleans,
and the sense of
urgency and desire to
help stand the city up.

Robbie Vitrano:
Fast food is arguably
the most successful
business infrastruc-
ture in human cre-
ation. So, what if we
could use that infra-
structure to help in-
stead of harm? Naked
Pizza's mission was to
demonstrate that fast
food can be part of the
solution to the global
epidemic of obesity
and chronic disease
associated with diet.
We considered a vari-
ety of different foods,
but landed on pizza as
a product that essen-
tially is recognized and
enjoyed universally.

Scott Stowell:
First of all, pizza
is awesome.

Robbie Vitrano:
I mean, pick a culture
and there's something
going on essentially
that is pizza-like. It's
recognized whether
it's flatbreads or naan.

Scott Stowell:
As soon as we heard
about it, I was like,
That sounds amazing.

Robbie Vitrano:
None of us had made
pizza. None of us really
had been in the food
business, and none of
us had done franchis-
es before. The idea
to create the world's
healthiest pizza was
driven by my partner,
Jeff Leach, in terms of
the idea of the ingredi-
ents, what went into it.

Randy Crochet:
We wanted to provide
a product that was a
bit more healthy—and
more importantly, cre-
ate a reason to have
a conversation with
our customers about
health and nutrition.

Robbie Vitrano:
We started focusing
on taking the com-
mon ingredients of
pizza and tweaking
them. Instead of hav-
ing processed flour
grain, we would use
10 different grains and
about half of them
would be whole, so
that would decrease
the glycemic index.

Vincent Vumbaco:
It tasted good.

Scott Stowell:
They only had one
location. It had
opened in New
Orleans after Katrina.

Zoë Scharf:
It was kind of a small
hole in the wall.

**Reverend
Earl Williams:**
It was named World's
Healthiest Pizza.

Scott Stowell:
Business was boom-
ing in that one loca-
tion, and then they
wanted to expand.

Vincent Vumbaco:
I was doing some nonprofit work and rebuilding after Katrina in Hollygrove, one of the most devastated neighborhoods. Reverend Earl Williams, the owner of the house that I was rebuilding, used to go to World's Healthiest Pizza on Tuesdays, because you could get two for one.

Reverend Earl Williams:
They donated a couple pizzas for our Bible study. I've been hooked ever since.

Vincent Vumbaco:
We'd have lunch together, as I was building his house, and that's kind of how I got introduced to Naked Pizza before it was Naked Pizza. Then I came to find out a couple years later that they needed some conceptual renderings. I found out about the job opening on Twitter. I followed up and had the job that afternoon, like a few hours later. It was a really super fast-paced, kind of crazy experience.

Robbie Vitrano:
I reached out to Valerie Casey, who was at Ideo at the time and was someone who had an overall well-developed sensibility about design.

Scott Stowell:
It was 2009, so we were in the middle of the crash and Obama had just gotten into office. I had been invited by Alissa Walker of *Good* to present at a conference called The Upside of Down. So we came up with this idea called the Give and Take Machine. It looked like a food truck, but it was kind of a mobile community center. I met Valerie because she was presenting there, too.

Robbie Vitrano:
When we started to get into the fine points of expression and elements that needed much more attention to detail, Valerie said we should go with Open.

Vincent Vumbaco:
Open really changed the direction of the visual identity of Naked Pizza, in my opinion, for the better.

Scott Stowell:
This was another one of those instances where I felt like I had all these ideas pent up for many years. The idea of doing a fast-food restaurant is just such a great project.

↑
prototype store rendering, February 2010

Scott's notes for Open's first presentation, April 2010

Open · NakedPizza · initial presentation · 27 May 2010

Pizza is about sharing.

Nobody has a "hamburger party."

Open · NakedPizza · second presentation · 14 June 2010

Here's a whole pie we can share.

Open · NakedPizza · third presentation · 26 June 2010

We've refined the system and the symbols to be simpler, warmer, and more direct.

↑
Open's first three
presentations,
May–June 2010

Robbie Vitrano:
The *A* in *Naked* is just
a simple triangle, so
it had the ability to
incorporate into a
mark, a collection, a
rainbow collection of
pizza slices, if you will.

Ryan Thacker:
Naked Pizza didn't
care that their
pepperoni was part
beef and part pork.
They just thought
the half-cow, half-pig
face looked weird.

Robbie Vitrano:
One of the most pow-
erful elements that
guided so much of
what we ended up
doing together was
the sentiment that
pizza is for sharing.

Scott Stowell:
Years before this, we
were pitching logo
ideas to the USA tv
network. I asked Gary
Fogelson, who was
working here at the
time, I was like, *Gary, I
need a concept image
that says, like, democ-
racy, and a bunch of
different things all add-
ing up to one big thing
that's populist and
American.* In five min-
utes, he sends back a
picture of a pizza. He
was joking, but I was
like, *Perfect. Done.*

Robbie Vitrano:
The notion of sharing
also confers a gener-
osity or a concern or
a relationship to the
people around you.

Scott Stowell:
Our core idea was that
pizza literally is a food
that's meant to be
shared. It's a circular
thing that has equal
parts. So basically we
said that with anything
they do, you have to
be sharing something
of value, whether it's
food, information,
a joke, whatever.

Ryan Thacker:
Naked Pizza already
had a wordmark, and a
wordmark in a square.
We were charged with
building the system
around it. We had to
take this thing that—I
don't know if it was
meant to have mean-
ing, but we gave it
meaning. I guess it was
a way of designing the
logo without getting
to design the logo, by
reverse-engineering
this idea of pizza being
this democratic thing
into the logo, then
engineering it into
the system. We gave
it the meaning that
we would have given
it had we made it.

Zoë Scharf:
Open had four people listed on their website as people who worked there, when in reality it was just Scott and Ryan. So I didn't know it, but I was calling Ryan—and Ryan every day—asking for an internship. It paid off. I think finally they got pretty tired of me calling so much.

Ryan Thacker:
I was the only designer at Open at the time. At least at the beginning of this project, I'm pretty sure it was just me and Scott.

Scott Stowell:
From the beginning, we wanted to do something that was totally modern.

Ryan Thacker:
We knew it wasn't going to be red and green. It wasn't going to be Papa John's.

Scott Stowell:
We didn't want to do any, as they say in the industry, "heritage cues," like, there was no, *This is an old-world pizza recipe*, and no gingham or wood texture or whatever. But we still wanted it to be warm.

Robbie Vitrano:
It was a bit counterintuitive for a company that was paying attention to ingredients not to show literal ingredients. But if Domino's can do anything, they can pay the day rate for the best food photographers in the world. It's probably not worth our while, and we're not going to get anywhere new by showing a beautiful shot of a tomato or an onion.

Scott Stowell:
We started off doing the style guide, which was done very quickly because they needed it right away.

Zoë Scharf:
Naked Pizza was very authentic. I tried to incorporate that mentality in things as small as the icons for the different toppings. There's a difference between using an icon of bacon or the actual animal, the idea being that a lot of kids just didn't even know that the food that they were eating came from this particular animal.

Ian Ohan:
The icons were cute. But the thing is, I almost found all that stuff finicky. As a business owner, I struggled with that.

↑
Ryan's topping sketches, June 2010

→
final topping icons, July 2010

Ryan Thacker:
The idea of the topping icons was to show the thing that it came from, not the thing. So it wouldn't be slices of pepperoni or sliced olives or whatever. It would be an olive, or a cow.

 ARTICHOKE
 BELL PEPPER
 BLACK BEAN
 BLACK OLIVE
 CILANTRO

 JALAPEÑO
 FIRE-ROASTED RED PEPPER
 FRESH BASIL
 GARLIC
 MUSHROOM

 PINEAPPLE
 RED ONION
 SPINACH
 SUN-DRIED TOMATO
 TOMATO

 HAMBURGER
 HAM
 SAUSAGE
 PEPPERONI
 CHICKEN

Ryan Thacker:
Naked Pizza had this winking emoji thing that they called the Chub.

Scott Stowell:
They were 100% attached to him. They were like, *Let's slap a Chub on there.*

Ryan Thacker:
They would put that face on anything.

Robbie Vitrano:
It was a little bit ironic, given that we were supposed to be talking about health.

Ryan Thacker:
It was from the first vinyl banner they ever hung on their first door in New Orleans. It had a lot of importance to the founders.

Robbie Vitrano:
Initially, we just used the keyboard to create it. Then by virtue of having the smile integrated with a bite of a pizza with that little fattened cheek holding a little bit of the pizza in the mouth, it just conveyed the personality that we liked.

Ryan Thacker:
There's a page of sketches, probably five pages somewhere, of every possible variation of that facial expression. There are probably several presentations somewhere of like, *It could be like this, or like this, or like this*, which goes on for 25 pages.

Ryan Page:
His face turned up in just the weirdest situations. Inappropriate situations. Franchisees using a generic smiley face in place of our special Chub smiley face was a very common mistake.

Robbie Vitrano:
It was likable, and people dug it, and it's just the kind of thing that created identity. It's not one of those stop-the-presses moments, but it just feels right and everybody likes it.

Ryan Thacker:
Who are we to tell them that they shouldn't have it? It's a weird thing. I like it in the end.

Robbie Vitrano:
The team gave that mark some personality and we certainly wouldn't be the first or the last ones to use a smiley face in our branding. But it became something entirely ownable.

↓
painting the original Chub at the first Naked Pizza, 18 April 2009

Ryan's Chub sketches at Open, 7 June 2010

the original Chub next to the new and improved version

Did you know? About 17% of U.S. restaurants serve pizza.

THIS PIZZA WAS MADE WITH LOVE (AND THE BEST INGREDIENTS WE COULD GET)

We feel sorry for the other 83%.

Ancestral Blend?

Our hand-stretched thin crust is made from a blend of grains and seeds, agave fiber and probiotics together with pure water.

NAKED PIZZA®

Welcome to the tribe

FOLLOW US ON TWITTER:

@NakedPizza

This is your pizza.

It is made with an Ancestral Blend™ of 12 whole grains, seeds, prebiotic fiber[1] & probiotics[2] with all-natural cheese & sauce. It is real food.

[1] this makes stuff that's good for your gut [2] this is that stuff

Think outside this box.

About the food you eat. Why you eat it. How it makes you feel. Inside this box is a delicious, all-natural pizza made from a diversity of real food you can taste.

We made it for you with our hands from 12 grains and seeds bound together with water topped with tomatoes and real cheese from a cow with no growth hormones.

It has fewer calories, more fiber, more protein, less fat and more taste. Rethinking food, plough to plate, is our generation's civil rights movement. Think before you bite.

www.nakedpizza.biz

←↑
Open's pizza box artwork, and a box of Naked Pizza at Open

↓
the napkin, photographed in February 2011

Ryan Thacker:
We had a bunch of fantastic ideas for how the box could be used, like a Dr. Bronner's label or something. Except without the crazy, mystical Christian stuff.

Randy Crochet:
Jeff and I thought we were extremely smart when we started World's Healthiest Pizza, because the name basically identified and conveyed who we were. What we found, however, is that we always had to explain why we thought we were the world's healthiest pizza. It started conversations but as we found later, the name created social stress, in that putting health and pizza together was just plain wrong.

Robbie Vitrano:
I remember very clearly the moment when we decided on the name Naked Pizza. I was on a mountain bike in Ketchum, Idaho. I remember calling where I could get a signal from the top of that mountain, and saying, *This is the right one for us.*

Ryan Page:
It left a lot of room for interpretation.

Robbie Vitrano:
It's a fairly easy way to get from nude to a pizza that had nothing to hide, and a pizza that was essentially free of bad things.

Ryan Page:
There were some design elements that Open gave us—and we gave franchisees—that ended up getting the brand in a little bit of trouble at times. We would see a picture on Facebook from a franchisee that would say, *Let's get Naked tonight after the baseball game.* When you start thinking about how the word naked is perceived in a school setting, and you're trying to gain the business of school lunch, it's a very challenging thing to talk to a principal with a straight face and try to sell your brand.

↑
getting Naked around the world, 2010–2012

Scott Stowell:
To get away with those *Let's get Naked* kind of jokes, we used the pizza icon as an asterisk and always included a little *Pizza at the bottom. So you're not getting naked, you're getting Naked Pizza. It would always drive Ryan crazy when they got that wrong, like, *I'm running Naked* or whatever. He would be like, *I'm running Naked Pizza?*

↓ →
the Naked Pizza
identity in action,
2010–2012

1. Pick a crust

And a size (small, medium or large)

Original 12-Grain

12 grains, plus prebiotic fiber and probiotics. No white flour.

$10 · $12 · $14

cal: 220 · fat: 8 grams · gi: 54

Skinny 12-grain

Thin crust version of our original 12 grain.

$10 · $12 · $14

cal: 220 · fat: 8 grams · gi: 54

Gluten-Free

Rice flour with probiotics and prebiotics.

$11 · $13 · $15

cal: 220 · fat: 8 grams · gi: 54

All pies are red sauce with mozzarella cheese unless otherwise specified. Our white sauce, a fine blend of Omega 3-rich canola with special herbs and spices, can be substituted at no extra cost.

2. Pick some ingredients

Topping prices: Small 1.25 · Medium 1.45 · Large 1.65

FLORA (you know, plants)

| black olive | red onion | bell pepper | tomato | mushroom | fresh basil | garlic | spinach |

| pineapple | artichoke | fire roasted red pepper | cilantro | black bean | jalapeño | sun-dried tomato |

FAUNA (for the carnivores)

ham	pepperoni	sausage	chicken	hamburger
cal: 220	cal: 220	cal: 220	cal: 220	cal: 220
fat: 8 grams	fat: 8 grams	fat: 8 grams	fat: 8 grams	fat: 8 grams
gi: 54	gi: 54	gi: 54	gi: 54	gi: 54

SAY CHEESE

cheddar	feta
cal: 220	cal: 220
fat: 8 grams	fat: 8 grams
gi: 54	gi: 54

Naked 101 Nutrition information is per (1 slice) serving. GI = glycemic index, a measure of the effects of carbohydrates on blood sugar levels.

or...
try one
of our
favorites

pima

Black Beans, Jalapeno, Cheddar, side of chilled Pico (Tomato, Onion, Cilantro, Garlic & Lime)

$11 · $14 · $16

cal: 220 · fat: 8 grams · gi: 54

superbiotic

Artichoke, Spinach, Bell Pepper, Mushroom, Garlic, Onion, Cilantro

$11 · $14 · $16

cal: 220 · fat: 8 grams · gi: 54

omnivore

Pepperoni, Hamburger, Ham, Bell Pepper, Mushroom, Black Olive

$11.25 · $14.25 · $16.25

cal: 220 · fat: 8 grams · gi: 54

mediterranean

Artichoke, Sun-Dried Tomato, Onion, Black Olive, Feta

$11.25 · $14.25 · $16.25

cal: 220 · fat: 8 grams · gi: 54

animal farm

Pepperoni, Sausage, Hamburger, Ham

$11.25 · $14.25 · $16.25

cal: 250 · fat: 8 grams · gi: 54

sonoran

Onion, Chicken, Fire Roasted Red Pepper, Mushroom

$11 · $14 · $16

cal: 220 · fat: 8 grams · gi: 54

greenhouse

Onion, Tomato, Bell Pepper, Black Olive, Mushroom

$11 · $14 · $16

cal: 220 · fat: 8 grams · gi: 54

smokehouse

Hickory-Smoked BBQ Sauce, Onion, Chicken

$11.25 · $14.25 · $16.25

cal: 220 · fat: 8 grams · gi: 54

the big easy

Sausage, Chicken, Garlic, Bell Pepper, Onion

$11.25 · $14.25 · $16.25

cal: 220 · fat: 8 grams · gi: 54

default

Mozzarella cheese

$8 · $10 · $11

cal: 220 · fat: 8 grams · gi: 54

3. And?

other naked stuff

EXTRAS

Mojomega Breadsticks

Tasty mozzarella and cheddar, chewy Ancestral Blend™ pull-apart bread with prebiotics and probiotics **$5**

cal: 220 · fat: 8 grams · gi: 54

Spinach Salad

Spinach, Bell Pepper, Mushroom, Black Olive and Red Onion (Dressings: Blush Wine Vinaigrette, Buttermilk Ranch, Rich Poppy Seed) **$6**

cal: 220 · fat: 8 grams · gi: 54

LIQUIDS

Jones Sodas: Cream Soda, Black Cherry Zilch, Vanilla Bean Zilch, Orange & Cream Soda; Abita Root Beer & Water **$2**

cal: 220 · fat: 8 grams · gi: 54

follow us on twitter
@NakedPizza

Visit **nakedpizza.biz** (on the internet) for an incredibly thorough and fascinating explanation of our very nutritious nutrition information.

greenhouse

---------------- bell pepper
---------------- black olive
---------------- onion
---------------- tomato
---------------- red sauce
ancestral blend*

ragin' cajun

---------------- pork
---------------- bell pepper
---------------- onion
---------------- chicken
••••••••••••••• sausage
---------------- red sauce
ancestral blend*

↑
*Start out naked/
Get dressed up*
strategy,
April 2012

exploded pizza
diagrams,
March 2012

Vincent Vumbaco:
Another way they
really represented
pizzas was to do like
an exploded view
of these things.

Ryan Thacker:
We did these exploded
pizza diagrams that
were pretty awesome.
They functioned as
wall art. They all had
sedimentary layers
of the toppings of
the different ridicu-
lously named pizzas.

Zoë Scharf:
I think Scott wanted
to name one of them
Slaughterhouse
and we didn't get
away with that. It
was a meat pizza.

Ryan Thacker:
If they think that
the Ragin' Cajun is
going to sell better
than whatever we
wanted to call it, then
it's their company.

Hayon Shin:
The Mediterranean
is my favorite.

Scott Stowell:
I remember having
a conversation with
them, and saying,
"Which pizza do you
want people to buy?"

Ryan Thacker:
They have all these
spreadsheets of what
makes them money
and what doesn't.
There's no money
in plain pizza, and
there's no money in
10-topping pizzas.
There's money in
three-topping pizzas.

Scott Stowell:
So we ended up doing
this whole thing for
them, which turned
into kind of an ad
campaign, which was,
*Start out naked. Get
dressed up.* Basically
it was trying to nudge
people into getting
a few toppings.

Ryan Thacker:
Pricing. That's one
thing they never
bought into. We had
said Naked Pizza was
smart, different, and
real, which led us, or
Scott, to be like, *Just
say it's nine dollars,
or 10 dollars.* None
of this $9.99 bullshit
that everyone does.

Zoë Scharf:
We made a list of
ideas that were
like, *Let's do $6 not
$5.99, Let's do .com
not .biz, Let's do this
thing, not this thing.*
Some of the things
they were on board
with. Some of the
things they weren't.

Ryan Thacker:
I remember getting
this really dense email
from them about what
the challenge was
and blah, blah, blah.
I remember in the
presentation high-
lighting the part of
their email where they
said, "Don't do this,"
and saying like, *No,
we think that's exactly
what you should do,*
and not getting fired.

Zoë Scharf:
It's the typical cli-
ent struggle, where
somebody knows what
they want but you
possibly know better
what's going to be
good for their brand.
You want to walk that
fine line of respect-
ing the client and
also producing work
that you're proud of.

Ryan Thacker:
That's the kind of
relationship it was,
where you're like,
*Actually, we think it's
a good idea. Here's
why.* They're like,
*Oh, cool. We hadn't
thought of it that way.*

Zoë Scharf:
If a client doesn't want
something, we can't
be resentful about
that. We can't be angry
at the client, because
this is their project.
This is their opportu-
nity to do what they
want, and if they want
Naked Pizza to be *.biz,*
then they can have
Naked Pizza be *.biz.*

Scott Stowell:
Dealing with a company with franchises was a huge part of the learning process for us. When we created our style guide, or what we called the cookbook, we were giving them rules that they're giving to other people who don't have the time or money or wherewithal to care about stuff that we cared about.

Ryan Page:
The cookbook was a general outline and recipe for the tools and the materials to introduce the Naked Pizza brand in a given market.

Scott Stowell:
We had to do a pitch book for India, so all the cows came out. And then we did Dubai, and there are no pigs in the graphics there.

Vincent Vumbaco:
Dubai is very much like the States, in that at that time, there was a lot of wealth and a lot of diabetes. I feel like Naked Pizza just came along at the perfect time for them and it was really the only healthy option in pizza over there. The store in the Dubai Marina was one of the highest-grossing pizza stores in the world.

Robbie Vitrano:
We ended up in Dubai because we had a very convincing request from a potential franchisee.

Ian Ohan:
I had no idea it was going to work in Dubai. I just wanted to do a business that was scalable and interesting.

Robbie Vitrano:
Ian literally hopped on a plane from Dubai and landed in Houston, rented a motorcycle and drove it to New Orleans, and came to the offices and said that Naked Pizza would be very, very, very successful in Dubai.

Vincent Vumbaco:
They have every kind of pizza you could imagine in Dubai, but the service, for some reason, was pretty horrible.

Robbie Vitrano:
When we got to Dubai we ordered pizza from other places and it arrived at various times, regardless of when we ordered it. Sometimes it arrived in 25 minutes. One pizza arrived two hours after we'd ordered it.

Vincent Vumbaco:
Naked Pizza successfully carried out the Domino's delivery method in Dubai, where even Domino's wasn't doing it.

CORN حار **TURKEY HAM** ديك رومي **POTATO** فلفل حار

↑ →
topping icons and cookbook page designed for franchises in Dubai, 30 November 2010

Ryan Thacker:
Yeah, some countries don't eat pigs. They had to make a turkey. I can't remember the other ones. We had to make a potato. I'm pretty sure I just took the top off the pineapple. No one ever questioned it.

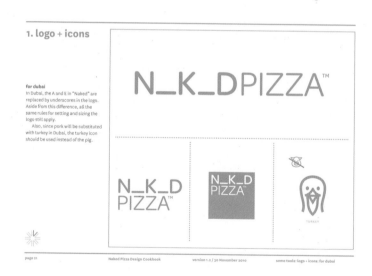

1. logo + icons

for dubai
In Dubai, the A and E in "Naked" are replaced by underscores in the logo. Aside from this difference, all the same rules for setting and sizing the logo still apply.
    Also, since pork will be substituted with turkey in Dubai, the turkey icon should be used instead of the pig.

N_K_DPIZZA™

N_K_D PIZZA™   N_K_D PIZZA™   TURKEY

page 21   Naked Pizza Design Cookbook   version 1.2 / 30 November 2010   some tools: logo + icons: for dubai

Scott Stowell:
In the Middle East, they can't call it *Naked Pizza*.

Robbie Vitrano:
The word naked is not publicly acceptable in Dubai.

Vincent Vumbaco:
They sort of played hangman with the logo, so rather than N-A-K-E-D Pizza, it's N K D Pizza, which then became NKD Pizza.

Scott Stowell:
They still have t-shirts that say, "I got NKD in Dubai." The censorship is evident, but basically the people who know it's supposed to say *Naked* are cool with it. And the people who are not cool with it kind of don't see that, and are also cool with it.

Robbie Vitrano:
One of our strategic decisions was to make our delivery guys heroes.

Ryan Thacker:
They basically wanted us to design a Batman-meets-NASCAR suit for guys who are speeding around on mopeds when it's a hundred degrees outside.

Robbie Vitrano:
I wanted our delivery guys to have uniforms that were superhero-like. The brief was to pay attention to Power Rangers and soccer uniforms.

Ian Ohan:
The drivers felt really good about themselves, which gave them pride. They look cool! They like it. I mean these are guys who can't afford many things.

Ryan Page:
The Palestinian immigrant who is shipping all of his money back home to his family and has this huge life opportunity to make something of himself—he gets treated well, he makes really good money. Just their enthusiasm, devotion, and passion for their jobs, I think that has pushed Naked Pizza to be so wildly successful there.

Hayon Shin:
I lived in Dubai for five years and I always saw Naked Pizza's green delivery bikes everywhere. They were impossible to miss.

Ian Ohan:
After we launched, every asshole in Dubai changed their brand to green. The green was a very powerful color. They copied our uniforms. They copied everything.

Ryan Page:
They did better in the five stores they had in the United Arab Emirates (UAE) than in all of the U.S. stores combined.

↑
NKD Pizza in Dubai, 2011–2012

↑
delivery drivers
at a NKD Pizza
event in Dubai,
January 2011

Ian Ohan:
We had a great brand.
We had a great
product. We had
great operations and
service. It was a great
opportunity to sort
of sweep the mar-
ket, which we did.

Ian Ohan:
Food and beverage is
hard. Everyone bought
the brand, but what
they didn't realize is
that they had to oper-
ate the business.

Ryan Page:
At one point, we had
20-something cor-
porate staff working
at the New Orleans
headquarters. Then,
overnight, pretty
much everyone left.

Vincent Vumbaco:
I don't think we can
really attribute it to
one thing. There were
so many issues, like
from supply chain, to
the cost of rent at our
locations, the cost
of construction, like
there was so much.

Ian Ohan:
They just expanded
too fast.

Ryan Page:
I think it's been harder
to compete in the
big cities. I live an
hour south of New
Orleans. We don't
have great pizza on
every corner. When I
visited Manhattan, I
was really just blown
away. There's pizza
everywhere. It's liter-
ally everywhere.

Ian Ohan:
They couldn't sup-
port franchises, let
alone their own stores.
They only have seven
stores left in the U.S.

Ryan Page:
The franchisee who
was running all the
stores in the UAE
broke off and got
away from the Naked
brand completely. He
and Robbie founded
and moved forward
with Freedom Pizza.

Ian Ohan:
It's a bit of a rebirth.
Now we literally
feel free to do what
we want to do.

Ryan Page:
The success and fail-
ure of Naked Pizza,
as a whole through
the years, was not a
result, in my opinion,
of the creative at all.
It was much more on
the business side.

Ryan Thacker:
The brand is still alive and well in Kenya.

Ian Cox:
In Africa, product and brand presentation especially stands out. Local brands have a long way to go on their branding, so when an especially strong, visual brand comes to town, you really notice.

Ritesh Doshi:
Anywhere else in the world, I was always able to get a pizza delivered in about 40 minutes, so why not in Kenya? Coupled with a fast-growing middle class, horrendous traffic, and people's work schedules, the opportunity to take healthy pizza to people at home and work was a no-brainer.

Ralph Obure:
The concept of home delivery is relatively new in Nairobi and other chains would take at least an hour to deliver. Once I waited two hours.

Ritesh Doshi:
It's great to have a brand that actually stands for something and means something in a market where international companies are just trying to capitalize on increased business but don't actually stand for anything.

Ralph Obure:
Other pizza chains in Nairobi had limited offerings on their menu and after having one of their pizzas you had basically had all of them. The Naked Pizza menu is diverse and each pizza has a whole different taste and flavor about it. This just makes me keep going time after time to try something new.

Ritesh Doshi:
Kids love the icons, especially of the animals. Most brands here have pictures of their products plastered all over the store and on their menus. By using clean, fresh, modern logos, we look and feel like a premium experience, but at a similar price point to the rest of the market.

Ralph Obure:
My friend and I were at Naked Pizza, having the best pizza we'd had in Nairobi, when the manager came up to us to ask our thoughts on the pizza and service. I remember thinking to myself that this was treatment I only expected in high-end restaurants, not a pizza place. On my subsequent visit he had actually implemented my suggestion of having fresh juice!

↓
Naked Pizza
in Nairobi, Kenya,
2014–2015

Scott Stowell:
I love seeing stuff like this. They're doing their own thing. I think this is one of the stories where we're actually a bit player in the end.

@nakedpizzakenya
on Twitter:
2 October 2015:
What's for lunch? Check out our lunchtime meal deals & get Naked with a colleague today! ;-) (*Pizza)*

Naz Şahin Özcan:
I am a designer
who always thinks
about what her
next meal will be.

I am writing this from a coastal
town on the Mediterranean
where I can fill a plastic bag
with perfect tomatoes for very
little money. This is nice, and an
unlikely thing in New York.

But in New York, I can
treat myself to a costly little jar
of yogurt made by hand in Red
Hook and it is worth every
penny. The yogurt maker sells
whey, a funky byproduct, to
nice restaurants, where it
becomes a poultry marinade or
a cocktail base. The chefs in
such restaurants turn vegetable
scraps into meals. They get
giddy at the sight of a car trunk
full of foraged leaves. They
organize field trips to hang out
with their suppliers and cook on
open fires.

As much as I love carefree
tomatoes, I have no complaints
about this zeitgeist.

I got a call one day from a former client I hadn't talked to in 15 years. She had become the president of something called the Brooklyn Bridge Park Development Corporation. Their job was huge: to turn six old piers and 85 acres of industrial waterfront into a new public park. The job they were asking us to do that day was very small. But it was part of a big story about designers, public servants, and regular people doing the best they can. And that story's not over yet.

12.

in order
of appearance

Wendy Leventer:
My title was president of the Brooklyn Bridge Park Development Corporation (BBPDC), but I did everything because there was no staff. My role was sort of chief cook and bottle washer.

Paul Seck:
I was the project manager and then principal in charge for Brooklyn Bridge Park (BBP) at Michael Van Valkenburgh Associates (MVVA).

Matthew Urbanski:
My title is principal at MVVA.

Rob Di Ieso:
I was project managing BBP at Open, similar to what I did for Yale and Brown.

Julia Zangwill:
I work in business development at AMC Networks.

Scott Stowell:
I hope to see you soon.

Nate Trevethan:
I'm a landscape architect with MVVA.

Nicholas Rock:
I worked at Open for the summer of 2006.

Ellen Ryan:
I was vice president of strategic partnerships at BBP. We all wore a lot of hats.

Lisa Silbermayr:
I am an architect, designer, and researcher.

Şerifcan Özcan:
I was a designer at Open. I just helped out when it was needed.

Tobias Frere-Jones:
I have a lot of memories of looking down at those piers from the Promenade.

Regina Myer:
I'm president at BBP and I am in charge of designing, building, and operating the park.

Michael Van Valkenburgh:
I am the president and CEO of MVVA.

Paula Scher:
I'm a commissioner on the Public Design Commission.

Jason Jude Chan:
I am Open's producer.

Mike Lampariello:
I'm director of operations at BBP.

Ryan Thacker:
I inherited BBP at Open from Rob, after all the heavy lifting was done.

Devon King:
I'm a senior supervisor. My job is overseeing all the custodians.

Danny Rodriguez:
I'm a senior technician.

Julie Golia:
I'm the director of public history at Brooklyn Historical Society.

Lindsey Ross:
I'm the permit coordinator at BBP.

Mike Cartagena:
I'm BBP's special projects and events coordinator.

Wendy Leventer:
Parks in this city are
super controversial.

Paul Seck:
When this project
started kicking around
in the late 1980s or
early 1990s, it was
about, *How do we
take this derelict
piece of land on the
waterfront and turn
it into something in-
teresting for people
in New York City?*

Wendy Leventer:
Everybody thinks,
*We're going to make a
park.* But there were
so many ideas about
what that should be.

Matthew Urbanski:
The Port Authority
controlled the prop-
erty, but was losing
money on it. They
felt that they should
monetize the asset.

Wendy Leventer:
A developer was going
to build high-rise resi-
dential buildings on
the piers themselves
and the community
went crazy because
it was going to block
their views. So that
deal was nixed.

Matthew Urbanski:
The immediate neigh-
borhood, Brooklyn
Heights, was unhappy
with that. People felt
like it should be de-
veloped as a park, and
the outcome of that
disagreement was
a counterproposal
that there would be
some development
of the site in order to
throw off revenue to
support the park.

Rob Di Ieso:
It would be funded
by the condos or
whatever else they
would build there.

Wendy Leventer:
The park would be
self-sufficient.

↑
the Brooklyn
Port Authority piers,
March 2006

Julia Zangwill:
My husband and I live
in Brooklyn Heights
and I remember when
abandoned warehous-
es occupied the space
that is now the park.

↑
protesters
at the BBP site,
May 2006

Scott Stowell:
People don't remem-
ber, but BBP was a
huge controversy.
Everyone hated it.
Nobody wanted it
because they thought
it was this giveaway
to rich people.

Rob Di Ieso:
People were just irate,
angry. They were like,
No, this is bullshit.

Rob Di Ieso:
Before we even got
to signage, a big
part of this project
was publicity.

Matthew Urbanski:
There was a competi-
tive process to select
a park master planner
to come up with the
financial plan, the
urban design, and the
maintenance plan. It
was all one big com-
mission. We at MVVA
won that and started
working on it in 2003.
That included a lot
of public outreach.

Wendy Leventer:
We spent a lot of
time really figur-
ing out what the
park could be, and
what it should be.

Matthew Urbanski:
Wendy had a lot of
experience with city
planning, and a lot
of experience with
development.

Wendy Leventer:
Years earlier, I had
worked on a proj-
ect called the 42nd
Street Development
Project, and we had
hired M&Co. when
Scott worked there.
They were just super
unorthodox—over-
flowing with great
ideas. I remembered
Scott, and I thought he
had a real connection
with regular people,
which is what we were
trying to do with BBP.
We didn't want to cre-
ate the High Line.

Scott Stowell:
Wendy was planning
a kind of kickoff event
with Mayor Bloomberg
and Governor Pataki,
and she wanted a big
sign that said, NEW
PARK COMING SOON.

Wendy Leventer:
Sometimes it felt like
the park was never
going to happen. We
wanted to remind
people that it still was.

Nate Trevethan:
We had never worked
with Scott before but
Wendy, our client,
had. She thought that
Open would be a good
fit to the team that
was already in place.

Scott Stowell:
I guess Wendy re-
membered there
was this kid in those
42nd Street meet-
ings back then.

Wendy Leventer:
We wanted to assure
people that this was
a park for everyone.

Scott Stowell:
Wendy called me
wanting one of those
vinyl banners. They
stay up too long and
look like garbage.
I said, *That's awe-
some, but no. We
don't want to do that.*

Wendy Leventer:
I was thinking so
literally. Like, *We
just need a sign*. We
wanted a sign for a
building. And he had
this whole other idea
that elevated it.

Scott Stowell:
We ended up meeting with Wendy and finding out about the park. We learned all about it, and basically understood that if you didn't have the hotel and the condos there, there would be no park.

Wendy Leventer:
The development that we had planned literally was not a single inch more of what was needed in the analysis of how to support the park.

Rob Di Ieso:
So there was a battle to be fought, to make sure that the public understood that, too.

Scott Stowell:
So instead of that banner, we proposed a different idea to Wendy, which was to make a website about the park, and then tease the URL on the building. So we made thisisyourpark.org to explain the whole controversy.

Wendy Leventer:
We also made postcards and we sent them to thousands of people in Brooklyn to let them know that the park was coming and it was for everyone.

Rob Di Ieso:
The idea was just to provide some level of transparency to hopefully sway the public into understanding.

Scott Stowell:
People would be like, *What is that?* Then go to the website and find out. And of course, if you are reading it, it's your park. There you go.

Wendy Leventer:
I remember having this really long conversation with Scott about what we were trying to achieve. The thing was being built with public money, but we were not going to make a park that was just a green lawn. We were going to make a park certainly for all of Brooklyn, but hopefully for all of New York City. We had to somehow communicate that without sticking a thumb in people's eye and we didn't know how. That used to keep me up at night.

Scott Stowell:
By refusing to make that vinyl sign, we got the job to do that website, and later Wendy offered us the chance to do their logo and website and all the signage for the park. But first they still needed something for that event.

Rob Di Ieso:
We were really into the idea of hand-painted signs, so we found a sign painter. We were like, *Hi, can you please paint* thisisyourpark.org *on the old pier shed?*

↑
thisisyourpark.org website and postcards, May–June 2006

Nicholas Rock:
We sent these postcards out in the top five languages in Brooklyn. One of my jobs was to work with the translation agency to translate the messages, and typeset them appropriately, and verify them so that we weren't saying something wrong or offensive. It was like, finding people who spoke the right Haitian Creole dialect. It was so eye opening as a young designer to realize that you do those things.

Scott Stowell:
Rob would ride his bike down there and watch them painting it. This was Memorial Day weekend 2006.

Rob Di Ieso:
No joke, it was literally like watching paint dry most of the time. I would leave and come back to see the progress.

Scott Stowell:
Rob went down there one time, called me from his cell phone and said, "Dude, you have to get down here. It's so messed up. We're going to get fired."

Rob Di Ieso:
The sign painter, he was very good, but he had made a mistake where he dropped the g down, so that it wasn't sitting on the baseline of thisisyourpark.org. It looked weird. I almost had a heart attack.

Scott Stowell:
I said, *First of all, nobody is going to fire us. They'll probably never notice.* Gerard, who ran the sign company, said he could just paint over the whole thing and paint a new g. But I wanted to preserve the layers of history you could see on the building, not cover it all up.

Rob Di Ieso:
Because it was a stencil font, we realized we could fix it.

Scott Stowell:
So we sat on the pier and redrew the g together. Gerard just repainted the top part.

Rob Di Ieso:
Then the postcards and everything else that we made for thisisyourpark.org had that new g. It was a unique logo made out of a very funny mistake. After the fact, once it was finished and fixed, I was like, *That's pretty cool.* But at the time, I was literally like, *Scott's gonna fire me.*

↑
the g (before),
May 2006

↓
the g (after)
at the kickoff event,
May 2006

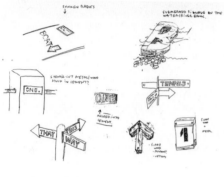

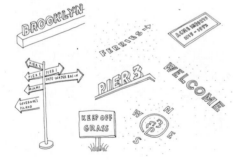

↑
Gary, Nate, and
Rob visit the BBP site,
October 2006

Gary and Scott's
signage sketches,
November 2006

Wendy Leventer:
The thing that I think
distinguishes Scott
from a lot of people
in the field is that he
makes design ac-
cessible. It's not all
mysterious and fancy.
He makes it a part of
the thing that it is.

Nate Trevethan:
We spent a lot of time
outside with Scott
and Rob walking on
the site, because that
was probably the easi-
est way to describe
what we were trying
to do as the design-
ers of the park.

Scott Stowell:
Unlike Central Park,
where everything is
designed to look like
this idealized version
of reality, to me all
the choices MVVA
made reveal how fake
everything is—areas
of trees will just stop.
Things that don't hap-
pen in nature. Because
the whole park is on
top of a pier, on top of
a river, so it couldn't
have existed naturally.

Rob Di Ieso:
We started looking
at a lot of signage
from other parks and
put together a plan
of things that this
park would need.

Paul Seck:
We had this meeting
where Scott came and
we talked about what
we were doing, and
how we were going to
move forward. Then at
the next presentation,
Open came back and
it wasn't, *Here are your
signs.* But, *Here's what
we think you need and
don't need.* We were
talking more about the
concept and approach
rather than the look.

Rob Di Ieso:
For design inspiration,
we salvaged a lot of
the existing signage
because the site had
a lot of history.

Nate Trevethan:
One thing we found
that we all liked were
these three-dimen-
sional letters that were
on five of the six piers.

Rob Di Ieso:
Rather than just wip-
ing the slate clean and
starting over, we want-
ed to make sure the
look of the park had a
callback to its days as
a functioning pier. The
nice thing about work-
ing with MVVA was
that they had similar
sensibilities to us.

Nate Trevethan:
We were always look-
ing for a language
of those kind of con-
structed pieces that
was unique to the
Brooklyn waterfront.
For instance, a lot of
the railing along the
water's edge is primar-
ily constructed out of
steel I-beams and steel
pipe—things that you
actually would have
found in the ware-
house sheds on-site
prior to demolition.

Paul Seck:
Open's signage, the
lighting strategy, the
landscape, structural
engineering, marine
engineering—all of
these things need to
tie together across
the whole process.

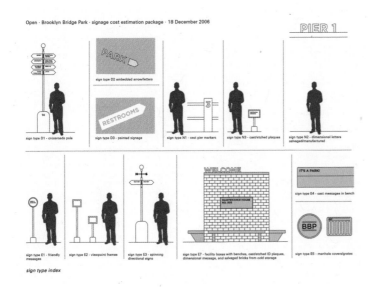

Open · Brooklyn Bridge Park · signage cost estimation package · 18 December 2006

PIER 1

sign type D2 embedded arrow/letters

sign type D1 - crossroads pole

sign type D3 - painted signage

sign type N1 - cast pier markers

sign type N3 - cast/etched plaques

sign type N2 - dimensional letters salvaged/manufactured

sign type E1 - friendly messages

sign type E2 - viewpoint frames

sign type E3 - spinning directional signs

sign type E7 - facility boxes with benches, cast/etched ID plaques, dimensional message, and salvaged bricks from cold storage

sign type E4 - cast messages in bench

sign type E5 - manhole covers/grates

sign type index

← preliminary cost-estimation package, December 2006

↑ BBP 100% bidding document set, February 2008

Scott Stowell:
It took 847 pages of construction draw-ings to make the park. Everything we did fit on five of them.

Ellen Ryan:
We wanted the sign-age to be welcoming. To be deferential to not only the landscape design, but to be mindful of views. We were looking to mini-mize it on some level.

Lisa Silbermayr:
The signs haven't caught my atten-tion. I guess there were more interest-ing things going on, like the sunset?

Ellen Ryan:
Open was not looking to make the signage the marquee part of the park, but instead have it work in concert with the natural way-finding of the paths and the plantings.

Rob Di Ieso:
The directional signs have a light at the top, and it was important that the base was concrete, because those giant concrete blocks were all over the original piers.

Matthew Urbanski:
The signs almost have a kind of play-ful quality to them. They're almost like if a regular person was asked to make signs for a park, they'd make little arrows pointing in different directions, like you'd see in a Road Runner cartoon or something.

Scott Stowell:
What Matt recognized was that we were in-terested in a similar thing, which is driven by not being fancy or too expensive.

Paul Seck:
The signage provided a little bit of a sur-prise and mystery, but felt welcoming and accepting.

Wendy Leventer:
I'm most proud of the design team. We tried to take the pressure off them I guess is the best way to ex-plain it. I saw my job as giving them room to do the best job that they could do.

↑ BROOKLYN sign idea, March 2008

Şerifcan Özcan:
One of the ideas we were super excited about was putting a huge sign that said BROOKLYN facing Manhattan, like the Hollywood sign.

Scott Stowell:
That never happened.

Tobias Frere-Jones:
I grew up about a block behind where this vantage point would have been.

Scott Stowell:
In 2007, Regina Myer became the president of the park.

Regina Myer:
This is, to me, not a controversial job. It's an amazing job. It's a job of a lifetime to create this fantastic place on the Brooklyn waterfront.

Scott Stowell:
Because we were brought in by Wendy, my concern was that we would get swept out with the person who brought us to the dance. I asked Michael to broker a meeting so we could present all of our thinking to Regina, and Michael could be there to bless us.

Michael Van Valkenburgh:
It wasn't hard to do this. Open's work was good.

Scott Stowell:
When Regina came along, the park was mostly designed. Some signage was, too, but none of it had been made yet.

Regina Myer:
My job was about implementation.

Scott Stowell:
Regina accepted us and we ended up staying. For a while it was hard to get stuff approved, though. Plus, after a while we had to redesign the BBP logo.

Regina Myer:
One of the early challenges leading up to when we opened was creating a park identity system that didn't talk about the organization that was running it. I wanted to separate the organization from the place.

Scott Stowell:
BBP is an independent, not-for-profit corporation, so it doesn't fall under the guidelines of the parks department. But we did have to present the signage to the Public Design Commission. Paula Scher is their signage person.

Paula Scher:
My job as a commissioner is to look at New York City projects that use city money and make aesthetic judgments to determine if they should be built or if changes should be made.

Ellen Ryan:
Scott presented and we immediately got approval.

Paula Scher:
Most of the signage projects that come to the Commission are pretty awful.

Ellen Ryan:
They would not have rubber stamped anything. So it was gratifying to know that we had their support.

BROOKLYN
BRIDGE PARK
DEVELOPMENT
CORPORATION

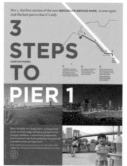

← original BBPDC logo, September 2007

Pier 1 poster with BBPDC logo, May 2010

BBP logo modeled by lawn technician Nick Fallon and Mike Cartagena, December 2012

Ellen Ryan:
The original logo being focused on the organization was a result of Wendy's— and my—aversion to branding the park.

Scott Stowell:
They were making a park out of industrial materials, so the idea of that logo was a plant, but made out of what could be metal. It was also meant to look like a seal or governmental thing. Regina hated it. The new logo is based on the old pier signs.

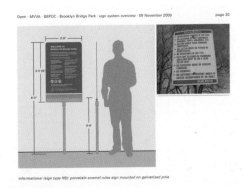

↑
sign system
overview,
October 2009

temporary
painted aluminum
rules sign,
March 2010

←
corrected
shop drawing
for the rules sign,
July 2014

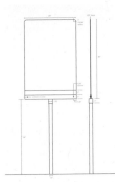

Regina Myer:
What was exciting
in those early years
was that the park
was moving from this
theoretical possibil-
ity to a real place. We
needed real signs, so
we had to worry about
real costs and materi-
als. Everything all of
a sudden went from
some ideas to, *Holy
shit, we need a sign.*

Scott Stowell:
When Pier 1 opened
in 2010, Regina hadn't
approved the final
signs, so what got put
up was temporary.
It was supposed to
be porcelain-enamel
panels and instead it's
just silkscreened on
painted aluminum.

Rob Di Ieso:
The reason we were
enamored with
porcelain enamel is
that it's super durable
and graffiti proof.

Ellen Ryan:
We never could bud-
get for it. The park was
in a constant state of
flux. It may change
depending on what's
constructed this year,
next year, in five years.
We had to think of it
as something that
was more variable
than you would have
with a finished park.

Rob Di Ieso:
We ended up with a
lot of metal signage
which got beaten
up. I was kind of into
it. I didn't mind.

Ellen Ryan:
Regina's a tough cus-
tomer. I give Scott and
his team a lot of credit
for helping to navigate
the demands of a client
who was juggling a
lot of issues and
events, and a massive
construction project.

Scott Stowell:
We've been work-
ing with Regina for
years now. I don't
know when it hap-
pened. I can't pinpoint
the moment. But I
think she trusts us.

Jason Jude Chan:
We're also more re-
sponsive to what they
want. And then there's
Mike, making sure
it's all nice and tidy.

Mike Lampariello:
When I started, the
relationship between
BBP and Open was a
little strained because
everybody was busy
and there wasn't time
to focus on this kind
of stuff. I noticed
some inconsistencies,
and I think slowly,
over the last two years,
we've checked a lot
of them off the list.
I want to see every-
thing installed the
way it was intended.

Ryan Thacker:
Everyone at Open also
got better at knowing
which battles to fight
and how to fight them.

Regina Myer:
We've all grown
together.

Signs throughout
Brooklyn Bridge Park,
2010–2012

Julia Zangwill:
The signs are
particularly useful
in understanding
how to navigate the
park due to it being
very spread out over
the waterfront.

Devon King:
I think what makes
Brooklyn Bridge Park
different from other
parks is the people
who come here.

Danny Rodriguez:
I see people—almost
every day, every
other day—taking
pictures of the signs.

Devon King:
Out here, you've got
some people that
are just into signs
and stuff like that.

↑→
historical markers and "footnotes," made in partnership with the Brooklyn Historical Society, 2013

Regina Myer:
We realized once we opened the park that people want another layer of information.

Julie Golia:
At the heart of the project was the goal of showing visitors that the waterfront has served many roles over time—from sparsely populated farmland, to an industrial juggernaut, to a post-industrial ghost town.

Jason Jude Chan:
They had these really long paragraphs that they wanted to print on the markers and of course it's our thing to be like, *No, no one's going to read that. Let's think of the person who wants to enjoy the park, but wants to get a little tidbit of information.*

Scott Stowell:
We walked around the park with Matt Urbanski and he helped us locate where these would all be. They're not anywhere you'd expect them to be.

Lindsey Ross:
A lot of people have been reading them.

Julie Golia:
In the end, the footnotes were my favorite design. They were playful, and pushed us to think creatively about how to distill our ideas down to a small number of words. That's always a good exercise for historians.

Scott Stowell:
I fully believe these signs happened because we called them *footnotes* in the first presentation. At every meeting they're like, *Well we've got to do the footnotes, right?*

Devon King:
I call them signs in the ground.

Matthew Urbanski:
We knew that the park wasn't that easy to get to, and you might need to draw people in with something more spectacular.

Michael Van Valkenburgh:
Rather than lamenting that the site is very long and that the piers create a series of islands, we saw this as an opportunity, as a way to create a range of experience: Pier 1 juts out into the river and is a mix of passive and active, Pier 2 is all active, Pier 3 is much more passive, Pier 5 is a soccer field, and Pier 6 is much less active.

Scott Stowell:
Pier 2 is the sports pier. There's a beach at Pier 4.

Ryan Thacker:
If Brooklyn Bridge Park had an Olympic venue, it would be Pier 2. But with goofy sports like shuffleboard instead of track and field.

↑
the Pier 2 bridge, roller rink, and restrooms (with the top 12 languages spoken in Brooklyn), 2014

Lindsey Ross:
It's a really inclusive way to say *bathroom*, and it gets a little bit of culture into the park.

Mike Lampariello:
Pier 2 has basketball, bocce ball, handball, all different things like that. The project actually started because we needed to have numbers to identify each of the individual courts, and then it slowly grew into, *Maybe it'd be interesting if we had something out there that was very visual.* Open came up with this incredibly intuitive wayfinding system.

Ryan Thacker:
This is all on a pier sticking out into the river. So you have to cross these bridges where the icons were introduced with the activity that they represented. It's kind of like a Disney World parking mentality. If you go through here, these are the three activities.

Mike Lampariello:
I don't think everybody realizes it's there.

Scott Stowell:
Our favorite thing is the fitness area. There are these outdoor fitness machines Brooklyn Bridge Park bought from Turkey.

Ryan Thacker:
The directions were apparently translated from Turkish with Google. Really bad grammar. And the names, I don't remember what the names were, but they didn't make any sense.

Scott Stowell:
We made up all these stupid names: *Arm Max 3000, Legatron, Ab Nauseam.*

Jason Jude Chan:
That was my favorite.

Scott Stowell:
We had to change it to *Ab Infinitum,* which is also funny.

Ryan Thacker:
They didn't know what they were going to call them, so we just named them for our presentation.

Scott Stowell:
Pendulum Plus. Hold the handlebars before getting on each pedal. Using arms and legs swing body side to side. Don't stop 'til you get enough.

Ryan Thacker:
BBP was kind of into our joke names so we got to joke name all of them.

Mike Lampariello:
I'm a believer that the tiniest details make the biggest difference. Ninety-nine percent of the public probably doesn't even notice, but it's certainly something that I see.

Scott Stowell:
So much work gets put into stuff like this and so few people ever notice. But this is the kind of stuff we wanted to do from the beginning. It only took us nine years to get some jokes in.

Mike Lampariello:
We're in an interesting position because the park's been built in phases. We have a lot of new or first-time visitors in a park that is changing every six months in a lot of ways, so it can be a little bit of a challenge, currently, for people to find their way.

Regina Myer:
We've really been trying to come up with a system that isn't so in your face but fits within our park design—that feels comfortable but gives park goers some more information.

Michael Van Valkenburgh:
Signs are a drag to me. Scott knows that I think there are too many signs. I find the historical stuff unnecessary, and if you go through the park today it is almost impossible to not always see a sign of some kind.

Nate Trevethan:
When you're on the water's edge you'd rather not see eight little yellow signs telling you to stay off the rocks. You'd rather just use your common sense.

Mike Cartagena:
We've got a sign that says KEEP OFF THE ROCKS. People still put their kids on the rocks.

Paul Seck:
I think the knee-jerk reaction was to have a big map that located you, that showed you where to go, and how to get to things. Scott talked everyone down off of the ledge, of having all of these big signs overwhelming people when they came into the entrances.

Scott Stowell:
Recently, we came up with an idea for signs made of galvanized steel pipes and printed panels that the people at BBP can change and switch out.

Paul Seck:
Our whole thing about entering into a park was that it needs to feel effortless. You don't want to be over-stimulated, you don't want to have all this information thrown at you. But there are people who want that.

Scott Stowell:
Our job is to improve the experience of people who use the park, no matter what.

Matthew Urbanski:
The park is like a book, where somebody keeps adding another chapter on the end. You had a really nice book, and then you get to the end, you get disappointed. With this one, you just wait a little while, and then they add another chapter.

↑
BBP book cart, 2015

Lindsey Ross:
Open helped us put together a book cart. There are these nice tables and chairs and umbrellas, and this little book cart. It's like a really nice, hidden space.

Devon King:
And it's quiet. You don't hear the BQE.

Lindsey Ross:
There are so many areas of the park, different nooks and crannies. To clean.

Michael Van Valkenburgh: I'm a landscape architect who lives in Brooklyn, New York.

Evidence of change—seeing and feeling it—shapes the reality that we experience. Embracing change, or at least planning for that change, is the essence of design.

As a landscape architect, I think about what pleasure can come from different combinations of plants at different times of the year. Change within a scene, at any single moment, also matters. But when is too much variety just chaos? In winter, do all the leaves fall off or are there evergreens?

Landscapes are loaded with emotional experience, kindled by the sensibility and technique of the designer. When done right, they can help people become more deeply engaged and alive.

This is Scott again. In case
you haven't noticed, there are
lots of underlined words (like
this: improvisation) in this book.
These are all things that you
might not know about. I didn't
want to interrupt the stories to
explain these words, so they're
here in the glossary. (There's a
little sponsored content in
here, too.) You could look these
up on your own, but some of
the explanations would be
hard to find—and a lot of them
are stories only I can tell.

16x9
This is the aspect ratio of HDTV, or as most people now call it, *tv*.

2x4
This design studio was founded by Michael Rock, Susan Sellers, and Georgie Stout in 1994. When I was at RISD, Michael was a teacher and Susan and Georgie were students, one year ahead of me. 2x4 and Open have both been at 180 Varick Street ever since Open moved in.

2001: A Space Odyssey

My favorite parts of this 1968 movie are the boring parts—the scenes that try to show what normal, everyday life might be like in that faraway year of 2001. And the most boring, normal moment is this quick look at the instructions for the "zero-gravity toilet."
see also: *Star Trek*

30 Rock
This is short for 30 Rockefeller Plaza, also known at different times as the RCA Building, the GE Building, one of the best tv sitcoms ever, and the Comcast Building.

4x3
This is the aspect ratio of standard-definition tv, or, as people used to call it, *tv*.

42nd Street Art Project

Our job on the 42nd Street Development Project at M&Co. was to make guidelines for signage on new (or improved) buildings. To clear the way for those buildings, every business on that stretch of 42nd Street was kicked out. But the development got delayed, leaving 42nd Street empty. A group called Creative Time came in to curate an exhibition of art in and around all those vacant buildings. I got to design the graphics, and the EVERYBODY sign got the best space in the show.
see also: Tibor Kalman

ADA
The Americans with Disabilities Act is a law passed in 1990 to help make buildings accessible to everybody. Guidelines for signage (including the size and color of letters, placement of braille, etc.) are part of that.

Adaptation
Directed by Spike Jonze, this very meta movie was based on the book *The Orchid Thief* by Susan Orlean. It's about what a movie about that book should be about, and it came out right when we were working on the Trio pitch.

After Effects
This is the most popular animation software, at least at Open. Trio, Bravo, and Jazz were almost entirely made in After Effects.
see also: effects house, motion design

AIGA

Founded as the American Institute of Graphic Arts in 1914, the AIGA now calls itself "the professional organization for design." I've been a member since 1993, when I paid two years of dues by designing a poster for free. In 2015, I missed the AIGA national conference for the first time since 1999—to get this book done.
see also: pro bono

Alive from Off Center

I discovered this tv show in the 1980s on WGBH. It was hosted by Laurie Anderson (and her "clone"), and every week it had something new: David Byrne, Meredith Monk, Philip Glass, Robert Wilson, all that stuff. For years I kept a stack of VHS tapes of episodes I'd recorded.

Laurie Anderson
After listening to Laurie's music and performance art for years, it was amazing to work with her on her host segment in *Art21* season one.
see also: *Alive from Off Center*

animation stand
This includes a camera, some lights, and a flat surface for artwork or objects to be filmed.
see also: effects house, film

aspect ratio
This is the shape of a screen. For years, tv had a 4x3 aspect ratio: The screen was four units wide by three units tall. Now tv has a wider aspect ratio: 16x9. Some movies are even wider.

Basecamp
Open (and this book) might not exist at all if we hadn't used this online project management tool to communicate with clients, track our time, and stay organized for the last ten years. And they paid for my honeymoon!

baseline
Most typography is organized in lines, like the words you're reading right now are. All the letters sit on an invisible horizontal line called the baseline. The descenders in letters like g hang below the baseline.

baseline grid
When making almost anything with a lot of type in it, many designers decide to lock the typography to an invisible grid, so that the lines of type can line up across the columns. All the type in Design for People is on a baseline grid, but it doesn't always line up across columns. This baseline grid is based on the lowest common denominator of all the line spacing in the book, so we could fit in as much copy as possible.

Saul Bass

Saul Bass is best known for designing film title sequences. But he also made many classic corporate logos and movie posters.

Battery Park City
This mostly residential neighborhood in Lower Manhattan was built starting in the 1970s and 1980s on land that used to be the Hudson River.

Battle of the Network Stars
This was a tv show from the 1970s that involved actors and actresses from other tv shows competing in weird sports like tug of war.

bespoke
This pretty much means custom or made to order. I think it was traditionally used to talk about clothing, like a tailor would make you a bespoke suit. I've thought about using it to describe Open's work, but it sounds too fancy.

bleed
When designing printed things, if you want the ink to go all the way to the edge of the page, you have to print it past the end of the page and then cut the page down to size. When ink goes off the edge of the page like that, it bleeds.

Blue Note album covers

What most people think jazz looks like, at least when it comes to graphic design, is totally based on Reid Miles' covers for Blue Note from the 1950s and 1960s.

bone folder

This tool is used in bookbinding to give folded paper a crisp edge. It isn't used for folding bones. It is usually made out of bone, though.

Irma Boom
Based in Amsterdam, Irma designs some of the most elaborately beautiful books ever. It's always nice to bump into her at Yale every year or so.

BQE
This is the Brooklyn-Queens Expressway. It's a highway that was built in the 1950s and 1960s. These days Brooklyn Bridge Park is located right below the section of the BQE that goes through Brooklyn Heights.

brand or **branding**
Many people use this word to describe what I prefer to call the identity of a company, idea, or organization.

brief
A brief is the information (ideally) given, either in person or in writing, to a designer before work begins. It's the assignment for the project, including what the client wants to get out of it.
see also: proposal, RFP

Dr. Bronner

I've never really been a fan of his soap, but the labels are excellent in a very crazy way.

Brutalism

This is a kind of modern architecture from the 1950s through the 1970s, which used lots of raw concrete as a material. A lot of people think the name comes from the idea that Brutalist buildings look "brutal," but it actually comes from a French term for raw concrete: *béton brut*.

bug

This is the tv network logo that usually sits in the lower-right corner of your screen during shows. For Ṭrio, we wanted the bug in the lower left, to line up with all our type. That was impossible, because NBC Universal's equipment had been programmed to display a bug in the lower right.
see also: lower third

bumper

A bumper is a very short thing between a tv show and a commercial break or vice versa.

card catalog

This is what people called the wood cabinets full of cards libraries used before online databases.

changeable identity system

Traditionally, identity systems were about consistency: the same logo, the same colors. For a while it was trendy to make identities that changed. I think the challenge of every identity project is the same: to figure out what should change and what should stay the same.
see also: brand

Citi Bike

This bike-sharing system made New York a whole new city for me—and everybody else. I'm proud to say they're an Open client, too.

cliché

By definition, a cliché is an overused, unoriginal idea. But they're overused for a reason, which is that most people understand what they mean.

CMYK

This stands for cyan, magenta, yellow, and black: the four colors of ink in four-color process. I don't know why *K* stands for black, but when I freelanced at the *New York Times Magazine*, I remember the art directors there called black *key*.
see also: RGB

Colors magazine

COLORS 8: RELIGION September 1994 ✺ Bhadrapad 2051 ☾ Jamada Al-

Working as art director of *Colors*, Benetton's "magazine about the rest of the world," was my last full-time job (for somebody else, anyway).
see also: Tibor Kalman, Rome

concrete

This is a material, commonly used in Brutalist and other modern buildings, made out of gravel, sand, and crushed stone, mixed with cement. The word concrete is also used to describe abstract art made with geometric shapes, music that includes real-world sounds, and poetry set in typography that reflects its content.

conference call

Before Hangouts or Skype, this is how a bunch of people would get together to talk when they couldn't—or didn't want to—do it in person.

Cooper Hewitt Museum

This is the Smithsonian's museum of design. They give out the National Design Awards.

Cooper Union

Founded in 1859 to provide education that was "free as air and water," I taught (and met Cat Kirk) at this school in fall 2010.

copy

In advertising, design, and publishing, this is the text—as in, *I need to finish the glossary copy*.
see also: dummy copy

crash

2008 was my third recession, but it was the first time I paid attention to how we got out of one.
see also: Barack Obama

crit or critique

This is a meeting in which people discuss each other's work, both in art school and here at Open.
see also: Rhode Island School of Design

deliverables

This basically just means *things you will make for a client*. We only ever use this word in the context of a proposal or contract.
see also: RFP

design for people

I don't remember when I started using this phrase, but the first mention of it I can find in an email is from February 2002, when Open was in *Fast Company* magazine's "Fast 50." It's been part of what we are ever since.

design furniture

This is not a thing. I mean, of course furniture is designed, and some of it (like Eames chairs, for instance) is super nice. But Chris Wilcha used this term as a way to describe all the stuff we had to crank out for Bravo. It sounded funny, but some people thought it was some kind of technical term. It's not. Don't worry about it.

dial

I don't think any tv has dials on it any more, but they used to. Some people still refer to tv channel numbers as being *on the dial* (also, some people still refer to channel numbers at all), and lower numbers are supposed to be better.

digital camera

This is what people used to take photos after film and before smartphones. I still do.

dingbats

A dingbat is a small decorative symbol (like ✏, 🖳, or ✳) used in typesetting.
see also: emoji

Discovery Channel

This tv network has been showing nature- and science-related documentaries and reality shows for years. In 2008, Discovery launched another network, all about the environment, called Planet Green. Open designed this very simple logo for Planet Green: ●.

doughnut promo

This is a type of promo that has a particular structure. Doughnut promos start and end with graphics, and leave a hole in the middle for clips from the tv show being promoted.
see also: topical promo

Don Draper

The main character of the tv show *Mad Men*, Don isn't always a great person, but he sure can do a great presentation.

dummy copy

Lorem ipsum dolor sit amet, consectetuer adipiscing elit, sed diam nonummy nibh euismod tincidunt ut laoreet dolore magna aliquam erat volutpat. Ut wisi enim ad minim veniam, quis nostrud exerci tation ullamcorper suscipit.
see also: copy

duotone

This usually refers to a photograph printed in a combination of two colors.
see also: CMYK, four-color process, surprint

DVR

The *digital video recorder* was what people used to record tv shows after VHS tapes went out of style and before everything became a digital file that you can access whenever you want.

Charles and Ray Eames

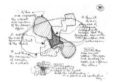

From the 1940s to the 1970s, the Eameses designed everything: buildings, exhibitions, furniture, movies, and their lives. When asked if designers could make things that were pleasurable as well as useful, Charles and Ray said, "Who would say that pleasure is not useful?"

Easter eggs

An Easter egg is a hidden surprise. This book is full of them. Actually, this page is full of them.

effects house

When I first started working on what's now called motion graphics, there was no After Effects—or any other software. We would bring our type to an effects house, where guys with huge machines would take 12 hours to make a word move a little. At least they had lots of free drinks and snacks!
see also: Talking Heads

Dave Eggers

The author of the memoir *A Heartbreaking Work of Staggering Genius*, Dave Eggers is also the founder of the *McSweeney's* publishing empire.

emoji

An emoji is a small decorative symbol (like 😊, 🍴, or ✨) used in text messaging.
see also: dingbats

The Ernie Kovacs Show

Back in the 1950s, Ernie Kovacs used the format and technology of tv to make visual jokes. My favorite was the time he labeled the colors of everything on his set so that people without color tvs could know what they were missing.

Etch a Sketch

Why is it so much fun to draw with a toy that's kind of hard to draw with—and erases your drawings when you shake it?

explainer

Traditionally, an explainer is a person who explains things. Now an explainer is a short article, infographic, or video that explains things.

fair use

This is a legal concept that says you can use copyrighted material if it's for academic, critical, or journalistic purposes.

fax

The best fax I ever got was from Pete Seeger, the legendary folk singer and political activist. He was excited about the *Broadside* box set we had designed for Smithsonian Folkways Recordings. We don't have a fax machine at Open anymore, but you can still send us a fax: +1 212 645-8164.

film

This refers both to the idea of movies and the actual film most movies (and still photography) used to be recorded on.

Flash

This was a programming language people used to make fancy websites with for a while. Now we just use HTML5 instead.

folio

The information—including some combination of a title, chapter or section title, and page number—that usually appears at the bottom of a book or magazine page is called a folio. Look! There's one right above this paragraph: *glossary / Design for People / page 230*.

four-color process

Most printed matter (including this book) is made with this type of offset printing, in which everything is made out of percentages of four basic colors.
see also: CMYK, surprint

Give and Take Machine

I presented this at a conference put on in San Diego by a group called CEOs for Cities. A response to the bad economy, this was Open's idea for a place where people could get together that wasn't all about spending money.
see also: crash

Milton Glaser

Milton might be the first designer I ever heard of. I copied his work in high school.

Gotham

This typeface, designed by Tobias Frere-Jones and based on old signs he photographed on his quest to photograph every block in Manhattan, is probably best known as part of the identity of Barack Obama's election campaigns.
see also: Port Authority

gradient

That's a gradient. It's pretty much just a gradual change from one color to another. I love bright, flat, pure, solid colors. So for a long time I was against gradients. Now I think they look nice.

Grand Prix

Designer Saul Bass drew storyboards for the famous shower scene in Alfred Hitchcock's *Psycho* (and designed its credits). But I prefer the split-screen racing scenes he directed in John Frankenheimer's *Grand Prix*. They (and the credits he designed to go with them) look as new today as they must have back in 1966.

Grapus

Grapus was a design studio founded by Pierre Bernard, François Miehe, and Gérard Paris-Clavel in 1970. They first started making posters together as students during the protests in May 1968. The studio operated for over 20 years, but never did work for any for-profit business. I first found out about Grapus when Pierre came to RISD and taught a Visiting Designers workshop during my junior year.

green screen

I was super into *Star Wars* as a kid (the first movie came out when I was eight), and I loved anything about how the movies were made. So I knew about blue screen at an early age. These days green screen is more common. It's used to film something that needs to be isolated or combined with something else, like a weatherperson or James Lipton.

grid

Graphic designers often use a grid to organize typography on a page. Even though you don't see the grid, the choices made in designing it can have a big effect on what you do see. You can see the grid used throughout *Design for People* in the background of this page.
see also: baseline grid

hand courier

This is literally a guy who would get on a plane with your package and deliver it personally.

Harold and the Purple Crayon

This 1955 children's book by Crockett Johnson was made into a short film in 1959 that looks a little bit like our *Art21* interstitials.

HD

This stands for *high definition*, as in HDTV. HDTV displays 1920x1080 pixels, which is about five times the resolution of standard-definition tv.

headline

Often called a hed by publishing people, this is the title of a magazine or newspaper article.
see also: copy

Heisenberg's Uncertainty Principle

This says that when observing certain quantum particles, you can't know everything—for instance, you could know where a particle is, but not how fast it's moving. I found out about this from *Star Trek*, where the transporter uses something called a "Heisenberg Compensator."

Hell's Kitchen

A restaurant kitchen is a lot like a design studio. The head chef (or creative director) makes a plan and works with other chefs (or designers) to make stuff. Then the head chef makes sure everything looks good before the customer sees it. I used to watch *Hell's Kitchen* all the time.

Helvetica

I don't know if this is the most popular typeface in the world, but it's the one most people know about. There's even a (very good) movie about it! For years, Open had a no-Helvetica policy. Any typeface famous enough to star in a movie is hard to use in a bit part in one of our projects.

high def or high definition

see: HD

High Line

This is an extremely fancy park in Manhattan, built on an elevated train line that had been decaying for years. It is nice, but I miss the elevated train line that had been decaying for years.

high res or high resolution

This is an image with lots of detail. In the case of a digital image, that means more pixels.

identity

Derived from *corporate identity*, this is how a company or idea or organization acts, looks, and sounds—a reflection of who they are inside. *Branding* sounds like a stamp on the outside.
see also: brand, changeable identity systems

Ideo

This design and consulting business is known as the first to use *design thinking*—using design with the goal of making things better—in a business context. Sounds good to me!

improv or improvisation

When I took classes (and performed) at the Upright Citizens Brigade Theater, I learned about *yes and*: listening, understanding what you hear, and adding something new to it. That's what improvisation is, and it works in acting, comedy, music, and just about everywhere else.

InDesign
This is the page-layout software I've been using since QuarkXPress.

infographics

I call them information graphics. Others prefer *data visualizations*. Either way, they turn information into stories. I'm pretty sure the first infographics we made at Open were for Chris Wilcha's MTV show *So Five Minutes Ago*, and they contained no actual information at all.

internship
An internship is a low-paying job students take to learn more about their field. A non-paying internship is a violation of U.S. labor law. I don't think it's wrong for students to choose to work for free—my M&Co. internship was unpaid—I think it's wrong for businesses to make them do it. Your work has value, especially when somebody else is making money on it.

interstitials
The graphic "palate cleansers" between the artist segments of *Art21* have always been called interstitials. They're basically bumpers, even though PBS doesn't have commercial breaks.

iPod
This device, first released by Apple in 2001, is like an iPhone—but without the phone part. The one I ordered the first day only played music.

Elizabeth and Manuel Morais
would like you to know about:
jantar

My wife, Carmen, was born in Newark, New Jersey, but her family is from Portugal. The first time she invited me to a family meal, I was surprised to be there for hours, checking my watch. *Jantar* means *dinner* (or *to dine*), but it also means coming together around a table in the company of others. Now, years later, I enjoy every hour—and don't wear a watch.

The John Stevens Shop

The Stevens Shop, in Newport, Rhode Island, has been drawing letters and carving them in stone since 1705. I first heard about them when I studied with John Hegnauer (who used to work at the Stevens Shop) at RISD and carved my own alphabet stone. When we got the Yale job, I knew I wanted Nick Benson at the Stevens Shop to make the new front entrance sign.
see also: sign painting, Trajan Column

Louis Kahn
I'm a fan of Kahn's buildings, with their simple forms and pure materials. During our Yale project, we watched *My Architect*, the film about him made by his son, Nathaniel. You should, too.

Tibor Kalman

Tibor was the cofounder of M&Co. He was my boss, there and at *Colors*. I have way more to say about him than could ever fit here, but here are two things I learned from him: First, *good enough* is never actually good enough. And second, sometimes *too good* is not that good.
see also: Rome

Wassily Kandinsky
In 1926, this Russian painter (and former lawyer) wrote *Point and Line to Plane*, a book that breaks visual art down to its most basic elements.

Ken Burns effect
This effect that moves images slowly across the screen in software like Final Cut and iMovie is named after Ken Burns, who makes films you can see on PBS. I wonder what Ken Burns calls it.

kerning
This is the adjustment of spacing between letters in a piece of typography.

Kickstarter
About 1,000 people ordered *Design for People* through Kickstarter, founded in 2009 to help original, creative projects happen. Thank you!

The Kids in the Hall
Along with *Monty Python* and *Mr. Show*, this will always be one of my favorite comedy tv shows.
see also: meta

Knockout
This typeface family, with 32 different weights and widths, was designed by Jonathan Hoefler in 1994, based on the kind of 19th-century American sans serif type often used for boxing posters. We used it for all our *Nation* covers.

Jeff Koons
I think the first time I saw Jeff Koons' art (in that case, a basketball floating in a tank of water) was in the 1989 Whitney Biennial. I learned more about him in *Art21* season five.

Jacques Lacan
Lacan was a French psychoanalyst. He came up with the idea of the *mirror stage*, which says when children recognize themselves in a mirror, it helps them understand that they exist.

Late Night with David Letterman

Late Night was a regular talk show that was totally not a regular talk show. Dave played with the show (and NBC, its tv network) like a new toy with no instruction manual. As a result, the hour from 12:30 to 1:30 am was always the highlight of my high-school all-nighters.
see also: *The Ernie Kovacs Show*, meta

Laugh-In
If I had been born 20 years earlier, this might have been one of my favorite comedy tv shows. It's not.

LCD
Short for *liquid-crystal display*, this is the technology that powers the screens of some tvs and lots of calculators. LCDs don't light up—they need a separate light source.
see also: LED

LED
Short for *light-emitting diode*, this is the technology that powers animated signs, old digital watches, and sustainable lighting—and provides the light source for LCD screens.

lenticular
This is the technique used to make those little novelty items with pictures that change when you look at them from different angles.

James Lipton
The host of *Inside the Actors Studio* since 1994, James Lipton was already 78 years old when we started working with Bravo. He wore sensible shoes to our green screen shoot, and he was up for anything—until we put him on a (slowly) rotating platform. He endured it for a while, but somewhere there's some footage of him quietly saying, "Please, make it stop." I really wanted to make a bumper using that.

lock up
This is a standard arrangement of elements, like a logo and tagline (like the Trio logo and *pop, culture, tv*) or more than one logo (like the Bike MS and Walk MS sponsor logos).
see also: wordmark

low res or low resolution
This is an image with not much detail. In the case of a digital image, that means fewer pixels.

lower third
When you're watching a documentary or news report and the name of the person speaking comes up near the bottom of the screen, that's a lower third. For the record, when we got the Trio job we totally knew what a lower third was.
see also: bug

Alvin Lustig

A graphic, interior, and textile designer who had an amazingly prolific career for years, mostly in Los Angeles, before dying of complications from diabetes in 1955 at the age of 40, Lustig is one of my favorites. I have a (very small) collection of his New Classics and New Directions book jackets.

M&Co.

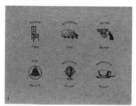

Cofounded by Carol Bokuniewicz, <u>Tibor Kalman</u>, and Liz Trovato in 1979, this design studio was the only place I ever wanted to work.

MacOS progress icon

mashup
This is a work of art (like a book, song, or video) made of different things stuck together. I think our <u>Yale</u> front entrance sign is kind of a mashup.

meta
In popular usage, the word meta is used to describe things that are self-referential, like a book that keeps talking about itself as a book.

MetaFilter
I've been a member of this, the original community weblog, since 2002.

Piet Mondrian
He was a Dutch artist best known for his paintings made up of horizontal and vertical black lines and solid areas of primary colors.

monoweight
For a long time, most <u>typefaces</u> had thick and thin parts, which reflected the influence of the brushes and pens used to draw letters by hand. Now many typefaces (like <u>Gotham</u>, or Graphik, which you're reading now) have much less contrast in weight, hence the term monoweight.
see also: <u>The John Stevens Shop</u>, <u>sign painting</u>

Monty Python
I watched it on <u>WGBH</u> when I was a kid.
see also: *<u>The Kids in the Hall</u>*

mood board
This is a collection of images meant to convey a vague impression of something.

motion design or **motion graphics**
These both mean graphic design that moves.

mouth trumpet
This is that thing where you hold your lips together and kind of hum, to try to make a sound like a trumpet. I'm pretty good at it. That year of playing the cornet in sixth grade must have helped. Try it. It's super annoying!

Movie of the Week

The idea of watching movies on tv used to be a big deal. In 1971, ABC started showing its own original movies on Tuesday nights. The <u>on-air package</u> used some of the technology that made those crazy scenes at the end of <u>2001</u>.

Mr. Robot
I love this tv show, but only one season has aired at this point. We'll see how it goes!

MTV
Short for *Music Television*, this is a tv network that was originally about music. When I met <u>Paul Rand</u> at <u>M&Co.</u>, he asked me what it was.

Museum of Television and Radio
Now called the Paley Center for Media, this is still the best place to go to watch old tv shows you can't find on YouTube. We did research for Trio there, and now you can watch Trio there!

Nathan's Hot Dogs
If you haven't been to Coney Island, you have to go. And when you go, go to Nathan's. I haven't been to either one in years. So why did Nathan's Hot Dogs randomly pop into my head while I was talking about <u>newspapers</u>?

newspaper
I don't read printed newspapers, except when I'm traveling. It's fun to pick up a newspaper in a café in Paris or <u>Rome</u>. But I do miss the feeling of reading and then finishing "today's paper."
see also: <u>newsprint</u>

newsprint
This is the cheap, off-white paper made from wood <u>pulp</u> that's used to print <u>newspapers</u> and some magazines, like *The Nation*.
see also: <u>Op-Ed page</u>

Nick at Nite

When Nick at Nite started, it was a way for Nickelodeon (a tv network for kids) to fill airtime when the kids were asleep. So they put on reruns of old shows that the kids' parents watched when they were kids. About a year after Chip and I moved into our studio, Nick at Nite asked us for some ideas. That led to a year of work doing a whole redesign of the network.

NTSC

This is the *National Television System Committee* standard for analog broadcast tv used in the U.S. from 1941 up until digital tv started taking over. NTSC specified the standard of 29.97 frames per second that a lot of tv still uses.
see also: scan line

Barack Obama

I've been voting since 1988, but it took me 20 years to pick a winner. President Obama's combination of idealism, realism, and relentlessness is a constant inspiration to me.

offset printing

The most commonly used type of printing, this is named offset because the image to be printed is first offset from the printing plate onto a cloth material, called a blanket, before being transferred onto paper. This allows the plates to last longer than traditional direct printing.
see also: CMYK, four-color process

on-air package

In the tv world, this is a way to say redesign, although *package* has more of a feeling of specific deliverables. A package could be just for one show, a special event, or an entire network.

Op-Ed page

This is the *New York Times'* opinion and editorial page. It often features illustration by designers.

Open

I've been doing business as Open since 1998.

pay attention

For years, I've been doing talks with this title. Everything is connected and everything is an opportunity—if you're paying attention.

PBS

This is the national public tv network in the U.S.
see also: WGBH

PDF

More and more, it seems like *Portable Document Format* files are what we at Open make more than anything else. Our presentations are PDFs. We send PDFs to the printer. We even designed a PDF annual report for Etsy.

Pink Lady...and Jeff

Apparently this was a variety show hosted by two Japanese singers (known as Pink Lady) and an American comedian (Jeff Altman). It was only on tv for five weeks, in 1980.

pitch

This is a situation in which a potential client asks a designer for some ideas in exchange for a reduced fee. Often it's a competition against other designers. Usually the winner of that competition would be rewarded with a large, well-paid project. I don't think a pitch is speculative work. It's an opportunity.
see also: pro bono

pixelated

This refers to a low resolution digital image.

pogo

This is the system of light, movable walls Louis Kahn developed for his Yale Art Gallery building.

Jackson Pollock

He is the best known abstract expressionist painter. One time Jason Polan drew Pollock's painting *One: Number 31, 1950*, for me.

porcelain enamel
This is the material used for those beautiful old house numbers and street signs you see in places like Paris. The surface is made of layers of powdered glass baked onto a metal backing. Porcelain-enamel signs last forever and look great even when they're showing their age.

Port Authority
The Port Authority of New York and New Jersey is in charge of the airports, bridges, seaports, trains, and tunnels in the New York City area. But when most New Yorkers say Port Authority, they mean the Port Authority Bus Terminal at Eighth Avenue and 42nd Street in Manhattan.
see also: 42nd Street Art Project, Gotham

PowerPoint
This presentation software is terrible, but most people use it. So we have to work with it, too.

presentation
This is our most frequent type of interaction with clients: us showing things, usually in a book or a PDF, in person, or on a conference call.

press check

It's great to be done with your work and put it in the hands of people who know what they're doing. A press check is a visit to make sure everything looks good while it's being printed. I loved going to Lane Press in Burlington, Vermont, to print *Good*. We had to stay up all night, but there were snacks. As Rob says, "It was miserable, but it was also kind of fun." Also, I've loved the smell of ink ever since I was a kid.
see also: proof

pro bono
This phrase means *for the public good*. For designers (and other people, like lawyers) it means *work you do for free, usually for a good cause.*
see also: internship, speculative work

Project Runway
I didn't watch when it premiered with our Bravo redesign, but since then, *Project Runway*'s combination of ridiculous constraints and thoughtful mentoring has inspired my work at Open and my teaching at SVA and Yale.

promo
A promo is basically a tv commercial for a tv show. Promos usually include clips from the show itself, edited together with graphics.
see also: doughnut promo, topical promo

proof
Printers typically provide proofs—a kind of facsimile of how your job will print—before going on press. Proofs used to be made from the film used to make the printing plates, so you would really know how your job would print. Now, printers often just send you a PDF of your digital files, which isn't actually proof of anything.
see also: press check

proposal
This is what a contractor might call a bid. It's a document we put together in response to an RFP that says what services we'll provide, what deliverables we'll make, and an estimate of how much time and money it would take to do it.

Public Design Commission
The 1898 New York City charter established a Municipal Art Commission to oversee monuments and public art in the city. 110 years later, it was renamed the Public Design Commission (PDC). A year after that, I presented our Brooklyn Bridge Park signage to them. At the time, the PDC met in the dome of City Hall. Getting there involved navigating some rickety wooden stairs. There was no smoking, but it felt like a smoke-filled room. They served popcorn.

pulp
Paper is mostly made from wood. The fibers in wood are processed into a material called pulp, and then into paper. Pulp can also be made from recycled paper fibers. As a verb, *pulp* means *turn into pulp*. So if a print job goes wrong, it might get pulped.
see also: newsprint

QuarkXPress
This is the page-layout software I used after PageMaker and before InDesign.

Paul Rand

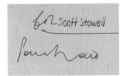

Lots of people say Paul Rand is the number one designer of logos ever. My favorite was his UPS logo. He wrote a few books, too. In the early 1990s, he was thinking about having Tibor write the foreword for one of them. I was just a couple of years out of school, sitting at my desk at M&Co., when Rand walked in. Besides seeing him eat egg salad, the highlight of that day was getting him to sign my copy of his book, *A Designer's Art*, which I kept next to my desk. I had already written my name in the front, so he just wrote *for* and signed his name under mine.

Robert Rauschenberg

As a fine artist in the 1950s, Rauschenberg started incorporating everyday objects into what he called combines. Later, he started combining images into silkscreen prints with different colors layered on top of each other. I own one piece of Rauschenberg's work: a limited-edition package for the Talking Heads album *Speaking in Tongues*, with images separated into cyan, magenta, and yellow inks on clear layers of plastic.
see also: CMYK, surprint

rear projection
This is a way of displaying an image by projecting it backwards on the back of the screen, so you see it the right way on the front.

redesign
Of course, this means *to design anything over again*. But it also means *to redo something completely*, like our Trio and Bravo projects.
see also: on-air package

render
As a verb, this is the process of creating watchable video files using animation or video editing software. As a noun, it's one of those files.
see also: After Effects, motion design

RFP
This stands for *request for proposal*. It's basically a document from a potential client, asking for a proposal for a design project.

RGB
Images on screens are RGB: They're made up of red, green, and blue light mixed together.
see also: CMYK

Rhode Island School of Design or RISD
When I first went to Providence, Rhode Island to visit RISD, I knew it was where I wanted to go to school. When I went there, I knew I was right. Thanks, RISD Financial Aid!

Road Runner
Created by animator Chuck Jones, this bird stars (with the hapless coyote, Wile E. Coyote) in the most existential cartoons ever.

Rome

I knew nothing about Rome before I lived above this pizza place for a year when I worked for *Colors*. Now I can't wait to go (or move) back.
see also: Tibor Kalman, Trajan Column

rubber stamp
I love printing technology. But I don't love "rubber stamping" anything without thinking.

sans serif
Serifs are very small details that appear in certain lettering and typefaces. Type with serifs is called serif type and looks like this. Type without serifs is called sans serif type and looks like this.

scan line
Older tvs (the non-flat-screen kind) displayed an image by shooting electrons at the inside of the screen in rows called scan lines, kind of like how 3D printers assemble objects. A standard 4x3 tv had only 480 scan lines from top to bottom.
see also: NTSC

Phil Schaap
Phil is the curator of Jazz at Lincoln Center and knows more about jazz than just about anybody else does. Working with him was fascinating— and kind of scary. When Phil was a kid, Count Basie's drummer Jo Jones was his babysitter!

Sears
When I was a kid, Sears was the biggest retail chain in the U.S. We got everything there: appliances, clothes, *Star Wars* action figures. Now they're owned by Kmart.

Segway
When this "human transporter" was invented, a lot of people thought it would change the world. I think the only benefit of a Segway over walking is to show people that you had $5,000 to spend on a Segway instead of walking.

sexiled
If you come home, your roommate has some-body over, and you're not welcome, you may have been sexiled. While this has happened to me, I had never heard the word until I read Nguyen Le's *Design for People* interview.

Sharpie

Next to the Uni-Ball micro point roller pen, the Sharpie is probably what I write with the most. I never use Sharpies in my sketchbook, though— the ink goes right through the page.

sign painting
I love that all hand-painted signs are made out of exactly the same stuff: just ink or paint and words. Plus, anybody can make them (with a lot of practice and the right tools).
see also: The John Stevens Shop, Trajan Column

signage
This is pretty much just a fancy way to say *signs*.
see also: wayfinding

silkscreen
I grew up learning about offset printing (and four-color process) from my dad, who worked as a printer for many years. I learned about silk-screen printing in school. It's done by pushing ink through a fine mesh screen onto a surface. The most common use of silkscreen is probably on t-shirts and other clothing. We used silk-screen to print the graphics on the walls of the Sciences Library at Brown.

sketchbook

I've been using these black, hardcover books for my ideas, notes, and sketches ever since I got my first one, during my freshman year at RISD.

slug
In publishing, a slug is a short description of an article or section of a magazine. We used the idea of magazine slugs to identify the different parts of our Bravo redesign.

Susan Sontag
To be honest, I don't know much about Susan Sontag. I know she was a writer, but I don't think I've read her work. Her name just popped into my head when I was trying to think of some "high culture" that might have been on Trio.

speculative work
What designers call spec work is any project that somebody asks you to do for free, with the promise of future payment or other reward (like "exposure" or a "portfolio piece"). Don't do it. Your work has value. That's why they want it.
see also: internship, pitch, pro bono

Standard Alphabets For Highway Signs and Pavement Markings, Metric Edition

I first got this book (by sending a letter to the Federal Highway Administration) when I was at M&Co. I had to get a fake highway sign made for a National Car Rental tv commercial Tibor was directing. The only way to get the typeface right was to copy it from this book. Tobias Frere-Jones also used this book to make **Highway Gothic** (which I used on the 42nd Street Art Project) and **Interstate**.

Star Trek
It's got diversity, optimism, and spaceships. What more could you ask for?
see also: warp core

Steadicam
This is a piece of equipment that a person can use to shoot very stable videos or films while moving around. The word is also used to describe the kind of long, smooth shots made using a Steadicam.

stock photography
I thought the rise of digital photography was killing stock photos, but now they're everywhere, thanks to websites needing cheap content. It's too bad they're as bad as ever.
see also: dummy copy

storyboard
This is a series of drawings or layouts used to plan out an animation, film, or motion design sequence before production.

strategy
This is the stage of our work before the design part, when we think about what we should actually make. There are huge consulting firms that sometimes do this and not the design part.
see also: IDEO

surprint
This is the printing of one color of ink on top of another, so the colors mix together.
see also: CMYK, four-color process

tagline
This is another word for *slogan*.
see also: copy

Talking Heads

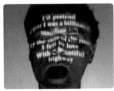

Started by a bunch of kids at RISD in 1975, this pop band was too weird for the mainstream and too normal for the weirdos. In other words, perfect. All of their songs were full of smart ideas that you could dance to. When I was an intern at M&Co., I got to work on their "(Nothing But) Flowers" video.

telecine
This is otherwise known as *film-to-tape transfer*.
see also: effects house

Tibor
see: Tibor Kalman

topical promo
This is a promo about a particular subject. Topical promos are often made for news shows.
see also: doughnut promo

Trajan Column

Put up in Rome in the year 113, this 100-foot-tall column has an inscription in what many people consider the best-drawn Roman letters ever.
see also: The John Stevens Shop, Rome, sign painting

Trollbäck + Company
This design studio in New York City, founded in 1999, is run by designer Jakob Trollbäck. They mostly make motion graphics for movies and tv. Right now I think my favorite project of theirs is the graphics for *Last Week Tonight with John Oliver* on HBO.

Tron
This 1982 Disney movie was one of the first to use lots of computer animation, which was mixed with plenty of traditional animation.
see also: animation stand

typeface
A typeface is a certain design of type, like Gotham or Helvetica. This text (and this whole book) is set in one called Graphik. Lots of people use the word font to mean *typeface*, since that's what your computer calls them, but they're actually two different things. Back when type was set in metal, a font was one particular size and style of a typeface, like *12 point Helvetica Bold*. Today the word font refers to the files you install on your computer to use typefaces. But if you say *font* to mean *typeface*, everybody will know what you mean.
see also: typography

typography
How can I explain typography? Well, you're looking at it right now. Let's just say it's the selection and arrangement of letters and words on a surface, whether that's a page or a screen or signage or pretty much anything else.
see also: typeface

Goffredo Puccetti
would like you to know about:

unspecialized
I used to worry about what kind of design work I was supposed to make. Some people say that designers should specialize in something, so others can understand what you do. It took me years to realize that there's power in not specializing in much of anything. I'm supposed to make the work I want to make. You are, too.

URL
This stands for *Uniform Resource Locator*, which is an address of something on the internet—like a website: *http://www.notclosed.com*.

UX/UI
Usually applied to things like apps or websites, these stand for *user experience* and *user interface*. Some people mix these up, but UX is more about how something works and UI is more about how something looks. Of course, those things go together—or should, anyway.

Varick Street

The main drag of what used to be called the Printers' District (and what some people now call Hudson Square), Varick Street has been home to Open ever since Chip Wass and I first signed a lease in November 1997. Of course it took until March 1998 for us to get the place fixed up and move in. Now the neighborhood is known as Hudson Square, and it's full of ad agencies, architects, and a lot more designers.

VHS
I just had to look this up. Apparently it stands for *Video Home System*. Anyway, this is what I used to use to record tv shows and watch movies. There are still some old VHS tapes at the studio. see also: DVR

Randy J. Hunt
would like you to know about:

walking
In his book *Walden*, Henry David Thoreau wrote that he'd prefer to spend a day walking 30 miles than to work a day to earn the money to take the train. I first heard this story when I was at *Colors*, but I still think about it whenever I take the time to pay attention and enjoy the trip, whether I'm on foot, on a Citi Bike—or on the train.

warp core
This is the reactor that powers warp-capable starships. Federation warp cores use deuterium and anti-deuterium reacting in a dilithium matrix. see also: *Star Trek*

wayfinding
In the context of design, this means helping people get where they need to go, primarily through the use of signage.

WGBH
This is the public radio and tv broadcasting organization in Boston, Massachusetts. see also: *Monty Python*, PBS

Wieden + Kennedy
I first got to work with this ad agency (the best ad agency) back in 1994, when Todd Waterbury brought me to Portland (Oregon, not Maine) to work on some projects for Coca-Cola.

Williamsburg

I moved from the East Village (in Manhattan) to Williamsburg (in Brooklyn) in 1992, and a lot of the cool stuff was gone before I got there. I moved to the West Village (Manhattan again) in 2004. Williamsburg boomed after I left.

Windows
I have never ever used a Windows computer.

winky
see: lenticular

WNYC

We got to design the logo for WNYC, New York City's biggest public radio station.

wordmark
A wordmark is a type-only logo with no symbol.

Yale
Paul Rand quit the Yale graduate program in graphic design in 1992 after Sheila Levrant de Bretteville took over as director. I'm proud to have been teaching in the program since 2000.

You're almost done. This is the
part of the book where you
can find all the stuff that didn't
fit anywhere else. There are
outtakes (from everybody who
was interviewed for the book),
an index, information about
the images, a page of thanks
from me, a page of suggestions
for you, and finally, the credits.
And speaking of thanks, thank
you for reading this book.
It means a lot to me. I hope it
means something to you, too.

etc.

Rachel Abrams:
The experience of watching these was like swallowing an encyclopedia in pill form.

Krishan Aghi:
The majority of my memories are flooded by stress, fear, and intense sadness.

Don Ball:
I love steering curious students to things that I know will expand their thinking and enrich their practice.

Tyler Banks:
Back in the days before the everything-that-happened-everywhere-always cataloging of the internet, there was an element to tv viewing where if you saw something, you felt like you might never be able to see it again and there may never be proof that this thing you experienced actually happened other than the eyewitness account of you and viewers like you.

Su Barber:
If we didn't want rules, we'd be artists.

Nicholas Benson:
We have an ideology that we follow closely. That's odd in this day and age.

Chase Booker:
I, like many people, fiddle with something way past the point of it being useful.

Rachel Bozek:
It's super interesting to see the other side of what was really going on.

Cara Brower:
I think I went home and ate like so much ice cream. It must have been 17 ounces.

Mo Caicedo:
I really had to think outside of the box in order to make the message clear.

Kate Davis Caldwell:
The '90s bring back sunny, nostalgic memories for me.

Casey Caplowe:
I think we were up for at least a day and a half, two days at one point. And I don't know exactly why.

Roane Carey:
I wish I could remember this!

Rob Carmichael:
It was chaotic—as things often are on deadline—but a total delight.

Mike Cartagena:
So a lot of people have visual problems.

Stephen Cassell:
I wasn't trendy enough to know that stuff.

Daralee Champion:
Sharing stories can be helpful when someone feels like no one understands what they are going through.

Jason Jude Chan:
Eventually, I was like, *I'm going to have to leave, you guys, because I've got to move to New York.*

Lu Chekowsky:
I had, like, a weird Britney Spears microphone, and a teleprompter. It was very staged.

Chris Cheng:
I left Google in 2012 after winning a reality tv show for marksmen called *Top Shot.*

Morgan Clendaniel:
The hardest part was that everyone cared about it so much.

Jorge Colombo:
I think I was still smoking a pipe in those days.

Eric Cornwell:
I must share with you a pet peeve and implore you not to let anyone use the phase *reach out* in any text attributed to me. To me, *reach out* implies a degree of difficulty that I don't associate with sending an email or picking up the phone, and suggests that the person reaching out is expected to fall short of actual *contact* or that word would be used instead. You are welcome to edit everything for clarity, drama, brevity, whatever, as you see fit, but please don't make me say *reach out.* Thank you.

Gabbie Corvese:
It was absolute madness, and probably a fire hazard. People fought for pizza.

Ian Cox:
In essence, it was a balanced, great-tasting meal in a pizza form.

Jesse Crawford:
I jumped right on the reality tv bandwagon when it started to grow in the early 2000s.

Randy Crochet:
As we grew, we became very cognizant that some customers did not want to be educated, so we moderated our message.

Thomas Dareneau:
Our thoughts don't follow straight paths. They take hard turns, move in and out, as well as up and down, and take us to places we never intended to go.

Gary David:
When Directv dropped the channel, I was a bit upset because it was something I truly enjoyed.

Anna De Paula Hanika:
. It was very much like, *Let us be your arms and your legs.*

Rob Di Ieso:
So that's the only thing I can really remember. Other than my absolute terror during the entire project of everything that could go wrong.

Ritesh Doshi:
I was visiting my parents in Kenya, where I grew up, and ordered pizza one night. It took 75 minutes.

Susan Dowling:
The world is changing. Technology is changing. Everything is changing.

Patrick Dugan:
It's a beautiful place, full of beautiful things.

Chappell Ellison:
My brother and I used to yell stupid things at each other in that voice from opposite ends of our house.

George Feese:
After learning a bit about design, I realize it's often difficult to balance humility with refinement.

Amy Feezor:
I don't need a park cluttered with signage. But I always appreciate maps.

Andréa Fernandes:
The best part was the focus on the good.

Michael Fischer:
It was sort of a fairly large mechanical space that was actually not being used for mechanical purposes.

Gary Fogelson:
The weird thing about working with Scott was that, I would say for at least like the first year that I worked there, I had no idea if I would have a job the next week, you know?

Peter Foley:
I can't say that I've consciously tried to add complexity.

Zach Frechette:
That was still in the golden era of, *Your job, Zach, is to just make the most fun, interesting publication that you can, and we're not going to worry too much about how much it costs to produce it.*

Tobias Frere-Jones:
I had some metaphor, but now I can't think of what it was.

Jason Fulford:
The subject list included: *elevator, tv static, Xerox machine, hamburger deluxe, take-a-number ticket, stoplight, dinosaur, trophy, marquee, drive-thru, coffee cup, wall clock, bookstore, dog, cat, baby, subway, equalizer, microphone, gumball machine, popcorn, satellite dish, balloon, outlet, stadium, watermelon, David Letterman, pancakes, soap.*

Christie Germans:
I am empowered to live my best life possible.

David Gibson:
I guess the moral of the lesson is that if you are a great, dedicated designer, you can do almost anything you set your mind to.

Sherri Giger:
We were actually excited about the possibilities it presented.

Milton Glaser:
You're asking me how my brain works?

Gina Goddard:
Nice color schemes, too.

Ben Goldhirsh:
I was just sort of a spectator on that ride, but it was a really fun ride to be a spectator on.

Julie Golia:
I have a very vivid memory of doing a signage location walk-through with the team on maybe the coldest February day in world history.

Elizabeth Goodspeed:
In the end, they raffled off an axolotl as a pet.

Logan Grider:
Nothing feels out of context.

Yotam Hadar:
I always had a plan to approach the Gallery and suggest that they would let students from the School of Art reprogram the LED display and allow custom, low-resolution artwork, but my two years at Yale passed by so quickly, I didn't get a chance to do it.

Greg Hahn:
It seemed like a good idea at the time.

Anna Hammond:
Oh my God. That is so weird.

Dehlia Hannah:
Just put it on a credit card! There's lot of benefits in Kickstarter, but monetizing social relationships isn't exactly the way.

Liz Harnett:
I've always said my job is a cross between stage-managing and air traffic control.

Carol Hayes:
I had never met Katrina, but envisioned her to be a very glamorous lefty intellectual, working from a '30s-style penthouse on the Upper East Side like someone out of a Dawn Powell novel.

Parvinder Heer:
I am constantly excited to see what's new.

Amelia Hennighausen:
People are often resistant to change.

Garin Horner:
For me, the graphics are the living breath that moves throughout the series.

Jason Hu:
That being said, there's a lot of things that leave something to be desired.

Samir Husni:
The design was the best icing I ever tasted on the best cake ever made.

Anastasia Rose Hyden:
I was a teenager and lived with my mom, who had satellite tv.

Gemma Ingalls:
I made it up to the office, but the door was wide open and no one was inside—not even Ruby, our resident French Bulldog.

Zak Jensen:
I remember Scott told me to wear pants. I guess as opposed to shorts, but I don't remember him making that distinction.

Natalie Jeremijenko:
I think what they're pointing to is that you work with graphic design to make statements bold, simple, inviting.

Laura Johnson:
The integration of all those different elements in a very compressed period of time in that kind of space was what we thought would be radical and more successful.

Chris Kairalla:
I could do a lot of different things and I could jump into a lot of different chairs.

Nikki Kalcevic:
I always want to put art in all caps instead of lower case.

Shreya Karia:
For me, functionality and ease is what I'm looking for.

Atley Kasky:
It was itself and was OK to be itself.

Bryan Keeling:
I'm usually the guy who has to sit in the chair and keep working to make the deadline. I'm the guy who doesn't stop working.

Alan Kimmel:
An exception to the blandness of more recent covers might be the one that features Bernie Sanders—but then he is my favorite politician!

Rob Kimmel:
Everything about it said, *Whatever you do, don't read me,* in a slow, raspy voice.

Devon King:
If you know your dog isn't supposed to be on the lawn but you're sitting in front of it, you can't be mad when you get a ticket.

Cat Kirk:
I was like, *Mom, it's on tv.*

Kate Kittredge:
There's really nothing cooler than researching neon.

Jason Klarman:
Everybody forgets all the things that didn't work.

Peter Knox:
I work in marketing and my wife's an architect, so we tend to get excited about good design when we see it.

Prem Krishnamurphy:
This was a multi-year process.

Mike Lampariello:
I fall into a few different worlds.

Steven Lavallee:
Least favorite: the bathrooms.

Nguyen Le:
I had never found what Bob Marley said so true until that moment.

Erika Lee:
My first impression was like, *Yes!*

Matthew Lee:
Only people who really need to get work done go to the stacks, so there's a kind of unifying solace in seeing other people there, even if you never talk to them.

Wendy Leventer:
First of all, I don't like it when people think that their audience is stupid. I hate that. I just think people are smarter than they're given credit for.

Daryl Long:
I'm going to say something negative, so negative it's just crazy inappropriate. I liked him better when he was chunky. I had to say something.

Louise Ma:
I feel like there's always a 1 to 3% chance that designing a newsletter can be really fun.

Tom Manning:
I'm Tom Manning, a designer, comic book writer and illustrator, scholar, and gentleman.

Bobby Martin:
Implementation is hard—and it's hard because you have to make decisions on things.

Martha Kang McGill:
Always say hello, and always say thanks at the end.

Graham McReynolds:
It was fun to go down memory lane.

Shimmy Mehta:
We already have this, that, this, that, and the other thing. We just need to find this.

Christina Milan:
It had street cred already by the time I hit the art scene.

Wesley Miller:
Through the process of collaborating closely with artists, we're able to engender new kinds of art history and conversation that privilege the creative process, uncertainty, contradiction, emotional and visual intelligence, and the unrecorded dramas of everyday life.

Linda Montanaro-Kramer:
I live in Brooklyn with my amazing husband and two dachshunds, fondly named The Weenies.

William Morrisey:
I'd like to hang out and eat pizza and design with those guys forever.

Kate Morse:
A staff member asked what I thought. I responded with, "I am getting that tattoo!"

Catherine Mulbrandon:
The quality of the graphics were uneven and I believe they lacked the in-house team to produce them month to month and had to bring people in.

Jonathan Munar:
Lesson learned: Don't completely disregard the formalities of defining business requirements!

Regina Myer:
I honestly don't think people care who runs things.

Leslie Myers:
Budgets and schedules are a day at the beach compared to design problem-solving at this scale.

Christoph Niemann:
I don't know exactly in which context it happened, but I get a sense of equal parts fun and wackiness.

Nyala Wright Nolen:
What I really learned is that budget and deadlines don't matter if you aren't putting out a good product.

Alberto Noriega:
The natural light, the landscapes, the everyday routine in the paintings assures that life is just fantastic.

Sue Noyes:
To me it means those of us who can should be involved.

Siobhan O'Connor:
I would describe it as mostly horizontal, with a few exceptions.

Emily Oberman:
Our client for the logo was a man named Michael Jackson who is not Michael Jackson, but a different—I mean, he is Michael Jackson, but a different Michael Jackson.

Ralph Obure:
I am a meat lover and the salad wonderfully balances out the meal.

Ian Ohan:
It was like a newborn baby that was all innocent and then it got beaten up.

Jane Olson:
There were a lot of different challenges that had nothing to do with the work.

Linda Ong:
There wasn't a lot of time to not move forward, if that makes sense.

Eve Moros Ortega:
Sometimes you look at art and you're like, *I don't know, really?* And then when you understand the idea more, you're like, *Oh, now I get it.*

Şerifcan Özcan:
Scott is the most democratic person that I've ever met in my life.

Ryan Page:
One particular issue is the sausage.

Uroš Perišić:
It was super exciting and easy. Well, nothing's easy, but it was super exciting.

Kim Phillips:
To show up, be present, and do what you can. Because if we don't, who will?

Simone Pillinger:
I should have sat and given this some thought.

Kevin Proudfoot:
I know that might sound cliché, but it is what it is.

Reem Rayef:
It would become this weird social space where everyone pretended to study until two in the morning while actually hanging out and eating the noisiest possible foods.

Anna Bishop Rehrig:
We wanted to start thinking, *How do we start even going into the real world?*

Dylan Reid:
It's like all of a sudden it was everywhere: on the subway, in line at the grocery story, tucked under the arms of co-workers and friends.

Jock Reynolds:
I'm a firm believer that I don't care how good your architect is, if you're not a good client, you're not going to get a good building.

Nicholas Rock:
Can you hear me OK? Because I'm driving.

David Rockwell:
There weren't a lot of things being thrown around the room.

Danny Rodriguez:
Where's the helicopter? Somebody was selling helicopter tickets on Pier 6.

Lindsey Ross:
Every day there's at least one shoot happening. We did *Ninja Turtles* recently.

Karen Rothmyer:
We had no phones, we had no internet, we had no anything.

Ellen Ryan:
It could have been an exercise that was just full of minefields and mistrust.

Frankie Salati:
They all started becoming kind of the same thing after a while.

Joanna Saltonstall:
We had to cut back on bathrooms and stuff like that.

Samantha Samuels:
For some things I really trust my memory, for other things, not so much.

Joel Sanders:
I would need to dig up their names.

Sara Sarakanti:
I never go anywhere without my dog, Nilla.

Buz Sawyer:
Frankly, once we started doing this, it took on a life of its own and it was just huge.

Zoë Scharf:
My biggest takeaway from working at Open that summer was how much work goes into simplicity.

Paula Scher:
Yeah, I remember there was some silliness. I usually try and stop that sort of thing.

Max Schorr:
It's a good question. It's a question that has so many different answers.

Barbara Schulz:
I personally do not have a favorite part of the design.

LaFrae Sci:
We treated the room like hallowed ground. The students sat on the floor, and always lowered their voices, and spoke in respectful tones—similar to church, actually.

Rich Scurry:
I liked that it was this clean wrapping for the more complex ideas discussed within the show.

Paul Seck:
Fun is such a loaded word.

Mark Serratoni:
I was excited about moving in a new direction.

Jena Sher:
The design world is kind of weird here.

Hayon Shin:
It was some of the healthiest, yummiest pizza around.

Hal Siegel:
Tibor scared the shit out of me.

Lisa Silbermayr:
I think I saw one and I thought that it was a nice idea, but didn't have a closer look.

Bekah Sirrine:
I'm so grateful to have been able to meet and work with so many amazing people on a project that's still so very close to my heart.

Christopher Sleboda:
It will always be open. It will never be closed.

Bryn Smith:
I'd describe *Good* in its early days as a magazine that made you feel like you were part of something, and that something was important.

Darrell Smith:
I always wondered if I would ever make it up there one day and how my legacy would be remembered.

Bob Stowell:
He knows a little bit about designing, yeah.

Elsa Stowell:
It seemed like he was going to get into things that would lead to what he is doing today.

Scott Stowell:
I just want to make a nice thing.

Dave Stoy:
It was a lot of long hours, but a great learning experience, with some great timeless work to show for it.

Jessica Svendsen:
This movement upward, progressing from darkness toward light, is a remarkable experience.

Dave Tecson:
It always seems like a lot of money until you go over budget.

Ryan Thacker:
I'm glad we did it, but I'm glad I don't have to do it anymore.

Nate Trevethan:
It's making sure people are comfortable not being overwhelmed by things.

Amy Troiano:
There was part of me that was happy I was 3,000 miles away and wasn't in every meeting they were going through.

Joaquin Trujillo:
I'm really bad at returning emails. I was like, *Come on. There's phones for a reason.*

Alice Twemlow:
I remember that we met Scott there, and that we were somehow standing in a kitchen area with Al Gore and Matthew Modine!

Matthew Urbanski:
You could say that you almost have to have a map in Central Park because it was designed literally to be confusing.

Beth Urdang:
It was very of-that-moment, in that it was using the past in a modern way.

Lindsay Utz:
We came up with playful ways to bring those ideas to life.

Michael Van Valkenburgh:
I do feel that the park has too many signs in it now and more are apparently coming.

Katrina vanden Heuvel:
In a new arrangement, there are always kinks, but there are great things that emerge.

Jon Varriano:
It's nice that they're all different while still feeling like part of the same family.

Lucia Vera:
There was an incident with a cake.

Robbie Vitrano:
It encapsulated without being the alpha and omega of what makes pizza a powerful mechanism or medium to deliver a message.

Corinne Vizzacchero:
I was so nervous, not in that cowering-terrified way you hear people talk about when working for their design heroes, but in an I-really-really-want-to-do-my-best way.

Vincent Vumbaco:
Sorry, we've got a crazy thunderstorm rolling though here.

Geoffrey C. Ward:
That's what happens when you have people in an institution and people outside all trying to work together.

Chip Wass:
That moment came, where this is the last day, and just that last minute. Scott's such an archivalist, that he whipped out a camera and had somebody take our picture, like, *This is the end.* It caught me off guard, and it was very moving. It became a moment, when I had just thought, *Ah, here I go, bye bye.*

Todd Waterbury:
That sounds like a bunch of five-dollar words kind of strung together.

Jack Watson:
I recall being struck by the fact that there was a serious program about contemporary art as told completely from the perspective of the artist.

Nancy Webster:
It always amazes me how fragmented our attention is and how signage almost has to hit someone over the head for them to see it.

Dan Wieden:
The work is the most important thing. And if you get the work right, the money will come, the people will come. And you can make change happen.

Chris Wilcha:
I remember someone having to explain to me what a bone folder was. You know those things? There was a lot of bone folding going on.

Reverend Earl Williams:
Another point I should mention that causes me concern is that they are now selling chicken wings, which is not the healthiest fare.

Lukas WinklerPrins:
I spend a lot of my time thinking about structures and movement through them, and enjoy expressing these things as equations and graphs.

Maia Wojcik:
I was sure that these people with good hearts and values would love it, and I wanted to perpetuate the good karma!

Robert Wong:
I remember I was really proud of those posters. I said, *Those are going to be in the book.*

Bryan Woo:
There isn't a lot of meandering around the park for me. Maybe it's just me, but in general, I don't meander a lot.

Eli Yamin:
At some point we couldn't use it anymore, which was disappointing because it was an amazing resource.

Kim Yao:
It's a very simple and dumb diagram.

Jeffrey Yoshimine:
There are several areas that I am partial to.

Lauren Zalaznick:
I think it is more that my natural inclination is to care about the process as much as I care about the outcome.

Julia Zangwill:
The fact that a small community over 25 years ago saw potential, took action, and was successful is truly inspiring.

Lesley Tucker Zurolo:
There were many challenges during the project.

preface page 10: photo by Elsa Stowell; page 15: photo by Levi Stolove

essay pages 17 and 32: photo by Scott Stowell; page 21 (EVERYBODY sign): photo by Maggie Hopp; page 28: photo by Sean Shapiro; page 29: photo by Sean Shapiro

1. The Nation designed by: Su Barber, Cara Brower, Carol Hayes, Scott Stowell, and Ryan Thacker; page 34: covers courtesy The Nation

2. Art21 designed by: Su Barber, Cat Kirk, Tom Manning, Scott Stowell, Ryan Thacker, and Amit Werber; page 63: Art111 video by Quinn Buckler, Aida Mohammad Ali Zadegan, and their graduating class at Cawthra Park Secondary School in Mississauga, Ontario, Canada; page 64: photo by Rick Meyerowitz

3. Yale designed by: Su Barber, Rob Di Ieso, Gary Fogelson, Zak Jensen, Nicholas Rock, and Scott Stowell; page 66 (top): photo by Elizabeth Felicella; page 70: photo by Cat Kirk; pages 71, 74, 75: photos by Chris Mueller; page 77 (top): photo by Chase Booker; page 78: photos by Chris Mueller

4. Trio designed by: Su Barber, Cara Brower, and Scott Stowell; page 86: photos by Chris Wilcha

5. Bravo designed by: Su Barber, Rob Carmichael, Rob Di Ieso, Gary Fogelson, Isaac Gertman, Drew Heffron, William Morrisey, Scott Reinhard, Douglas Riccardi, Dmitri Siegel, Scott Stowell, Julie Teninbaum, and Corinne Vizzacchero; page 106: photos by Tim Barber

6. Jazz designed by: Su Barber, Cara Brower, Rob Di Ieso, Gary Fogelson, Drew Heffron, Zak Jensen, Şerifcan Özcan, Scott Reinhard, Scott Stowell, and Ryan Thacker; page 114: photo courtesy Rockwell Group; page 127: photo by Joanna Massey; page 128: photo by Clay Patrick McBride

7. Brown designed by: Rob Di Ieso, Gary Fogelson, and Scott Stowell; page 130: photo courtesy Architecture Research Office; pages 131, 135 (top left, bottom right), 136, 137 (top), 139: photos by Chris Mueller; pages 140 (top right, second row left, third row): photos by Elizabeth Goodspeed

8. MS designed by: Rob Di Ieso, Şerifcan Özcan, Nicholas Rock, and Scott Stowell; page 147: ad courtesy National MS Society; page 153: photos courtesy National MS Society; second from top by Ray Ng; page 154: courtesy National MS Society; page 158: photos courtesy Kate Morse; page 159: photos courtesy National MS Society, top left and third row right by Ray Ng, bottom right courtesy Todd Waterbury

9. Good designed by: Rob Di Ieso, Gary Fogelson, Carol Hayes, Tom Manning, Şerifcan Özcan, Nicholas Rock, Scott Stowell, and Ryan Thacker; page 166 (bottom left): photo courtesy Atley Kasky; page 172: frames from The Big Idea with Danny DeVito, directed by Henry Joost

10. Google designed by: Louise Ma, Şerifcan Özcan, Scott Stowell, Rich Watts, Ryan Thacker, and Lucia Vera; page 179: photos by Ryan Thacker; page 187: (top and center) photos by Elizabeth Goodspeed; page 188: photo by Braz Brandt; page 190: photo by Sean Shapiro

11. Naked Pizza designed by: Zoë Scharf, Scott Stowell, and Ryan Thacker; page 194: photo by Infrogmation of New Orleans; page 198 (top), page 199 (bottom), page 200, page 201 (top left, top right, bottom right), 205, 206: courtesy Naked Pizza; page 207: photos courtesy Naked Pizza Kenya; page 208: photo by Şerifcan Özcan

12. Brooklyn Bridge Park designed by: Chase Booker, Rob Di Ieso, Gary Fogelson, Elizabeth Goodspeed, Cat Kirk, Erika Lee, Martha Kang McGill, Şerifcan Özcan, Scott Stowell, and Ryan Thacker; page 218–221, 222 (top): photos by Sean Shapiro; page 222 (bottom): photo by Mike Lampariello; page 223: photos by Instagram users (first row) @missyclicks and @dannewoo, (second row) @peterknox and @ajthegent, (third row) @legwinn and @ladyandprince, (fourth row) @a_ivi_p and @jessesdu

glossary Citi Bike: photo by Ryan Thacker; Charles and Ray Eames: © Eames Office LLC (eamesoffice.com)

back cover photo by the guy who takes the passport photos at Gateway Newsstand

Any images not mentioned on this page came out of a bag, box, camera, DVD, envelope, hard drive, notebook, server, or sketchbook at Open or at Scott's house.

to Mom and Dad, for everything

to Carmen, for saving my life

to Steve and Alyson, for taking care

to Kathryne, for seeing the world

to Emily Oberman, for that thing you did at the place that time; to Chris Vermaas, for hey look what I bought; to Leslie Mello, for *che palle*; to Chip Wass, for cue the montage; to Barbara Glauber, for breakfast; and to too many friends to list here, for you know what you did

to Sally Hawkins, for History Day; to Mom again, for making me show up; and to Steve Thompson, for walking there on a Saturday

to Bob Bourke, for graphic design; to Merlin Szosz, for integrity; to Tricia Hennessy, for craft; to Doug Scott, for intent; to Janet Zweig, for concrete; to Pierre Bernard, for leaving one end open; and to RISD (and idiopathic neuropathy), for financial aid (and everything else since then)

to Jay Connolly (and Joanne Weisman) at The Editors, Lisa DeFrancis at DeFrancis Studio, and Tibor Kalman at M&Co., for telling me what to do

to Douglas Riccardi, for M&Co.; to Keira Alexandra, for 80 Warren Street; to Tibor again, for not paying Carmen $1.00 more an hour; to Paul Ritter, for not going to Rome; and to Carmen again, for being there when I got back

to David Carson, for RISD; to Warren Lehrer, for Purchase; to Michael Rock (and Sheila Levrant De Bretteville), for Yale; to Steve Heller, for SVA; and to Mike Essl, for Cooper Union

to all of my students, for teaching me

to David Gibson, for signage; to Drew Hodges, for business; and to UCB, for improvisation

to Todd Waterbury, for Wieden + Kennedy; to Bob George, for the ARChive (and David Bowie); to Matthew Duntemann, for Nick at Nite; to Hal Siegel, for *The Nation*; to Rob Odegard, for Art21; to Jena Sher, for Yale; to Stuart Selig (and Linda Ong), for Trio; to Henry Myerberg, for Jazz; to Jelly Helm, for *Good*; to Valerie Casey, for Naked Pizza; and to Wendy Leventer, for BBP

to everybody at Open, for putting up with me; to Emily Cohen, for keeping us in business; to the National Design Awards, for waking me up; and to Jason Jude Chan, for turning it around

to Ian Adelman, Michael Bierut, Roy Burns, Jean Claude Cancedda, Carol Coletta, CyberPoint International, Chad Dickerson, Nick Finck, John Fisher, Randy J. Hunt, Peter Kilpe, Lindsay Kinkade, Debbie Millman, Carmen Morais; Elizabeth and Manuel Morais, Gina Moreno Valle, Emily Oberman, Linda Ong, Phoenix Urban Design Week, Goffredo Puccetti, Dominic A.A. Randolph, Michael Riley, Tosh Sano, Max Schorr, Rita Siow, Maria Verastegui, and Chris Wilcha, for your generous support

to Alice Twemlow, for making this book happen (in more ways than one); and to everybody who worked on this book, for making it better

to Charles Adler, Chappell Ellison, and Grace Hawthorne, for Kickstarter advice; to Tristan Jones, Louise Ma, Christian Schwartz, and Jejon Yeung for modeling; and to everybody who spread the word, for spreading the word

to everybody who was interviewed, especially Michael Fischer (for doing your interview twice); to everybody who contributed essays; to Joeffrey Trimmingham, for helping Chuck; to Nyala Wright Nolen, for wrangling Wynton; and to Heloïse Bernard, for typing for Pierre

to Shamus Adams, Rob Di Ieso, Gary Fogelson, Atley Kasky, Graham McReynolds, Şerifcan Özcan, Mark Serratoni, Ryan Thacker, Lucia Vera, and Vincent Vumbaco, for sharing; and to Eve Moros Ortega, for letting us look in your email so we could find out you wanted to fire us

to Stefan Bucher, Grace Hawthorne, Steve Heller, and Adrian Shaughnessy, for publisher advice; to Morgan Clendaniel, Carol Coletta, Steve Duenes, Cliff Kuang, Diana Murphy, Emily Oberman, and Josh Tyrangiel, for writer advice; and to Jason Jude Chan, Chappell Ellison, Kaye Ellison, Barbara Glauber, Avi Granite, Martha Kang McGill, Carmen Morais, and Emily Oberman, for repeatedly reading what I wrote

to Christian Schwartz and Mark Record, for type help (and SMALL CAPS); to Jeff Baker at Shapco, for great work (I hope!); to Ben Rosenthal, for letting us know about phthalates; and to Anshul Jain, Saurabh Mahajan, Brenda Sutherland, Douglas Waterfall, and the rest of the InDesign team at Adobe, for ebook advice

to anybody I forgot to include on this page; and to you, for taking the time to read it

Sound Patterns (1953) is one of many albums of field recordings of everyday life that Folkways Records released, mostly in the 1950s and 1960s. Its 31 tracks include "Monkey (Happy)," "Monkey (Same Monkey, Angry)," and "Street Cries, Hot Dogs in Times Square."

Frederick Wiseman's films (1967–) all start with weeks of filming inside an institution. Wiseman doesn't plan ahead, preferring to find a story by seeing what happens—and then spending months editing it together.

Forget All the Rules... (1981), by Bob Gill, is one of the first design books I ever read, and it still inspires me now. Once, I heard Gill trash our WNYC logo, live on WNYC. At least he noticed it!

Harvey Wang's New York (1990) is a book of portraits of regular people in New York City, most with a job (like a blacksmith, a sign painter, or a tv repairman) that not many people do.

Where the Suckers Moon (1995), by Randall Rothenberg, is the true story of Wieden + Kennedy's work with Subaru— from the first meeting, through the pitch, to the end. Tibor shows up in chapter 13.

Printed Matter (1996, revised 2001 and 2010), by Karel Martens, is the most beautiful book of graphic design I can think of. Designed by Jaap van Triest, it's boldly experimental and disarmingly modest—just like Karel and his work.

Tibor Kalman: Perverse Optimist (1998), edited by Michael Bierut and Peter Hall, is one of the best design monographs ever, and not because I'm in it wearing priest underwear.

Helvetica (2007), directed by Gary Hustwit, is a documentary about a typeface. It's also an accessible and engaging history of graphic design— the perfect introduction to graphic design for any designer's nondesigner friends.

How to Think Like a Great Graphic Designer (2007), by Debbie Millman, isn't really the instruction manual that its title makes it sound like. It's a collection of surprisingly personal conversations with some super successful graphic designers.

Studio Culture: The Secret Life of the Graphic Design Studio (2009), edited by Tony Brook and Adrian Shaughnessy, is full of interviews with people who run studios around the world, about how they got started—and how they keep going.

Stories We Tell (2012), directed by Sarah Polley, seems like it's a documentary about a family. Then it seems like it's a documentary about making a documentary about a family. Then it turns into something else.

StartUp (2014–) is a podcast about starting a company: the company that makes the *StartUp* podcast. I've always believed that nobody knows what they're doing. *StartUp* showed me that I was right—and let me know that's OK.

directed by:
Scott Stowell

edited by:
Chappell Ellison,
Bryn Smith,
and Scott Stowell

interviews by:
Chappell Ellison,
Bryn Smith,
and Christina Milan

contributing writers:
Douglass G. A. Scott, Karrie Jacobs, Pierre
Bernard, Maira Kalman, Emily Pilloton, Chip
Wass, Alisa Grifo, Wynton Marsalis, Amina Huda,
Willy Wong, Alissa Walker, Charles Harrison,
Naz Şahin Özcan, and Michael Van Valkenburgh

copy chief:
Rachel Bozek

copy and transcribing team:
Melissa Beveridge,
Aabye-Gayle D. Francis-Favilla,
Erin Petenko,
and Helene Salmon

additional editing:
Martha Kang McGill
and Carmen Morais

additional transcribing:
Rev

produced by:
Jason Jude Chan

designed by:
Scott Stowell,
Martha Kang McGill,
and Ryan Thacker

additional design and production:
Chase Booker
and Cat Kirk

typefaces:
Graphik (and one line of Produkt)
by Christian Schwartz/Commercial Type

This is an Open book.
notclosed.com

Library of Congress
Cataloging-in-Publication data
is available upon request.

ISBN 978-1-938922-85-5

METROPOLIS
BOOKS

Metropolis Books
ARTBOOK | D.A.P.
155 Sixth Avenue, 2nd floor
New York NY 10013
phone +1 212 627 1999
fax +1 212 627 9484
artbook.com
metropolisbooks.com

paper:
Rolland Enviro Print, which contains 100%
recycled post-consumer fiber; is EcoLogo/UL,
Processed Chlorine Free, FSC®, and Ancient
Forest Friendly certified; and is manufactured
using renewable biogas energy

   Ancient Forest Friendly™ BIO GAS

printed by:
The Avery Group
at Shapco Printing
Minneapolis, Minnesota

first printing
December 2015